CONTENTS

ERRATUM

Page 135, column 1, line 21 should read:
"his Cabinet colleague, Jonathan Aitken"
not "Alan Clark"

We sincerely regret and apologise
for this error.

THE CROWN AND PARLIAMENT

What Does the Queen Think of Parliament?

Parliament must be important because the Queen thinks that it is even if nobody else does. As the richest and most powerful person in the Kingdom who performs a pivotal role in the appointment of Prime Ministers and who looks down from the throne on Archbishops of Canterbury as well as having six royal palaces together with personal wealth beyond all our dreams, she should know.

The Queen is so interested in what goes on in Parliament that she has appointed one of its members, Timothy Kirkhope, a government Whip, to be Vice-Chamberlain of the Royal Household. By order of Her Majesty, Timothy sends her written reports of each day's proceedings in Parliament. She is, we are reliably informed, as interested in the outsized egos of MPs as in the more prosaic aspects of the daily routine of Parliament.

When the Beast of Bolsover, Dennis Skinner MP is suspended from Parliament, as he is from time to time, or if Tarzan, Michael Heseltine MP, goes ape, as he once did, and picks up the Mace and brandishes it over his head, the Queen is told about it. Every now and then Timothy pops over to the Palace to give the Queen an oral report.

Thus it is that Timothy Kirkhope MP, unknown to the whole world and probably unrecognised by most Members of Parliament, has come to represent on a formal as well as informal basis one of the links, indefinable but indissoluble, between the Monarch and Parliament. Certainly if Timothy, a person of much delicacy and sensitivity, were ever to stumble across or hear of some indiscretion, some impropriety or, how shall we put it, some hanky-panky in the Royal Household, the nation can rest assured that he would never dream of exposing it by succumbing to the temptations of cheque-book journalism or the urge to kiss and tell the *News of the World*. Such revelations are, perhaps, best left to intruders, uninvited as well as invited, into royal bedrooms. Timothy, you see, is bound by the Official Secrets Acts as well as by the notions of good manners which enable us to distinguish between a good chap and a yob. More of good manners later....

Regal Talk with MPs

One question to which people are desperate to know the answer is what do MPs and the Queen talk about when they get together? Well, when I was a civil servant in the Ministry of Housing and Local Government and Richard Crossman MP, an Oxford academic with a huge brain, was the Minister in charge of the Department, he said to me one day: "I'm seeing the Queen today. It's going to be a terrible ordeal. I'm told she only talks about babies and horses and I don't know anything about either." I replied: "If you haven't got time to mug up on Dr Spock tell her that the government is thinking of nationalising the Tote. She'll think you're barking mad and ask her mum who's a horse-racing fanatic for advice. Then the conversation should really hum and you'll be at home in the middle of the bloody great row that ensues."

Of course times change and with them the Queen's loves and hates. A few years ago I took tea with her (Earl Grey tea, it was) at St Joseph's Hospice in Hackney. Her Press Secretary was present. There was no baby or horsy talk. Most of the conversation was about how the monarchy and the Labour Party faced a similar problem – how to cope with the odious reptiles who write for the tabloid press and misrepresent everything we say.

However, if anyone wants to know in detail what the Queen talks about, what interests her about the common people whom she rules and what makes her tick, the obvious people to ask are those Prime Ministers who are still alive and who, when in office, had regular audiences with her – Sir Alec Douglas Home, Edward Heath, Jim Callaghan, Margaret Thatcher and John Major. Unfortunately all of these Prime Ministers have accepted the absolute confidentiality of their audiences with the Queen. A further problem is that documents and papers which would shed light on these matters have a hundred year bar on publication. This compares with a thirty year bar on the publication of Cabinet papers, which are surely more important than Queenly affairs.

The Queen, incidentally, has automatic and immediate access to Cabinet papers, which is not to accuse her of actually reading them. So we've a long wait before we hear of what is currently transpiring between the Queen and John Major. Is the approach of this commoner from Brixton business-like or does he flatter the Queen and flaunt himself in front of her as Disraeli, the Prime Minister, with thick black ringlets, fancy waistcoats and powder, did to Queen Victoria?

Tensions Between the Crown and Parliament

Inevitably relations between the Crown and Parliament have had their ups and downs. They reached their lowest point in 1649 during the English Revolution when Parliament challenged the very authority through which the King, Charles I, reigned. Eventually Parliament drew up a list of all the worst crimes known to man and charged Charles with being a "tyrant, traitor, murderer and a public and implacable enemy of the Commonwealth".

The trial began on 20 January 1649 in Westminster Hall, that monumental edifice begun in 1097, not long after the Norman Conquest, which still dominates the Houses of Parliament today and which makes the rest of the Palace of Westminster with its fussy lines look like a serious architectural mistake. 300 feet long and 100 feet high with a magnificent hammer-beam roof built in oak, it was in this Hall that Edward II abdicated, Richard II was deposed and Sir Thomas More was tried and sentenced to death, his trial being later commemorated in the film *A Man for All Seasons*.

Charles entered the Hall dressed in black with only the Star of the Garter and the George and blue ribbon around his neck to relieve the

What the team thinks: ex-Prime Ministers will never tell

monotony. Six days later the judges found him guilty and ruled that he should be executed. Finally on 30 January Charles, his hair silver, his beard now grey, walked "with calm dignity and religious resignation" from St James's Palace to Whitehall where a scaffold had been erected outside one of the windows of the Banqueting House, whose ceiling was and is adorned with paintings by Reubens. Then two masked executioners did the bidding of the Commonwealth. Oliver Cromwell, the King's tormentor, weighed down by the cowardice that often accompanies shame, was attending a prayer meeting elsewhere when the chief executioner held up an object dripping with blood and let forth the traditional cry: "Behold the head of a traitor".

Although the trial had, from the outset, been manifestly unlawful and a terrible example of the exercise of arbitrary cruelty, the outcome did give credence to the popular maxim that no country can lay claim to being a democracy without first lopping off the head of at least one king.

The judges for the trial, who were also the jurors, consisted of 135 Commissioners appointed on the authority of the House of Commons, although at the end when it came to passing sentence only sixty-two had the stomach to sign the death warrant. The Commissioners included in their number Members of Parliament, members of the Army, country gentlemen and landowners, a lawyer's clerk, a shoemaker, two brewers and Sir Edward Baynton, the Wiltshire magnate who "had been in trouble during his stormy life for duelling, adultery and peculation".

If the poet Andrew Marvell who witnessed the bloody deed and later wrote *An Horatian Ode to Cromwell* is to be believed, our King displayed throughout such courage as we would expect from one of royal blood:

He nothing common did or mean
Upon that memorable scene:
But with his keener eye
The axe's edge did try:
Nor called the Gods, with vulgar spite
To vindicate his helpless right,

But bowed his comely head
Down, as upon a bed.
A bleeding head, where they begun
Did fright the architects to run;
And yet in that the State
Foresaw its happy fate!

As for Cromwell, the only Lord Protector of the Kingdom and dictator that our country has ever had, he was buried in Westminster Abbey, only to have his dead body dug up later so that he could be posthumously hanged. But in 1899 a statue to his memory as the guardian of our liberties was set up outside Westminster Hall. Although in a prominent position, he somehow seems as lonely a figure as he ever was.

Yet had not Cromwell appointed his hopeless son Richard as his successor and thereby made a mess of things, England might have become the first modern republic, in which event Cromwell would truly have been remembered as our chief of men.

Relations Improve

With the restoration of the monarchy, the Glorious Revolution of 1688 when William and Mary landed at Torbay, and the Act of Settlement in 1701 which sought to establish a constitutional monarchy subordinate to Parliament, relations between the Crown and Parliament improved – a bit. Later still with Parliament's assertion of absolute power the Kings and Queens of the Kingdom may not have liked it, but none of them was prepared to stand on principle and take the same road as Charles I along the Mall to the scaffold. However, despite all the talk of the democratic nature of the agreement of 1701 the Crown still controlled the executive, the great government machine which ran the country throughout the eighteenth century. Ministers in Parliament were still the servants of that machine and not, as now, its masters.

Today it is Tory MPs who can be expected to give total support to the monarch. It was not always thus. When George I (1714-27) came to the throne he faced the universal hatred of Tory MPs and peers. Indeed the only reason that they could stomach this vile Protestant foreigner from the House of Brunswick was that they thought that he was all that stood between them and popery. To High Tories he was a robber and tyrant; to moderate Tories he came from an evil dynasty. Even Whig MPs, on whom George I shamelessly showered favours, were far from infatuated by a King who could not speak a word of English and who liked nothing more than punch and fat women.

George II (1727-60), who did not set foot on British soil until he was thirty years old and who was described by the historian Macaulay as "a bad son and worse father, an unfaithful husband and an ungraceful lover", prevented Pitt the Elder, who was to become one of our greatest Prime Ministers, from becoming Minister in Parliament for several years. He acted out of pique after Pitt made a superb speech in Parliament criticising the King for making the English taxpayer pay the wages of German troops.

George III (1760-1820) before he went blind, deaf and mad inevitably made enemies in Parliament when he intrigued against his own Ministers. To the astonishment of Parliament he sent meddling messages from the royal closet to Lords of the Bedchamber, bishops and Scottish peers who sat in the House of Lords and who depended on his patronage, ordering them to bring down the coalition government of Charles James Fox and Lord North. Sure enough they carried out the dirty deed on behalf of their King.

George IV (1820-30) so angered Parliament over a squalid domestic dispute with his wife Queen Caroline that MPs and peers turned on him and refused to do his bidding. Theirs was an arranged marriage when he was Prince of Wales and she was Princess Caroline. She was, some maintained, good looking but, according to the Earl of Malmesbury who met her, was also "coarse to the last degree, a slattern even to such a point as to excite disgust, and in her conversation vulgar and indelicate beyond all degree". The couple shared the same bed for just a few months.

Pains and Penalties

When he became King, George IV, himself an adulterer of public renown, demanded that Parliament remove Queen Caroline's name from the liturgy and then introduce a Bill of Pains and Penalties to grant him a divorce on the grounds of his wife's adultery. That the Whigs in Parliament took the Queen's side did not matter. That the public took her side, and in the process brought the country to the brink of revolution, did. Daily for three months while Parliament debated the Bill the public took to the streets in huge numbers and the military threatened another Peterloo massacre, as happened in 1819, when the yeomanry opened fire on unarmed members of the public who were demonstrating their support of parliamentary reforms and were mown down. The Queen, one chronicler tells us, dressed in a black wig with voluminous curls, an Episcopal gown with a ruff and a hat topped with ostrich feathers, encouraged the mob to rebel. Every day she drove to Westminster Hall accompanied by undesirables of all kinds, including prostitutes and pickpockets. According to the historian Arthur Bryant, "Revolution now seemed certain. Night and day the streets resounded with shouts of 'No Queen No King'". Parliament took fright, deserted the King and abandoned the Bill, thus enabling husband and wife to continue with their adulterous relationships. A second English revolution was thus averted.

Parliament Triumphs

Spats continued between Parliament and the Crown during the reign of Queen Victoria (1837-1901). When Palmerston was Foreign Secretary between 1846 and 1851 he had to put up with constant interference from the Crown, most of it inspired by Prince Albert, the Queen's consort. Worse, when Palmerston became Prime Minister in 1859 Victoria and Albert went behind his back and began using members of the Cabinet to intrigue against him. For a while it looked as though Palmerston's administration would be brought down, much as the Fox-North coalition had been brought down by George III.

Happily, in 1861 Prince Albert unexpectedly died. Queen Victoria lost some of her stomach for political intrigue, although she continued to take a keen interest in matters diplomatic. True, she later tried to balk the ambitions of Gladstone whom she loathed, and he was not best pleased with what he felicitously described as her "armed neutrality". However, to all intents and purposes Prince Albert's death marks the virtual elimination of the Crown from politics.

A few years later the second Reform Bill of 1867, which gave the vote to people in the towns and which presaged the rise of organised political parties, completed the process of excluding Kings and Queens from exercising real political power and cleared the way for the monarchy to become a soap opera. Henceforth public opinion would matter more to governments and MPs than the views of Queens and Kings.

However, it took the courtier nerds behind the scenes at Buckingham Palace over 100 years to tumble to what had happened and to take up the challenge of marketing the monarchy as symbols of decency, duty, faithfulness, selflessness and all the virtues to which the institution could scarcely lay claim before. The result was the Windsor Soap Opera. Never again would Parliament and the monarchy fall out – or so it seemed.

Parliament and the Soap Opera

Trouble started up again between Parliament and the monarchy when the Soap Opera which was meant to be about the fantasy, glamour, style and savoir-faire of a royal family turned into the mucky story of a family in crisis whose parents were out of touch with the modern world and whose children were selfish and crippled by self-pity. For a time MPs were able to laugh and snigger privately in the tea-rooms of the House of Commons, perhaps the most sophisticated gossip shop in the world, as the Windsors imploded inside their own contradictions.

However, it became their public business

when the heir to the throne, Prince Charles, separated from his wife, admitted to the sin of fornication and in the most graphic of metaphors confided to the world that he would like to be reincarnated as Camilla's Tampax. Later he went out of his way to tell the public that he had been bullied into a loveless marriage with his wife as a result of pressure from his father. Sympathy at these revelations disappeared amongst members of his own class who thought him a cad for betraying his mistress in a kick-and-tell story.

Any doubt that the crisis was serious was removed when the Prime Minister scuttled to the Despatch Box in the Chamber of the House of Commons and assured MPs that all was well

as far as the succession was concerned, when even the least intelligent of MPs could see that this was far from so. That the crisis was running deep in society was confirmed in opinion polls and implicit in the question of our first woman

Prime Minister, Margaret Thatcher, now Lady Thatcher, which she put to one of her former policy advisers: "What are we going to do about the Royal Family? They are so stupid".

Even if they wanted to, MPs could not close their eyes to the position of the monarch as the Defender of the Faith and head of the established Church, the Church of England. Even in a Church for which the only principle has long since been the absence of a principle – with a belief in the Ten Commandments perhaps, and in God, so to speak – there would undoubtedly be some who would object to having as their supremo a fornicator, perhaps a divorced fornicator and, worst, a re-married fornicator with a supplicatory fornicator as a wife.

So much for the troubles which Charles was presenting to Parliament. But what of those that now accompanied his wife, the Queen to be, everywhere she went? When the government asserted that if Charles became King his separated wife would become Queen, even those MPs who are normally slow on the uptake blinked. How, they wondered, could Diana resolve the conflicts inherent in being

three persons in one – in part a fairy princess who is magical and untouchable, in part a tortured Goddess like Brigitte Bardot in search of fatherly love, in part a self-conscious object of desire like Marilyn Monroe in search of understanding from powerful men. Maybe such a person – mad and sad perhaps but probably not bad – is not fit to be Queen or fit to be Queen Mother, should her son William leapfrog over Charles and become King.

Parliament Starts to Ask Questions

MPs are aware that the Queen's main formal constitutional duties in Britain are slight in the extreme and just three in number.

The Queen has to ensure the continuity of government. So when a Prime Minister dies or resigns the Queen, guided by those whom political parties select as their leaders, or, if there are complications, by the advice of Privy Councillors and the three officials who make up what is termed the 'golden triangle' – her own Private Secretary, the Cabinet Secretary and the Private Secretary of the departing Prime Minister – summons the chosen person to Buckingham Palace and asks him or her if he or she can form an administration. To this question, which has been set in aspic in over a century and a half of constitutional practice, two answers are possible – "Yes, Ma'am" or "I will enter into consultation to see whether I can report to you that an administration can be formed".

Although the Queen has seen off eight Prime Ministers in her reign and will probably see off John Major too, this task can hardly have occupied much of her time over the past forty-odd years.

The second official task for the Queen is to attend the State Opening of Parliament. Taken from Buckingham Palace in a horse-drawn coach to Parliament, the Queen makes her way on foot to the Royal Robing Room. There with the help of the Lord Chamberlain she takes off her tiara and replaces it with a crown. Then, having polished her spectacles,

Eyes down for a full House: The Queen opens Parliament

she moves along the Royal Portrait Gallery through the Princes Chamber, which contains a statue of Queen Victoria together with wood engravings of all of Henry VIII's wives, and into the debating Chamber of the House of Lords where she ascends the throne, watched by courtiers, sycophants, bishops, peers and, in the far distance, MPs. Embarrassingly, she then delivers what is known as the Queen's Speech, a very dull affair indeed, written for her by advisers to the Prime Minister and read from notes in her disconcertingly tinny and squeally voice. Constantly she refers to "My Ministers" though they have long since ceased to be such. Before the ceremony ends the ladies of the realm, each one wearing a tiara, curtsy to the Queen, the diamonds sparkling in unison as they do so to form a flash of man-made lightning which rips across the Chamber. The ceremony occupies the Queen for half a day once a year.

Royal Assent to Bills

Third and finally, the Queen has to give her assent to Bills which have passed through all their stages in Parliament before they can become law. In truth, and for the most part, she delegates this task to her Council of State composed of Privy Councillors with time on their hands. Five grown men in flowing robes and Nelsonian headgear, including the Lord Chancellor, sit on the Woolsack in the House of Lords, their strange garb fitting the Ruritanian atmosphere. A voice intones the names of the relevant Acts of Parliament. Half a dozen men and women of the nobility loll on the benches, also dressed up in funny clothes. And despite the fact that this is England, our England, one man keeps on talking in Norman French and assuring us that the Queen assents to each Bill. There standing at the entrance to the Chamber of their Lordships, not allowed beyond the bar of their House and dressed in shabby lounge suits, is a desultory gathering of MPs from the House of Commons, the elected rulers of Britain, at the scene like peasants of old invited to watch a public hanging.

All in all this does not add up to a lot of work for the Queen. Realising that vulgar personages might one day ask whether such idle hands deserved all the monies which Parliament votes the monarchy today through what is known as the 'Civil List' and all the accretions of personal wealth which have only come to sovereigns and their predecessors by virtue of their office, the constitutional theorist Walter Bagehot set about searching for a role for the monarchy. Eventually he came up with the answer that in the modern world the duties of a constitutional king or queen are "to advise, to encourage and to warn" Prime Ministers and governments. As a justification for the huge expenditure meted out to keep the Soap Opera going this simply will not do. Nobody really thinks that the current Prime Minister John Major is anxious to be guided by an ageing woman whose traditions lie in a forgotten era, whose sense of duty is touched by snobbery and who is, to put it politely, unimaginative to the point of being dull.

Against this background the Queen and the government badly misjudged things when a fire at Windsor Castle in 1992 destroyed or damaged 104 rooms and 2,800 square metres of roof. On behalf of the Queen, the Secretary of State for National Heritage told Parliament that the taxpayer would foot the bill, now expected to be £35 million. The public took a different view and so did Ann Clwyd MP, Labour's Shadow Heritage Spokesperson, who suggested that the Queen was rich enough to dig into her own pocket. The Queen appeared to panic and six months later announced to Parliament through the Secretary of State for National Heritage that she would open the State Rooms in Buckingham Palace to the public for eight weeks each summer in the hope of raising seventy per cent of the restoration costs.

As the Soap Opera turned to farce and respect for the Windsors as a family if not for the monarchy as an institution fell even further in the esteem of Parliament and the public, the Queen, in a measure that can only be described as desperate, was persuaded to put right an injustice that rankled, when she agreed to pay some tax on her vast private income. The Prime Minister said she was a willing penitent but nobody believed him.

Then the powerful Public Accounts Committee in Parliament poked its nose for the first time into the way in which some £20 million of taxpayers' money was spent each year on the royal palaces. Concerns were expressed about accountability and the need for public visibility in the spending of the monies. When one member of the Committee, Alan Williams MP, who as it happens is a staunch monarchist, suggested that the Royal Family did not need five of its six palaces, another member of the committee, Michael Shersby MP, accused him of conducting a vendetta against the Royal Family. When Williams, a thoughtful former Minister of the Crown and as far from a headbanger as you could get, asked why five members of the Royal Family who carried out only twelve public engagements a week between them should occupy no less than eighty rooms in the palaces for themselves and their staffs he was told: "Grace and Favour accommodation is provided to members of the Royal Family in accordance with long-established practice. It is in keeping with the style and dignity of the monarchy and national prestige that the more immediate members of the Royal Family should be appropriately housed and a London residence is needed to entertain and undertake official duties on behalf of the Queen".

The Committee was also told that within the royal palaces there were 272 self-contained households and apartments of which just eight were occupied by members of the Royal Family, 174 by staff of the Royal Household, forty-nine by the Queen's private staff and staff of other Households and organisations (including the Mistress of the Robes, the Keeper of the Privy Purse, Sarjeant of the Vestry, the Insignia Clerk, the Reprographic Operator, the Royal Librarian, the Assistant Curator of the Royal Library, the Headbookbinder of the Royal Library and the Deputy Headbookbinder of the Royal Library (whoever he may be), and forty-one by pensioners, of whom thirteen were Military Knights at Windsor Castle whose duties comprised attending church services in uniform on Sundays and the annual ceremonies of the Order of the Garter.

Hangers-on

In addition to giving the Royal Family £20 million a year for their palaces, together with monies to meet the costs of the Royal Yacht, the Queen's Flight of aircraft, travel by train, overseas travel, and postal and telecommunications services, Parliament provides the Queen and some of her hangers-on with monies from the Civil List to enable them to carry out their public duties. In the Queen's case this is topped up by monies from the Privy Purse, financed from Revenues from the Chancellor of the Duchy of Lancaster. Although Parliament makes no provision for Prince Charles and his wife, they get three quarters of the revenues from the 127,000 acre estate of the Duchy of Cornwall in South West England and London. This means that in recent years the Prince and Princess have cornered for themselves over £2 million a year.

Every year when the sums paid out to individuals were increased, members of the common herd and tumultuous swine from amongst the Queen's subjects, together with a

THE CIVIL LIST	
Annual amounts payable 1991 to 2000	
Queen	£7,900,000
Queen Mother	£640,000
Duke of Edinburgh	£360,000
Duke of York	£250,000
Prince Edward	£100,000
Princess Royal	£230,000
Princess Margaret	£220,000
Princess Alice	£90,000

small band of MPs, used to kick up a stink. To avoid the annual and unseemly row Margaret Thatcher, when Prime Minister, settled the amounts to be paid out of the Civil List to the Royals for ten years ahead.

Meanwhile at hearings of the Public Accounts Committee Alan Williams MP continued to complain that Parliament has no way of monitoring how monies paid through the Civil List and the Duchy of Cornwall are spent by the beneficiaries. It seems that the time cannot be far away when the Queen will have to account for every penny she spends on toiletries and the Princess of Wales will have to justify spending £7 on a tube of toothpaste – Rembrandt, presumably, and presumably also because it is designed to keep royal teeth white. Some monarchists and constitutional theorists say that the problem with this approach is that it will most likely detract from the mystery and mystique of the monarchy, factors which have hitherto added potency to its appeal. As Walter Bagehot wrote, "When there is a select committee on the Queen, the charm of royalty will be gone. Its mystery is its life. We must not let in daylight upon magic."

Depending on which source you look at, the Queen's personal wealth when put at £7 billion makes her very rich indeed but when put at £50 million renders her almost a pauper.

Enemies of the Queen

Since the death of the poet Shelley in the Gulf of Spezia in 1822 republicanism has lacked a cultured voice in Britain. Except for a few MPs it is not part of the political agenda. However, the subject crops up rather more than the monarchy would like as the following recollection from Enoch Powell, one-time MP for Wolverhampton and then for South Down in Northern Ireland, shows:

It is 1919. I am with my mother and father in the front seats of the otherwise empty top deck of a Birmingham tramcar. I start up singing my favourite (was it my only?) song, "God Save the King". 'Don't sing that here,' scolds my mother. 'Oh, let the boy sing it,' says my father. 'He may not be able to much longer.'

One would expect most of the Queen's enemies in Parliament to come from Nationalist parties, from Scottish Nationalist MPs, Welsh Nationalist MPs and Irish Nationalist MPs who wish to break up her Kingdom and secede. One Irish Nationalist, Gerry Adams, the Sinn Fein MP for Belfast West between 1983 and 1992 and a barman who was interned in Northern Ireland without trial and later sentenced to eighteen months' imprisonment for attempting to escape from Long Kesh prison, never came to Parliament to take the oath of allegiance to the Queen. Had he done so, then like other MPs he would have been eligible for tickets for one of the Queen's Garden Parties for himself and his lady. "Care for a slice of Battenburg, Mr Adams?" However, bearing in mind that Sinn Fein is the political wing of the IRA the very thought of it must have created nightmares for the Queen's security staff. The whole British establishment could so easily have been blown to smithereens in one go on a fine summer's afternoon.

Some MPs are discreet to a degree about their republicanism or hostility to the monarchy. No one has ever seen the lips of Ann Clwyd, the only woman MP who represents a constituency in Wales and whose first language is Welsh, move when what she regards as the English National Anthem *God Save The Queen* is sung.

Although forty-four per cent of Labour MPs privately say they want to abolish the monarchy, only some twenty or thirty are prepared to admit this publicly and stand up and be counted. Chief amongst them is Tony Benn MP, formerly Viscount Stansgate and a Cabinet Minister and Privy Councillor who has sworn a special oath of allegiance to the Queen. Not known before as a republican, Benn's views changed in the 1970s. One day in May 1977 when I was working as his PPS he disappeared, only to return shamefacedly and admit that he had been to Westminster Hall to hear the Queen's Jubilee address. He reported it thus:

Westminster Hall had been all set up for the Queen's Jubilee address, and I went and sat in the second row on the right-hand side plum behind the Prime Minister. Next to him was Maggie Thatcher, then Harold Wilson, Ted Heath and Harold Macmillan; then Willie Whitelaw, David Steel, Denis Healey and so on.

I had had very mixed feelings about going but I am glad I did because it was another reminder of how totally undemocratic British democracy is, both in its outward appearance and in reality.

I watched the Lords troop in; it was like Madame Tussaud's with all these figures I hadn't seen for years, some of whom I thought were dead – Derick Heathcoat Amory, Hailsham and others all coming down the steps from the top of Westminster Hall, many of them looking very poorly.

Prince Charles was in a morning coat, looking like a tailor's dummy. I shiver at the

Once a toff... Tony Benn has a soft spot for the Crown

thought that that man will one day be King. Finally the Queen and the Duke of Edinburgh came in.

The Lord Chancellor read the most grovelling address about Her Majesty's tremendous contribution, how the monarchy was responsible for the rights of our people. George Thomas said much the same thing, and then the Queen addressed us. She spoke as if Britain were a constitutional monarchy rather than a democracy. The Crown always talks about a constitutional monarchy, the establishment talks about a parliamentary democracy, but nothing talks about a democracy as such. Still, I'm glad I went, just to get the feel of it.

It was very cold and I muttered 'I've got cold feet', and Maggie Thatcher turned round and said, 'So have I.'

In 1994 Jack Straw MP, Labour's Shadow Home Secretary, in calling for a slimmed-down Royal Family, seemed to be suggesting that they should leave their yachts behind and get on their bikes like some of their Scandinavian counterparts. However, rest assured that if Labour does win the next election there's a fair chance that Straw will be sucking the toes of the Royals much as deferential Labour Ministers in the past have done.

Perhaps the last word should be left to Philip Ziegler, the official biographer of Edward VIII, who wrote:

The strongest argument for the monarchy is that the alternatives are so appalling. A powerful president, making decisions of policy, would withdraw so much power from the House of Commons as to be unacceptable, to MPs at least. One might seek out some elder statesman, infinitely wise, armoured in rectitude, far above the political strife, but if such an animal exists it is lying remarkably low. What one would end up with as president would be some clapped-out politician, kicked upstairs to get him out of the line of succession or rewarded for decades of mediocre service. The result would be less effective than the present system, very little cheaper and not half as picturesque.

THE COMMONS VERSUS THE LORDS

There are two Houses of Parliament. One is variously called the House of Lords, the Upper House or, when referred to in the House of Commons, the Other Place. The House of Lords dazzles the senses as a real palace should. The magnificent deep rich colours of its glittering, gilt debating Chamber contrast sharply with the drab interior of the Chamber of the House of Commons. The one befits nobility, the other is adequate for commoners. Likewise the ermine and robes of their Lordships, worn on formal occasions, serve only to highlight the scruffiness of MPs in crumpled suits and terrible outfits chosen by women, who for the most part lack the dress sense of Lacroix. Teresa Gorman, for example, appears to believe that, like the Queen, she must dress in the citrus colours in order to stand out from the crowd.

The House of Lords has 1250 members, most of them hereditary peers – Royal Dukes, Dukes, Marquesses, Earls, Viscounts, Barons. The hereditary principle works, so Lord Somers told their Lordships in a debate in 1991, because Bach would not have been such a superb musician had it not been for the fact that his father, brothers, uncles and practically his whole family were professional musicians. Lord Somers, no student of history he, then rather spoilt his argument when he claimed that the Kings and Queens of England were proof of the ability to pass on the characteristics of hard work, decency, wisdom and intelligence through the genes. There must also presumably be limits to the value of the hereditary principle in those cases when the original titles of today's

noble Lords were granted to unscrupulous robber barons and aristocratic pirates and thieves who then received royal patronage for their misdeeds rather than their good deeds. The evil that men do lives on after them.

The Monarch, debarred from attending

The House of Lords

COMPOSITION OF THE HOUSE OF LORDS	
Archbishops and bishops	26
Peers by succession	758 (17 women)
Hereditary peers of first creation	15
Law Lords under the Appellate Jurisdiction Act 1876	21
Life peers under the Life Peerages Act 1958	376 (60 women)
TOTAL	**1,196 (77 women)**

LORD GREYSTOKE'S HERE FOR THE POLL TAX VOTE

the proceedings of the House of Commons because of attempts by her predecessors to usurp its powers, can pop along to the House of Lords any time she wants. Members of the Royal Family can and do speak in debates in the House of Lords. In 1994 the Duke of Gloucester spoke passionately in a debate in defence of St Bartholomew's Hospital which the government wanted to close. He began his speech thus: "My Lords, I am speaking this afternoon as president of St Bartholomew's Hospital, an honorary position that I hold with great pride, as did my father before me... I am frankly amazed that its future should be in any doubt... I beg for a stay of execution for Barts, an institution whose crime it seems is to have tried too hard, if not too politically, to serve its community." He was snubbed by Ministers, who sat stony faced, hissing through their teeth as the Duke magnificently destroyed their arguments.

The hereditary principle also ensures that there is a massive inbuilt Conservative majority of peers in the Lords but this, we are told, is not abused because as Baroness White, in perhaps the most pointed criticism ever directed at the House of Commons, put it: "We're genuine seekers after truth". In practice the House of Lords does not oppose legislation from Labour governments outright unless it deems it to be unwanted by the country at large or has not appeared in Labour's election manifesto. This principle was established by Lord Salisbury in the last century. He was not daft, and realised that a Prime Minister who was not a Conservative could always threaten to recommend the Queen to create enough new hereditary peers to overcome the Conservative majority. Much better, he reasoned, to have a Conservative majority which could always amend or delay legislation from those of other political persuasions.

The power of Conservative 'backwoodsmen' in the Lords to come to the aid of the Party was seen at its best in 1988 when Margaret Thatcher's government faced defeat over an amendment in the Lords to the 'Poll Tax' Bill which proposed that payment instead of being on a flat rate basis should be on the basis "of ability to pay". The Prime Minister was having none of it. If the amendment were carried it would be seen as a victory for the 'Poll Tax' rioters who in her eyes were lower than vermin and in need of condign punishment. So her Whips in the Lords, people who apply pressures of varying degrees to make their Lordships vote in a certain way, people who may make offers that some cannot refuse, issued calls to backwoodsmen from all over the Kingdom to do their duty. Spectacularly 317 of them, old fogeys, some with their valets and maids waiting for them in London hotels, together with middle-aged men with red faces and pot bellies, the squirearchy of England, turned up to defeat the amendment.

For some it was their only visit to the House of Lords. The Prime Minister was

COMPOSITION OF THE HOUSE OF LORDS BY RANK (15 JULY 1994)	
Royal Prince	1
Archbishops	2
Royal Dukes	3
Dukes	25
Marquesses	35
Earls	170
Countesses	5
Viscounts	107
Bishops	24
Barons	752
Baronesses	67
Ladies	5
TOTAL	**1,196**

delighted; others saw it as an abuse of the constitution. History may well record that this episode was not the success claimed at the time. What we may well have witnessed was the night that the Prime Minister's fate was sealed because the vote ensured that the 'Poll Tax' would become the most hated tax for centuries and that the Conservative Party would be associated with it as long as she was its leader. Without knowing it, these backwoodsmen who loved her so much had signed the Lady's death warrant. John Major, Thatcher's successor, was to be the only person to benefit.

Life Peers and Bishops

In addition to the hereditary peers the House of Lords contains Life Peers, bishops from the established Church, the Church of England, but not from any other Church or religion, and Law Lords. The Lords Spiritual, as the Bishops are called, consist of the Archbishops of Canterbury and York, the Bishops of London, Durham and Winchester and twenty-one other diocesan bishops of the Church of England according to seniority of appointment. In the Chamber of the House of Lords the bishops' bench is the only bench with an arm rest, put there to stop them falling off when drunk.

Amongst the Life Peers appointed by Prime Ministers are a host of those who were once MPs and either lost their seats or retired from the hurly burly of real politics. As Sir Ian Gilmour MP, a former Cabinet Minister and Tory wet who was an object of Margaret Thatcher's contempt put it, the House of Lords "provides a haven for electoral casualties" and "embalms without burying a number of useful politicians".

Many of the Life Peers are fearful snobs, who, whilst denying it to their last breath, clearly enjoy the company of the nobility. Former Labour MPs, horny-handed working-class sons of the soil, are the worst offenders. Why, I ask myself, do Joe Dean and Ted Graham, former Labour MPs (now Baron Dean of Beswick and Baron Graham of Edmonton), now look so happy in their robes and ermine? Also amongst the Life Peers are a

The House of Lords provides a haven for electoral casualties

crashing off his boat into the river. By hook or by crook the Lords usually wins. As indeed it has done over the political rows in this century over whether to retain it in its present form or keep it but change it and make it fit for a democratic society, or simply abolish it. At one time it looked as though the Lords would wither away, leaving the Commons triumphant. But now rejuvenated, almost re-invented, the Lords is still able to drive democrats from the Commons to apoplexy. MPs have proved impotent in what was going to be their final victory – the abolition of hereditary peers.

The years 1909-11 saw a fearful row between the Commons and the Lords which ended with the Lords facing decay and collapse. The row concerned the refusal of the Lords to approve the Budget of the Liberal government led by Asquith which laid the foundations of the welfare state. The Lords would have none of it. It was the end of civilisation as they knew it. Asquith responded with a Parliament Bill which tore away the power of the Lords to thwart Budgets. In the constitutional crisis that followed, eventually the King reluctantly agreed to create as many peers as it took, possibly 500, to get the Bill through the Lords. Enough of their Lordships relented and the Bill went through by seventeen votes. The preamble to the Bill spelt death for the Lords in stating: "it is intended to substitute for the House of Lords as it at present exists a second Chamber constituted on a popular instead of a hereditary basis".

As the twenty-first century approaches

number of women, not seen in the House of Lords between its inception and 1958, with the passing of the Life Peerages Act. In 1963 women were allowed to become hereditary peeresses in their own right under the Peerage Act and sit in the Lords too. However, for Margaret Thatcher, being appointed a Life Peer was not enough and she insisted on her husband, Denis, being given a hereditary peerage, presumably for the benefit of her son Mark, the boy who reduced his mother to tears when he got lost in the desert.

War Between the Commons and the Lords

Life is conflict: life is strife. No one knows this better than MPs and members of the House of Lords. Every year war, in which no prisoners are taken, breaks out between the Commons and the Lords – on the cricket pitch at Lords, over the chess board, in sailing boats on the Thames and down the ski-slopes of the Alps.

In 1994 Stewart Randall, a Labour MP and the Commodore of the House of Commons Yacht Club, was the victim of a foul manoeuvre by their Lordships during a race and was sent

DECLARED POLITICAL ALLEGIANCES OF THE HOUSE OF LORDS (1994)	
Conservative	473
Labour	114
Lib-Dems	54
Cross-bench	283

the House of Commons has failed to act on the preamble. By the 1950s abolition seemed unnecessary, the Lords having become "a wasted and powerless assembly". As one observer put it cruelly, "the Lords was dying in its sleep". Not so. While so many MPs hope or expect to become peers the Upper House is safe and well.

In 1968-69 the Lords agreed to a proposal for reform put forward by the Labour government of Harold Wilson which would have turned them into a useless talking shop. It was not so much an act of self-emasculation as the administering of a lethal injection. With exquisite irony the Bill was wrecked in the House of Commons through an alliance of two old devils, Michael Foot MP (Labour) and Enoch Powell MP (Conservative). Miffed that their suicidal plans had been rejected, the Lords re-incarnated themselves, took heart and began making a nuisance of themselves and creating problems for the House of Commons. They defeated the Tory government of Edward Heath (1970-74) twenty-six times and the ensuing Labour government (1974-79) no less than 350 times. Later the Lords sniped at measures put forward by Margaret Thatcher's government (1979-91) and mauled a couple of Bills put forward by John Major's team (1991 to the present day).

Preening themselves in the title of being the only real opposition to Tory government from 1979 to the present day, their Lordships set up their own Study Group in 1986 to discuss their future. Perhaps not surprisingly they gave themselves a clean bill of health. That came as quite a relief to all the other noble Lords, who, desirous of constancy and continuity as they prepared to meet their maker, did not want to be caught up in cantankerous arguments about change. Even Labour peers were happy with the opulence and comfort of London's best club for gentlemen and ladies. For the pensioners amongst them the Lords is a nice little earner, enabling them to draw £31.50 a day in an attendance allowance, £70 for each overnight stay and £30.50 a day for secretarial expenses. Is it any wonder that Labour MPs and Conservative MPs who have devoted their lives selflessly to public service in the House of Commons less selflessly offer themselves up to Prime Ministers for late-in-life peerages? Is it any wonder that Prime Ministers in the House of Commons use their patronage in this sphere ruthlessly, rewarding the back-scratchers, the placemen, the faithful retainers and those for whom the cry "My Party right or wrong, my Prime Minister good or bad" has guided their actions? Thus has the House of Lords become both an annexe of the House of Commons and a greaser's paradise which derives what semblance of sanity it has from some of the more thoughtful cross-benchers who positively disclaim party political allegiances. Remember that the late Harold Wilson said that a week is a long time in politics.

Should the Conservatives win the next General Election things will stay much as they are. Should Labour win, reform is promised in which hereditary peers will lose the right to vote, but in politics there's no such thing as a solemn and binding promise.

Heath comforts himself after twenty-six defeats

PARLIAMENT AND THE CHURCH

The idea that a Church should be under the control of and accept its doctrine from a bunch of atheists, agnostics, fraudsters and many attached to most of the other deadly sins may seem at first to be bizarre. Yet ever since Henry VIII's celebrated divorce and the Reformation which split Western Christendom that has been the position of the Church of England, our Established Church.

It is not just that the Sovereign is the 'Supreme Governor' of the Church of England

Ann Widdecombe ducks out of the Anglican Church

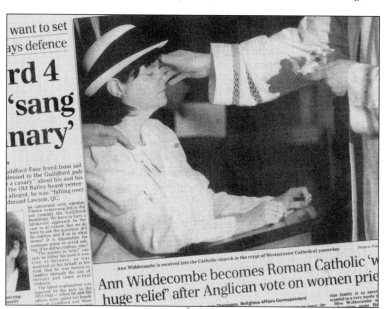

and as such must be in communion with it, and in the Coronation oath promises to uphold "the Protestant reformed religion established by law" and "to maintain and preserve inviolably the settlement of the Church of England, and the doctrine, worship, discipline and government thereof". In fact the Monarch also takes an oath to preserve the Church of Scotland. Queen Elizabeth II took this oath at a meeting of her Privy Council immediately after her accession. The Church of Ireland was disestablished in 1869 and the Church of Wales in 1914.

Godless and Empty

Nor is it simply that bishops of the Church of England sit in the House of Lords as of right, or that the Chaplain to the Speaker of the House of Commons says prayers in the Commons at 2.30 pm Mondays to Thursdays and at 9.30 am on Fridays to a Godless and almost empty Chamber.

No, the real problem is that while the Church of England may proclaim that it holds its commission from Our Lord Himself, since Tudor times it has been under the control in fact of the Crown and then Parliament. Under the Submission of the Clergy Act 1533, before any Canon of the Church of England became law the Crown had to assent. Under the Church of England Assembly (Powers) Act 1919 which set up what is in effect the system today, Parliament has to assent.

For while the law-making body of the

Church of England is the General Synod which is composed of the House of Bishops, the House of Clergy and the House of Laity, Parliament has to approve its laws, either by an Act of Parliament or by both the House of Commons and the House of Lords voting by simple majority for a 'Measure' proposed by the General Synod.

The General Synod cannot enact Canon Law if it conflicts with an Act of Parliament or a Measure sanctioned by Parliament. But whilst a few MPs, mainly on the Conservative side, may be practising Anglicans, most are not. Yet all the other MPs – sleeping members of the Church of England, Baptists, Ulster Presbyterians, Buddhists, evangelical nutters, sceptics and Godless Marxists – have a vote. It is difficult to think of any other self-respecting organisation in the Kingdom which would allow itself to be hijacked in this way.

Accountability

This hijacking clearly was not voluntary at the start but now has the approval of the Church. In July 1994 the General Synod of the Church of England defeated a motion to cut the links between Church and State by 273-110. Rather optimistically the Bishop of Lichfield said: "The Church and State links can enable us to remind politicians that they are accountable, not just to voters, but to God".

The Archbishop of Canterbury wants his Church to remain under the control of Parliament, as does the heir to the throne, Prince Charles. Of course this creates a few problems both for MPs and the Church. As a self-confessed adulterer Prince Charles is surely not the kind of 'Supreme Governor' of the Church which Archbishop Carey would want. After all it was the Archbishop of Canterbury who in October 1994 fulminated against the amoral society, called for firm moral guidelines and spoke of "the enormous pain and damage inherent in .... sexual licence and family break-down". His speech might well have been aimed at the Supreme Governor designate of his own church as well as at all those MPs (referred to in Chapter 13) who approve, or not as the case may be, the laws of his church whilst failing

miserably to live up to them.

Thus in October 1993 MPs met to discuss and vote on the labyrinthine theological arguments on the ordination of women. Ann Widdecombe MP, a clever, opinionated supercilious prig who left the Church of England to become a Roman Catholic simply because of the ordination measure, told the House of Commons: "I believe it is theologically impossible for women to perform the specific role of the sacramental priesthood. If a woman represents Christ as victim and priest at the Holy Communion, there may just as well be a man who represents the Virgin Mary in a nativity play". The 'Measure' to ordain women was approved by 215 votes to twenty-one. Amongst those impertinent enough to vote with the 'Ayes' was the author of this book, who is an atheist; amongst those impertinent enough to vote with the 'Noes' was Rev Ian Paisley, who is a Minister of the Martyrs' Memorial Free Presbyterian Church, Belfast.

Grave Obstacle

Shortly before the vote the Archbishop of Canterbury met the Pope at the Vatican where he was told that the issue of the ordination of women was a "grave obstacle" to reconciliation between the two Churches. MPs, who

Keep women in their place: Ian Paisley votes with the 'Noes'

knew about this, took no notice whatsoever of the Pope's views.

It should not be thought that Parliament always approves Measures put forward by the Church of England. MPs can and do shamelessly exercise their ultimate control. In 1927 a Measure concerning the Prayer Book put forward by the Church of England was rejected by MPs by 247 votes to 205. Similarly the Incumbents (Vocation of Benefices) Measure of 1975 was defeated. In 1984 MPs threw out the Appointments of Bishops Measure. And in 1989 they blocked the Clergy (Ordination) Measure but subsequently agreed to it in 1990. The original rejection of the Measure led to a call by the former Bishop of Aston for the disestablishment of the Church. He argued that Parliament has neither the moral nor theological basis for the vexed question of governing the Church of England today.

Selling Souls

The Church of England also sells its soul to Parliament by allowing the Prime Minister to interfere in the appointments of archbishops and diocesan bishops. The system that has evolved is that the Queen appoints these bishops and archbishops on the advice of the Prime Minister. After much disquiet in the Church and discussions with the then Prime Minister, Jim Callaghan MP, the General Synod of the Church of England set up a Crown Appointments Commission in 1977 to assist the Prime Minister in making his recommendations to the Queen.

So now the Commission, made up of members of the Church of England, agrees two names for nomination to the Prime Minister in the case of these appointments. The Commission can give the two names in order of preference but the Prime Minister retains the right to recommend to the Queen the second name or to ask the Committee for a further name or names. In the case of the appointment of the Archbishop of Canterbury the Commission is chaired by a lay churchman chosen by the Prime Minister. So the Prime Minister, who may be an atheist, sceptic or member of some barmy religion other than the Church of England, has a real element of choice.

It seems that in Britain Parliament leaves its fingerprints, footprints and bodyprints all over the Kingdom of God. For his part God has special representatives from amongst MPs and peers. This despite the fact that less than ten per cent of Britons are churchgoers and the nation is now a healthy mix of ethnic creeds. The Church of England and its precepts, however, officially prevail. These consist of fifteen members of each House of Parliament who sit on what is called the Ecclesiastical Committee. This was established in 1919 and gives advice to Parliament on issues that concern God through the Church of England. The peers are nominated by the Lord Chancellor, the MPs by the Speaker. So there is a direct line from God to the Speaker. One of the members of the Ecclesiastical Committee today is Michael Alison MP who as the Second Church Estates Commissioner in the Commons is God's favourite MP. He answers parliamentary questions on certain Church matters.

Talking to MPs through their House Magazine the Archbishop of Canterbury has blessed all these arrangements, saying:

Our history as a nation is permeated with the Christian religion, which is also reflected in much of our art, literature and architecture. Many things which characterise the established nature of the Church go back much further than Henry VIII's break with Rome. That break itself was not simply to do with a divorce. It was also the culmination of the desire of the people of this country for a Church which more accurately reflected their national character... My feeling is that our sense of national identity would be weakened more grievously than many people realise if the rich fabric in which religion and society are woven together in so much of our national life were to be unravelled.

Some say that "Arch", as one of the characters in David Hare's play *Racing Demons* called Dr Carey, means what he says but in the Church of England you can never be sure.

THE ROAD TO WESTMINSTER

It must be obvious from what you have read so far that the power which MPs in the House of Commons wield is astonishing because it is limitless, in theory at least. They, we, are more important than the Queen, more important than the Lords of the Realm, more important even than God in as far as his views are expressed through the Church of England. MPs rule, OK. They, we, have it in our power to decide on the future of the monarchy, to determine whether to abolish or reform the House of Lords, to define right and wrong and dictate the morals of the nation.

If you feel you can cope with these responsibilities and much more besides and if you would like to treat with monarchs, dukes, barons, bishops and the other 650 rulers of Britain elected to the House of Commons, then politics is for you. And if politics is for you your first goal should be to become an MP. After that it should not be difficult for you to work your way through the system. Be warned though. With experience will come understanding; with understanding will come power and with power will come the knowledge that things are not always as they seem.

Political Parties

To become an MP the first thing you must do is join a political party. And because you want to become a big league player this means becoming a card-carrying, paid up member of either the Conservative or Labour Party. You can see the first problem immediately – which one? Obviously before making your choice you will want to know something about the history and practices of British political parties. In order that you do not waste time cluttering your brain with an excess of detail, the following paragraphs will set out everything you need to know as well as enabling you to answer that all-important question. You would be well advised to memorise them. It is politics for all seasons and every occasion.

In the beginning God and the established order ruled Britain through the Tories – the name started out as an abusive term for politicians of the Church of England who opposed Catholics and non-conformists alike, who were regarded as outlaws and bandits, fit only to live in Ireland. Then along came the Whigs, composed in the main of corrupt, aristocratic families who nevertheless thought that there were limits to oppression. In the nineteenth century Tories stood for Queen, Country and Empire, law and order, custom and continuity, while Liberals who made common cause with Whigs laid claim to doctrines of enlightened progress, what we now call civil liberties, and the laissez-faire standards of the classical economists, particularly that of free-trade. A virus born of the industrial revolution and spread throughout the country by democracy killed off the Liberals. The twentieth century saw the rise of the Labour Party, led by an unholy alliance of Methodists, revolutionaries and utopians, who told working-class people what was in their best interest. The important thing in all this history for the aspiring MP to remember is that it means that today, the middle-aged female flower arranger in the church at Penton Mawsey, a village in Hampshire, is likely to vote Tory, whereas a coal miner in Barnsley inclines to Labour.

Castrating the Wets

In the 1980s Margaret Thatcher, the Prime Minister, muddied the philosophical waters when she decided to castrate the one-nation members of her Cabinet, whom she derided as "wets", and then embarked, with evangelical zeal (and shamelessly stealing the clothes of eighteenth-century Liberals), on a crusade to turn Britain into an enterprising, cut-throat, competitive country. In seeking to change the world, its driving political ideology and everything in it, Margaret Thatcher used every weapon at her disposal, including her favourite handbag. Waving it under the noses of her Cabinet colleagues she sneered "I'm the only man amongst you lot", though as one of her colleagues pointed out she was not averse

to using feminine wiles: "a few tears, the odd tantrum, then a bit of coquetry". In the end, traitors in her Cabinet cheerfully cut her throat. Her successor, John Major, although elected to carry on with her enterprise, tried to temper her philosophy by denying the truth of her assertion that society does not exist. He argued that what society needed above all else was more lavatories on motorways. This became known as the Big Idea, the politicians' equivalent of the philosophers' stone.

However, the success of the Thatcher revolution shook the very foundations of the Labour Party. It showed that if Labour MPs ever wanted power for themselves again they had to change their ways. Political analysts made it clear that no belief was too sacred to be jettisoned. Spin doctors, ad men and media consultants were brought in to explain how changing one's mind was both therapeutic and a sign of maturity. Puppies and yuppies from the world of communications ordered Labour MPs to re-invent themselves.

A woman called Barbara Follett, the wife of a best-selling novelist (known in the trade as Ken Wallet), introduced members of Labour's Shadow Cabinet to double-breasted suits, shirts with collars and a slap of make-up. New words and phrases entered the language, like 'folletting' and 'to be folletted', that is to say 'to know how to dress, speak and act'. 'Socialist' became a proscribed word in Labour's lexicon, except for use by the new Leader of the Labour Party, Tony Blair MP, when its meaning would be lost in his smile. Dissidents were at first comforted, then mocked and finally, as a result of the behind-the-scenes machinations of Labour's media manipulators, characterised as irresponsibly non-conformist and pushed into the margins of politics.

As the differences between Labour and the Tories became blurred Labour MPs, facing a crisis of identity, began asking the Tony Hancock questions – Where am I? What does it all mean? Where am I going? In order to dissuade them from following the example of Tony Hancock and committing suicide, Tony Blair is thinking of setting up a 'Policy Hotline' which Labour MPs can ring at any time of the

day or night so they can know what it is that for the time being they are supposed to believe in passionately. Cynics in the Shadow Cabinet say that the most frequent user of the hotline is likely to be Tony Blair himself.

Whether or not the 'Hotline' is ever installed, Tony Blair has already seen to it that Labour has now joined the Tories as the party of the fast buck. The What's In It For Me Party, indeed. In 1994 the Labour Party joined forces with Littlewoods Pools and every member was sent a Standing Forecast for "The Quick 'n' Easy Way for your chance to win OVER £2 Million". An advertisement in the official Labour Party magazine told party members how it worked. "Simple. The Labour Party will receive at least twelve per cent of the stake money from your entry PLUS ALL SUBSE-QUENT RENEWALS. This offer applies only to entries which begin with the special coupon provided featuring Labour's 'Red Rose' symbol." This attempt to fund the Labour Party, whose roots lie in Methodism and Christianity, through a gambling organisation surely takes it part of the way down the road to Hell.

So there it is. The barriers between Conservatives and Labour are now like Chinese walls – so invisible they may not even exist. Of course as the parties move closer together so the rhetoric that proclaims the differences between them becomes louder. This is what political analysts call the theory of inverse rhetoric – politicians shrieking more and more about less and less. Should you wish to explain all this to your gobsmacked friends in fashionable political jargon, just say that politics is no longer about competing ideologies but about elites competing and hungry for power. Perhaps they'll be impressed.

However, in many ways these changes make it easier for a would-be MP to decide which political party he or she should join. No longer is it necessary to worry about complicated issues of conscience, philosophy or conflicting views. The need now when someone knocks on your door and asks you to join a political party is simply to work out which of the two parties is likely to be in power when you yourself will be in your prime. Thus the ability to predict election results accurately is now far more important than faith for a new recruit to a political party. If as a new recruit your predictive powers in this field are not good, don't worry – you can always decide the issue by the toss of a coin.

Qualities Needed by an Aspiring Candidate

"What do I do if I am an idealist" you may ask. Quite frankly if that is your problem then politics is definitely not for you. The Church maybe, a social worker possibly, but not politics. The art of government is to keep the show on the road. The government in a complex, modern technological society like ours cannot be expected to cope with whingers, dreamers, people who want to change things, shakers and movers or, unholy of unholies, those who believe that when they leave this world it will be a better place than when they entered it, thanks to their efforts.

Opinion polls show that the public sees the typical MP as being remote, irrelevant, ineffectual, selfish, over-ambitious and on the make. So if you do not want to look out of place in the House of Commons you must at least pretend to have some of these attributes. If they come naturally, better still. Certainly if you do not have a large house and a comfortable life-style with a bit of bombast people will wonder what is wrong with you. So as an aspiring candidate you should be prepared to conform to these nostrums.

Becoming a Candidate: Preliminaries

To become a member of the Conservative Party you will be asked to pay your local Association a contribution of £20 a year, a figure recommended by the bosses at Conservative Central Office in Smith Square, London. If, however, you were to round the sum up to, say, £100 when you sign on then your generosity and enterprise will not go unnoticed so that when, eventually, you express an interest in becoming an MP, you may well be fast-streamed. Thereafter make yourself useful. Go to barbecues and fetes set in the grounds of the country mansions of leading figures, pay over the odds for raffle tickets, donate prizes and above all attend morning service on Sundays, preferably as a member of the Church of England. If you are Jewish this could prove awkward but just think – Disraeli got past all the barriers put in his way by Anglicans. In church, put notes rather than coins in the collection. If you are young, borrow off Mumsy. Remember that every penny you spend now will help to guarantee you a handsome real rate of return on your outlay in future, not just in your salary and expenses as an MP, but by having business put your way and through company directorships later in life. If you are super-rich make your money do the work and speak loudly for you.

The subscription for becoming a member of the Labour Party is £18, renewable annually with a reduced fee for pensioners and non-earners of £5. On no account offer to pay over the odds or you will be accused of bribery, brownnosing and God knows what else. Labour's HQ in Walworth Road will send out endless demands for money and if you can afford it by all means contribute, but expect snide looks and comments rather than favours if you do. At all stages of your career in the Labour Party before you become an MP (that is, when your constituents will have expectations of you), you must not merely live and act as though you are ordinary but must have proof which you can express in emotionally moving terms of your working-class roots and the grinding poverty of your youth, or if that manifestly did not exist, the grinding poverty of one of your forebears.

If you are middle-class like Tony Blair then you have to invent working-class roots. Despite the fact that Blair looks like a London barrister, sounds like a London barrister and is a London barrister, lives in London and sends his children to independent Roman Catholic schools in London, none of this appears in his Curriculum Vitae or in his *Who's Who* entry. There he gives his address as Myrobella, Trimdon Station, Co Durham and his clubs as the Trimdon Village Working Men's Club and the Fishburn Working Men's Club. Thus does a member of the Islington chattering classes educated at Fettes College, a public school in Edinburgh, and St John's College, Oxford, become a man steeped in the sweat of the people of the North East of England. Mr Blair is ironically, or perhaps appropriately, married to the daughter of the actor Antony Booth who played the 'scouse git' son-in-law of TV's Alf Garnett. To this end, if you have a double-barrelled name then change it. Anthony Wedgwood Benn MP, formerly Viscount Stansgate, whom Michael Foot MP used to call "Wedgy" in the days before they came to hate each other, showed the way when he changed his name to plain Tony Benn.

Before you attempt to become a candidate offer to do some of the chores in your local party, preferably those which will eventually bring you an office of distinction for your CV. In both parties you should go for the job that nobody wants, i.e. that of Membership Secretary which involves persuading other people to bang on doors, make new recruits, and in the case of the Labour Party, argue with HQ which has a central list about who is and who is not a member locally. These days the job of Membership Secretary is a thankless task precisely because political parties are organisations fast running out of members. The Conservative Party which had 2.8 million members in 1953 is facing the prospect of under 100,000 by the end of the century.

The average age of your membership will be an alarming sixty-two, and only five per cent will be under the age of thirty-five. If you can recruit youngsters, boisterous without being yobbish, flirtatious but controlled in their sexual appetites, you will be exalted like the man who made loaves and fishes multiply. Because lots of potential new recruits are put off by the party's super, super-rich image, HQ will be grateful if you could place emphasis on the ordinariness of your members. Now there's a challenge and possibly a contradiction in terms. The world will be your oyster.

In the Labour Party you will find life difficult too as Membership Secretary, but again success will be rewarded. According to the votes read out at Labour's Annual Conference there seem to be something in excess of five million members. In fact there are just 300,000 individual members. The rest are fantasies which occupy the minds of Trade Union bosses. Labour has a lot of pensioners and members of interest groups of every kind – the Child Poverty Action Group, the Low Pay Unit, CND, the Badger Defence Union, Liberty, Amnesty, etc, etc – but very few ordinary members. In most constituency Labour parties you can become a Branch Secretary within weeks; in some you may be offered the job at your first meeting. Do not under any circumstances refuse.

You should beware of becoming the Treasurer of your local party or having anything to do with finance. Because political parties have no members they have no subscriptions. Yet they need lots of money to survive. A General Election may come round only once every five years but it can cost a political party anything between £6 million and £20 million. So the parties have to dig around for money.

More than a fair share of money for the Labour Party comes from trade unions whose members pay a political levy. Some trade unionists expect their political levy to go to the Labour Party; others believe that it should be used for political campaigning which suits their special needs.

Local constituency Labour parties often rely on sponsorship money given to their MPs by trade unions. Although under what is called the 'Hastings Agreement' the money does not go into the pocket of the MP but into the coffers of the local party, its very existence can encourage Labour MPs to support their trade union, right or wrong, and temper their real views on various issues. One MP, Ann Clwyd, recently lost her sponsorship by the TGWU because she disagreed with the Union's view on party democracy. Why Ms Clwyd should have thought that she could ignore the rule that he who pays the piper calls the tune baffled most MPs.

Labour also organises fund-raising dinners at up to £500 a head. Perhaps not surprisingly, these are not attended by old age pensioners or single parents but by members of the trendy metropolitan chattering classes anxious to press the flesh of Labour leaders. Most of these people could probably find better uses for £500 than to spend it on an indifferent meal in the West End, attended in the main by affluent no-hopers. Mega-crook Robert Maxwell also gave money to the Labour Party, which belatedly it returned.

The Conservative Party raises substantial funds from commercial and industrial companies. Controversy has arisen, however, because although these donations have to be declared in companies' accounts, shareholders are never asked beforehand if they want to make them. More controversy was aroused when it was revealed that both companies and individuals were channelling money into the Conservative Party through off-shore bank accounts. It emerged that rich foreigners, some of whom had never lived in Britain and would never live in Britain and who were not eligible to vote in British elections, were funding the Conservative Party.

Confirmation came that the Greek shipping billionaire, John Latsis, a supporter of the infamous Colonels who ruled Greece between 1967 and 1974, had given £2 million to Conservative Party funds; that a fugitive from

British justice, Asil Nadir (now basking in the Cyprus sun of his youth), gave the party nine cheques for £440,000 between 1985 and 1991 and later assumed that this would enable him to get criminal charges dropped against him; Li-Ka-shing, Asia's richest man, and C H Tong, whose father bought the liner Queen Elizabeth, provided funds; and so did Octar Botnar, former chairman of Nissan UK, who resided in Switzerland and was wanted for questioning by the Inland Revenue over a £97 million tax fraud.

On the basis that there is no such thing as a free lunch, why were these donations made? Should people without the vote be allowed to influence the result of elections in Britain? If the money is being given for some expected economic gain should that be allowed to override the rights of citizenship? Happily, in 1992 Prime Minister John Major assured prominent Asian businessmen, many of whom were Conservative Party donors, that he did not intend to change tax rules to their disadvantage and bring Britain on a par with the United States by taxing them on income earned abroad. Phew! Now this kind of reciprocity – donations for tax relief – really does make sense. It's grease like this which keeps the world going round.

The Conservative Candidate

After you have worked yourself silly filling in and addressing envelopes, delivering leaflets, canvassing and acting as a dogsbody for the existing candidate or sitting MP, you should go for the job. If you are a Conservative this means getting onto the 'Candidates List' held at HQ, Smith Square. The whole process is overseen by the Vice-Chairman of the Conservative Party, sometimes an MP and who may be a woman, who combines the qualities of an MI5 agent searching out your past misdeeds which could damage the party, a seductive charmer and a Rottweiler in pain. His decision is final. So before you see him find out everything you can, likes and dislikes, strengths and weaknesses and his position in the political spectrum, including his or her relationship to the Prime Minister or, if the Conservatives are in opposition, the Leader of the party. However, before you get to see the Vice-Chairman you will have to fill in a form telling all about your past life, being economical with the truth where it helps.

Unless you are insane or bankrupt you will then have an interview with the area agent before you lay bare your soul to the Vice-Chairman. Above all else he needs to be reassured that you are, or have the potential to be, a good family man with a proven track record at work. Stockbrokers, insurance salesmen, estate agents and barristers need have no worries these days, just as landowners, farmers and captains of industry had no worries in the past. He also needs to reassure himself that you believe in low inflation, the enterprise culture, law and order, the defence of the realm, and individual responsibility.

If by accident you are a woman then you've got problems. Currently there are only twenty women Conservative MPs and many Conservative Associations still see a woman's role as that of helping her man. Unlike the

Labour Party which has plans to ensure that half of all their MPs are women within ten years, the Conservatives abhor positive discrimination and believe in selection by ability.

So here you are at the last hurdle, the Candidates' selection weekend, a truly forbidding experience which uses the methods of recruitment to the higher echelons of the Civil Service and those through which the Army selects its officers. It's a combination of psychological profiling, role playing, group discussions, mock debating and social undressing. For men Armani suits, tweeds and a dinner jacket are essential; women have to go with the soberest fashions of the day. Obviously the whole process is geared to putting extroverts, intelligent yobs and those whom Prime Ministers refer to as bastards on the Candidates List.

Now when an MP retires or a by-election comes up you can apply to the local Conservative Association to be considered. A baptism of fire in a safe Labour seat such as Islwyn in Wales, Glasgow Pollok or Tottenham is your first step. There will not be much competition and the Selection Committee will invite you to make a short speech followed by questions. Another interview for both you and your lovely lady wife may follow, and of course you will have to address the whole Association.

In a safe Labour seat the qualities of your spouse or fiancee for the day may not matter so much, but in a marginal or safe Conservative seat the squirearchy, old ladies in large hats, blimps and a few cocky young men may give your partner a torrid time, mentally undressing her and dabbling in the very stuff of her soul. In a safe seat you may face 400 or more rivals but most of them will be living beyond their ability.

The important thing to remember is that activists from Conservative Associations in rural areas can be primitive, primordial even, when it comes to certain sections of humanity – the unemployed who have failed to get on their bikes, scroungers in queues in post offices who look fit to work, criminals who should be scourged, birched, caned, locked away for ever or hanged, social workers, gays, lesbians and single parents.

So bear in mind that the success of Michael Howard MP, Peter Lilley MP and John Redwood MP in damning, leering and sneering at these people is not based on personal prejudice but on an in-depth research of the psychology of their audiences. Get the nuances right at your selection conference and the response will be electric, even if your voice reminds people of some of the sillier vicars. Even before you are elected the faithful will be talking about you as a future member of a Conservative Cabinet.

The Labour Candidate

Advancement in the Labour Party used to depend heavily on one's ability to perform in the halls – not dance halls but draughty Methodist halls where most Labour Party meetings take place. If these do not exist in your constituency then most likely you will meet and seek to curry favour in the classrooms of local primary schools with tiny seats, in cavernous rooms above pubs, in tenants' halls and in other places where the conditions are uncomfortable and inhospitable enough to discourage all but the most ambitious. Very few constituencies own large Victorian buildings with a bar which undercuts every pub for miles around, like Hackney South & Shoreditch. Fewer still are like Norwich which has comfortable premises which speak almost of modernism.

Getting on one of the two central lists of candidates – an 'A' list for sponsored candidates and a 'B' list for others – kept by HQ at Walworth Road is a much easier affair in the Labour Party than getting on the Candidates List in the Conservative Party. Providing you do not have a very bad criminal record, can read and write and support the aims and objectives of the Labour Party (since nobody knows what they are any more this is no bother these days), you should experience no difficulty. Of course some people who do not meet even these limited qualifications slip through the net.

One such was John Prescott, now an MP and Deputy Leader of the Labour Party. It is difficult to see how Prescott passed the literacy test. On his own admission he cannot write joined-up sentences, do joined-up speech or put together joined-up thoughts. I've had wonderful conversations with him in the tea-room of the House of Commons without understanding a word of what he was saying.

John Prescott's wonderfully idiosyncratic use of the English language was beautifully illustrated in a speech he made on 26 February 1995 to a conference at London University when he said: "London beat the racists in Tower Hamlets and the rest of the party proud of you doing it were and we much talk about outside the rest of London.... Let us say something to the unemployed, yes you are after full employment years and we can go back forward now back to full employment."

Labour constituencies are divided up into Branches which coincide with local government Ward boundaries. After you have been in the party two years you get your Branch to nominate you for the 'B' list candidates. This will be done automatically – no interviews, no fuss. The Branch then passes the nomination to the

"We can go back forward now back to full employment." John Prescott makes himself clear

General Committee of the constituency party which is made up of delegates from Branches. You would need to be desperately unpopular to be asked to come to an interview before they passed your name on to Walworth Road. Even though there is a thought police at Walworth Road, its members are too busy expelling fundamentalists to bother about the names on the 'B' list so your application is rubber stamped. And that's it.

Now when a vacancy arises you write to the Secretary of that constituency party with your CV expressing an interest, and she (it tends to be a woman because men shy away from time-consuming, unsung jobs) will distribute it to local Branches as well as to a number of organisations affiliated to the local constituency party such as the Fabians, the Socialist Education Association and trade unions. If they like the look of you they will invite you to a meeting along with other candidates, for an interview and session of questions. At the end of it they will almost certainly nominate one of you to the General Committee as their choice of a candidate.

The General Committee will draw up a shortlist of up to six people, from all the nominations received from Branches and affiliated organisations, and call a huge meeting of all members of the local party where each of the six of you will speak and answer questions. Any member who cannot get to the hustings meeting can, if he or she wishes, vote by post. If perchance you want to knock out a sitting MP the procedures are nasty, complicated and designed to frustrate you. Better forget that unless you have the cunning and stamina of Machiavelli, and a hide like a rhinoceros.

If you are a Machiavelli and solvent, it is possible under the new rules of one person one vote and postal ballots to buy a constituency. Of course you must not get caught, like the group that in 1994 wanted to rid Manchester Gorton of Gerald Kaufman as their MP and replace him with a sympathetic Asian candidate. After a court case they lost. Kaufman won. Basically the plan of the plotters was to get a rich sponsor to put up some £5,000 and pay to sign on 200 or 300 new members, enough to win any constituency ballot. They might have got away with it if they had adhered to the following rules:

1 *Do not sign on as party members people who do not exist*
2 *Only sign on people who live in the constituency*
3 *Forget the dead*
4 *Sign them on well in advance of the re-selection*
5 *Sign on the new members in dribs and drabs. The sudden appearance of 100 new members in a Branch whose existing total is forty raises suspicions*
6 *Don't sign the cheque for the membership subscription yourself*
7 *Don't do it in Gerald Kaufman's constituency. Not for nothing did "Spitting Image" project him as a determined, ruthless 'psychotic' behind bars from the film "Silence of the Lambs"*

Until Tony Blair told the Labour Party that he had no objection to people becoming wealthy it was a positive advantage for a candidate to be poor. Now you have to look as though you are capable of doing a job. If you are a woman you have to be into power-dressing and if you are a man you have to be able to afford at least one double-breasted suit. Drabbies, that is social workers in anoraks and housing officers with chips on their shoulders who dress down and talk miserably, will find it difficult in Blair's slick, modern party to become a candidate. Ironically, if you are going to win the nomination you will need the votes of drabbies, who in some seats may constitute ten per cent of the voters. So be nice to them and ignore their ghastly footwear.

To have served an apprenticeship as a councillor is a distinct advantage. As a Labour councillor you will have spent a lot of your time engaged in hideous machinations, nasty deals and trade-offs, stabbing your colleagues in the chest and pulling knives out of your back. Party members will therefore know that you've got what it takes to be an MP.

Obviously, though, a councillor in Hackney wanting to become an MP should apply for a seat in Newham, Haringey or Islington and a councillor in the Cynon Valley should apply for a seat in Merthyr, the Rhondda or Cardiff. In their local areas all their personal vices and their public humiliations will be known to the host of ambitious shits opposed to them who laughingly call themselves colleagues. However, seeking a seat in a constituency where your grandfather's gravestone is not in the cemetery or where there is no mill or mine where he once toiled, where you were not born and bred and in which you do not now live, is a high-risk strategy in the Labour Party.

So parochial are many constituencies, particularly in the North (and the position is getting worse), that they would prefer someone who is thick and local to someone who is intelligent and lives on the other side of the valley. In Scotland different considerations apply. There you should be at least sixteen stone in weight with a cholesterol stomach, call yourself "Jimmy" and be unemployable if you want to win. For although Labour's Leader Tony Blair is an Anglo-Scot, no constituency north of the border has yet even tried to understand what his 'modernising vision', whatever that might be, is about.

The General Election Campaign

Only one person can run the election campaign and it's not you. It's your agent. For three weeks he is your God and you would be a fool to question any of his or her decisions. If he or she tells you to get into a tracksuit and go to the local park ("Brian first out of the starting blocks"), for a photocall then you do it. Even if you are an atheist and he or she tells you to pray at the Catholic church, join evangelical hot gospellers in shrieking Hallelujah or kneel down before Mohamed, then you do it. If he or she sends you up a fireman's ladder moving ever higher in the sky towards eternity then you do it.

You have to accept that however hard you flog yourself canvassing, pressing the flesh, speaking to small groups, visiting schools, hospitals and old people's homes, using the loud hailer in street markets, issuing press releases, nothing you do is likely to affect the result. If you are a student of psychology then you will know that even if you did nothing at all the result would be the same. Even a sitting MP with four election victories behind him is kidding himself if he or she thinks they have a large personal following. If they're honest they will know that their persona is worth no more than 500 votes. As a new candidate your persona is worth nothing at all.

What may matter in a marginal seat is the number of canvassers who work for you during the campaign. And in a sense that is your only real job, to get as many people out on the knocker canvassing for you as possible. Evidence from the General Election in 1992 suggested that having lots of helpers canvassing over the telephone is highly productive. This enables your team to contact all those people who will not open their doors to strangers. It also enables canvassers in inner-city areas to avoid the snarling teeth of savage dogs which

all too many people, afraid of burglars, keep.

Two academic studies show that in the 1992 General Election the Labour Party had more canvassers, about 160,000, nation-wide than the Conservatives, approximately 140,000. This was one of the main reasons why Labour achieved a larger swing in many of the key marginal constituencies in that election. So ingratiate yourself with canvassers and knockers-up on the day; suck up to community leaders who might encourage some of their members to work for you; and although it is illegal for the candidate to treat people during election campaigns, buy drinks fast and furiously for all and sundry.

In an average constituency with 60,000 to 70,000 voters you will have some £7,000 to spend. In a safe seat this is ample. In a marginal seat it is quite inadequate to pay for all the leaflets, election addresses, posters, stickers, balloons, hired halls and rooms, cars, jazz bands and all the other paraphernalia you need. So although exceeding your limit is a serious electoral offence that could disqualify you if you win, you have to cheat in a marginal seat. There is no alternative. You and your agent are responsible for your electoral returns setting out your expenditure. Let your agent do the cheating and the creative accounting.

He will be an expert at it. For example, he or she knows the friendly printer who will make out invoices which bill you for less than you actually pay. He or she will know how to hide the cost of the professional agents which HQ sends down to help you; how to put the police off the scent if they start an enquiry when your ungracious political opponent reports you. If your conscience pricks you, remember this is big league stuff, the first battle for the control of Britain, the outcome of which will determine not only your future but the future of two political elites who have only one purpose in life – the pursuit of ultimate power. At a General Election a political party has no time for those with scruples or wimps liable to wet their pants or knickers with fear.

You must expect to hate every minute of the campaign. Your stomach will be turning over however seasoned a campaigner you are, whilst your body will test itself to the limits of destruction. If you get six hours' sleep a night you are not working hard enough. Every day someone from amongst your political opponents will tell you, often to your face, that you've lost your marbles. When they do so you must smile sweetly as though you mean it and thank them for listening so carefully to your arguments. At the end of each merciless day, if you are a Conservative go off for a few tinctures or glasses of wine with your supporters, and if you are a Labour candidate anaesthetise yourself from the horror in a pub.

At the Count on election day when it is all over and miraculously you have been elected one of the 651 rulers of Britain and are just a day away from joining Britain's most exclusive club, be generous in victory and tell everyone present that you enjoyed every minute of the fairest and best-conducted campaign in which you have ever participated. Only Tony Benn, who is calling for annual elections to Parliament and has absolutely no concern for the sanity of politicians, will be able to say that he enjoyed the campaign without lying through his teeth. Anyway, congratulations!

The By-Election Campaign

If in a General Election nobody notices the candidate as all eyes are glued to the TV and what the party leaders say, the same is not true of a by-election. For a start, if you are a member of the governing party there is no such thing as a safe seat. Moreover, such is the decency and sense of fair play of the British people that in by-elections Liberals are often allowed to win seats normally held by the Conservatives with huge majorities. In by-elections the candidate does matter, so much so that in the Labour Party the shortlist is drawn up not by the local party but by the National Executive Committee, i.e. top people from HQ. This change came about when local parties in London put forward candidates for by-elections who attracted the label 'loony left' and for whom the excitement of dreaming about the revolution was more important than winning.

The only candidate to enjoy a by-election: Lord Sutch at the hustings

In short, they put forward Third Division players, boys and girls guaranteed to lose rather than men and women from the Premier Division calculated to win.

In a by-election the candidates are subjected to intense national scrutiny. Their past lives are picked over in minute detail and every millimetre of their flesh is examined like buzzards finishing off their prey. Top journalists are sent down from London to laugh at them, humiliate and then destroy them. Their friends are paid to rat on them. Police records are checked; past relationships exposed; hot pokers are pushed in their eyes. MPs will descend on the constituency like locusts.

The party machines will run the campaign using high-tech electronic gadgetry. Each candidate will be assigned a minder who will be a sitting MP. Although the minder will deflect hostile questions, hold the candidate's hand and, if the minder is Frank Dobson MP, try to get the candidate happy with his stream of risqué jokes, it's a nightmare for an accomplished politician and unbearably cruel for anyone else. Currently, if you are a prospective Conservative candidate, better to have your balls cut off than put yourself forward for a by-election. If you are a dim-witted Liberal or a Labour hopeful go ahead but it will hurt, whatever the result.

THE MAKE-UP OF THE HOUSE OF COMMONS

So now you are one of the rulers of Britain. As such your chest will naturally swell with pride when you first step into New Palace Yard, walk past the policeman into the Members' Entrance, climb the stairs, stroll past marble busts of Randolph Spencer-Churchill and William Henry Smith, enter the Members' Lobby which is guarded by statues of Winston Churchill and David Lloyd George, two great warriors of modern politics, and then get your first glimpse of the Chamber of the House of Commons where you may become a nobody, or alternatively, and with just a little application, part of the remembered history of Britain. If you want to get to the top you cannot start too soon.

In the early days if you are pushy your fellow MPs will criticise you, mostly behind your back. However, if you are not pushy no one will think the more of you. The truth is that right from the start you have to be pushy, you must be ambitious and you must let your colleagues know that you can perform and are a person to be reckoned with. Always bear in mind the two cardinal axioms of parliamentary life. The first is that politics is a struggle. The second is that those who advance the furthest are those who select themselves.

In the Conservative Party it is important from the outset that you show that you are officer class and not a member of the other ranks. In the Labour Party you must, these days, show that you belong to the managerial class and that you are a master of the manipulative arts,

able to suggest that you could be awkward but would like to be compliant. It helps if you can find yourself a patron, someone of Ministerial rank or, if you are in opposition, of Ministerial calibre with whose views you are broadly in agreement or whose life-style makes you feel comfortable. Be prepared to suck up to your patron. Defend him or her in the tea-room, praise him or her every time he or she makes a speech, asks a question or intervenes in a debate, however feeble the performance. Never outshine your patron. Study your colleagues well and remember that every one of them is a competitor, a potential enemy.

Gentlemanly Daggers

As a Conservative MP you can expect your colleagues to thrust daggers in your back in the time-honoured gentlemanly fashion. As a Labour MP be prepared for your colleagues to stab you in the front. Ironically, Conservative MPs are a collective bunch where the men do what their leaders tell them. Even when Conservative MPs are involved in huge internal rows in public they seem to have an ability to regroup and get back into good order quickly. The survival instinct comes naturally to them. Labour MPs on the other hand form a collection of untamed ambitious individuals, too many of whom do not even realise what they are doing when they press the self-destruct button. The great goal towards which the Parliamentary Labour Party has been moving in the past fifteen years is the repudiation of its reputation as the last bastion of individualism in British society.

If all this sounds a bit daunting do not let it get you down. Without a super-ego you would not be where you are as a ruler of Britain. Polish and burnish that ego. As for talent, it helps but is not essential. After all John Major, the Prime Minister, and Tony Blair, the Leader of the Opposition, hardly merit comparison with Disraeli and Gladstone. In an age of political mediocrity everyone, including the men from nowhere, have a chance of making it to the top. If you are a good-looking woman you can take heart too. Look, for example, at Virginia Bottomley MP, a member of the Cabinet, and Harriet Harman MP, a member of the Shadow Cabinet. Although it is a terrible thing to say, if they had been less well-favoured physically by God it is doubtful if either of them would even become a PUSSY, i.e. a Parliamentary Under Secretary of State, the lowest rung on the Ministerial ladder. On the other hand, Margaret Beckett, who is not con-ventionally good looking is exceptionally able. Could it be that her challenge for party leadership was hindered by her lack of glamour?

Background of MPs

You would be well advised to make a mental note of the names, occupations, social background and political leanings of the other 650 MPs. They feel insulted if not instantly recognised.

The election proved to be an expensive business for the Natural Law Party who lost 309 deposits (£154,500) and the Greens who lost 253 deposits (£126,500); less for Labour who lost one deposit (£500) and the Conservatives who lost four deposits (£2,000). Candidates lose their deposits if they get less than five per cent of the total votes cast.

John Major had the largest Conservative majority, getting 36,230 more than his nearest rival in Huntingdon, while Walter Sweeney MP had the smallest Conservative majority of just seventeen in the Vale of Glamorgan. Llewellyn Smith MP had the largest Labour majority of 30,067 in Blaenau Gwent, while Janet Anderson MP had the smallest Labour majority of 120 in Rossendale and Darwen.

The two 'golden oldies' in Parliament are Edward Heath MP (born 1916) and Sir Trevor Skeet MP (born 1918), both of them Conservatives. The five oldest Labour MPs, all born in 1923, are Andrew Faulds, Mildred Gordon, Eddie Loyden, Stan Orme and Robert Sheldon. The babies of the House of Commons, born in the 1960s in the age of pot and flower power in their mothers' milk, are ten in number, six of them Conservatives, two Labour and two Liberal Democrat – Harold Elletson, Michael Bates, Matthew Banks, David Fabour, Liam Fox, William Hague, Gregory Pope, Angela Eagle, Nick Harvey and Matthew Taylor.

Educational Background

If you are a Conservative the whole point of sending your children to public school and to Oxford and Cambridge is that there they will

POLITICAL AFFILIATIONS OF MPS 1992 ELECTION		
	VOTES	**MPS ELECTED**
Conservative	14,100,000	336
Labour	11,600,000	271
Lib-Dems	6,000,000	20
Ulster Unionist	271,000	9
Plaid Cymru	156,000	4
SDLP	184,000	4
Scottish Nationalist	629,000	3
Democratic Unionist	103,000	3
Popular Unionist	19,000	1
	33,062,000	651

meet a high proportion of tomorrow's rulers of Britain as well as the bulk of those who in later life will be rewarded as the richest movers and shakers of our society. Just under two-thirds of all Conservative MPs (208 of them in all) went to public schools and a third attended Oxford and Cambridge colleges. The most favoured public school amongst Conservatives is still Eton, with no less than thirty-two Conservative MPs having been educated there. Only two of the forty Labour MPs who went to public schools attended Eton – Mark Fisher MP, the son of a Tory MP, and Tam Dalyell MP. In fact the House of Commons is proof indeed of Tam Dalyell's aphorism that Eton educates people beyond their ability. Some would argue, however, that at times of crisis it is a comfort to know that we are ruled by those who have not only besported themselves on the playing fields of Eton but who also know the words of the school's boating song. Of the other Labour MPs, 166 of them were educated at universities but only forty-four at Oxford or Cambridge.

Occupations

If you are a Conservative MP then the chances are that the first person you bump into will be oleaginous and arrogant, i.e. a lawyer. No less than thirty-nine Conservative MPs are barristers and another twenty-one are solicitors. Seventy-five Conservative MPs claim to be "company executives", but in reality most of them are low-grade managers of their own little companies, insurance salesmen, estate

agents and the like. And so it is with most of the thirty-seven who call themselves "company directors". Ten Conservative MPs are "farmers" while six refer to themselves as "housewives". None of the latter seem to have hands which suggest that they do the washing-up. Labour's biggest block consists of skilled manual workers – forty-three in number. It's best to defer to these people, some of them built like granite, a lot of them now going to seed as the good life gets to them, because conventional Labour mythology has it that these are the only real jobs that exist or ever have existed. The other large Labour block consists of thirty-eight school-teachers, most of them with blinkered vision. There are also a lot of Polytechnic Marxists (twenty four), now ashamed of their earlier political leanings.

Knowing an MP's previous occupation is useful because it often provides clues as to the whereabouts of the MP when he or she cannot be found at their place of work in Parliament. This situation arises because a number of MPs carry on with their old job when they enter Parliament. Obviously two incomes are better than one. Some people think that being an MP is a full-time job and that those MPs who earn more from a second job – it's called moonlighting in the world away from Parliament – are not just being greedy but are practising a fraud on the public. The easy retort to this is that having another job enables MPs to keep in touch with the real world and makes them better able to serve their constituents. Besides,

OCCUPATIONS OF MPS			
	Conservatives	**Labour**	**Liberal**
Professions	131	115	12
Business	128	22	2
Manual Workers	4	59	0
Miscellaneous	73	75	6
TOTAL	336	271	20

some MPs have better life-styles than others or more demanding spouses to keep.

Anyway, stockbrokers like Sir Peter Tapsell excuse themselves from time to time to do their work in the City. Then there are the practising barristers like Sir Ivan Lawrence MP and Paul Boateng MP. Twice in recent years Sir Ivan has, without any suggestion of breach of duty, absented himself from the Courts in favour of the House of Commons, expecting on each occasion to be given a Ministerial job in a re-shuffle by the Prime Minister. Alas, each time Sir Ivan was disappointed. As a front-bench Labour spokesperson, Boateng's position is ever more bizarre. Then there are the professional comedians cum media stars like David Mellor MP and fat cats like Greville Janner MP, QC, who fill their pockets with pickings from non-parliamentary activities. And so it goes on.

Women

When they first started building Parliament in the reign of Edward the Confessor, women did not count for much in our society. Not much has changed in the 800 years that have passed, except that in 1918 women first got the vote. Nancy Astor became the first woman MP. Bizarrely, she was an American. Today there are just sixty women MPs – a record, but not much of a record when you consider that over half the population is female. Of these sixty women MPs thirty-seven are Labour, twenty are Conservative, two are Lib-Dems and one is a Scottish Nationalist.

Labour hopes that through mandatory shortlisting, and insisting that half of the winnable seats that come up when Labour MPs retire have a woman candidate, the number of its women MPs will increase substantially. Through the quota system Labour hopes that fifty per cent of its MPs will be women by the end of the century. The Labour Leader Tony Blair seemed to misjudge the mood of the party for positive discrimination in this field in 1994, when his spin doctors put it around that he was lukewarm about the idea. The Labour Conference of that year brushed aside the reservations of the doubters like Blair.

In the Conservative Party, the policy of

Nancy Astor, the first Woman MP

local autonomy and selecting candidates on merit has come under criticism by some of its women standard-bearers like Emma Nicholson MP. Another failed former Conservative candidate called Harriet Crawley, who had a more famous father, comments bitterly that in the Conservative Party "women are judged unseen from their CVs".

Surprisingly, you will find that as many Labour MPs are as much at home in what is essentially an unattractive male club as Conservative MPs. Even today, women MPs look out of place both in the Smoke Room of the House of Commons where Conservative MPs take their gins and tonics, and in the Strangers' Bar where hundreds of pints are swilled every night.

Race

If you are observant you will quickly notice the absence of black faces in the House of Commons. There are just six – five Labour and one Conservative. This may have something to do with the fact that Labour's 'B' list had only thirty-two black names on it in 1991 and its 'A' list only six black names on it, while the Conservatives' Candidates List in 1991 had only thirty black names on it. It may also have something to do with the racial preferences and prejudices of white voters. Scratch an Englishman and you will find a racist underneath is still something of a truism. For the Conservatives John Taylor, an admirable black candidate, came unstuck partly through prejudice in Cheltenham; while for Labour, Ashok Kumar who was the Labour MP for Loughborough for a very short period following a by-election was advised to "go and get a seat in Leicester".

Although prejudice against Jews was on the increase at the time of the 1992 election, with the rise of the BNP in parts of Britain and the desecration of Jewish cemeteries on the part of those looking for scapegoats for the recession, twenty Jewish MPs were elected – eleven Conservatives, eight Labour and one Lib-Dem.

Ethics

Sooner or later, and probably sooner, you are going to have to grapple with the ethical problems of being an MP. It's not that the job is evil in itself – far from it – rather that at every twist and turn you are likely to be asked to act in ways which could trouble your conscience. Although for centuries MPs have been lining their own pockets there is a public tradition of honour in the House of Commons. Like your colleagues you will see yourself as a person of great integrity. Like them you will refer in debates to other members of your party as "my Honourable Friends" and to members of the opposition as "the Honourable Member".

Like the other 650 MPs you will not want to transgress the rules of proper conduct lest you find yourself berated by the Speaker or hauled before the Select Committee on Members' Interests or, worse, before the Privileges Committee which can result in your being rebuked, censored, forced to resign as a Minister, or even forced to quit Parliament. But like the rest of your colleagues you will quickly become aware that there are lucrative grey areas where the rules are pleasantly ambiguous, opaque even.

Although it is far too early to introduce you to all the scandals that will come to worry you, just ask yourself how you would respond to the following scenarios.

❖ *An MP uses his position to get a friend or relative admitted to Oxford or Cambridge, or some other prestigious institution*
❖ *A Cabinet Minister uses his influence to obtain a contract for a firm in his constituency*
❖ *An MP is retained by a major company to arrange meetings and dinners at which its executive can meet parliamentarians*
❖ *An MP hires his wife or other family member to serve as his secretary*
❖ *At Christmas, an MP accepts a case of wine from an influential constituent*
❖ *An MP is issued a first-class airline ticket as part of a parliamentary delegation. He exchanges the ticket for an economy fare and pockets the difference*
❖ *An all-party group on the aged secures the services of a full-time research assistant at the expense of Age Concern*
❖ *A Member on retainer to a PR company representing a foreign government submits several written questions for the Order Paper on British industrial development in that country*
❖ *An MP requests and receives a House pass for a lobbyist, to act as a research assistant, although his services are paid for by an outside source*

These scenarios were put to 100 MPs by political analyst Maureen Mancuso at in-depth interviews. The 100 MPs, who were guaranteed anonymity, represented a cross-section of Parliament. In 1993 Mancuso published the results in *Parliamentary Affairs, a Journal of Comparative Politics.* In putting these scenarios to the MPs Mancuso was concerned to find out:

❖ how many MPs are prepared to do things in the interests of their constituents which are questionable, dubious or wrong;
❖ how many MPs are prepared to do things where they have a conflict of interest but from which they will benefit personally.

Bearing in mind that a number of MPs not wanting to show themselves up in a bad light may not have told the truth, the whole truth and nothing but the truth, the responses bear startling witness to a sadly damaged Parliament. If that is the way in which MPs see themselves then you may cease to wonder why a more cynical public, looking in from the outside and deluged in the press, on radio and TV with scandalous stories, sees Parliament as irredeemably sleazy. On the basis of MPs' responses to the scenarios Mancuso divided you and your colleagues up as follows:

Ethics – MPs Assess Themselves
1. *Ethical entrepreneurs*   35 per cent
2. *Ethical muddlers*   21 per cent
3. *Ethical servants*   12 per cent
4. *Ethical puritans*   28 per cent

Ethical entrepreneurs are MPs prepared to take high risks, who put profit before honour and who are prepared to condone almost any activity unless it is so gross as to constitute bribery, the blatant misappropriation of public funds and criminality. They see "perquisites and advantages" as perks and bankable rewards in a job which demands personal sacrifice. Ethics are not something that worry them. Two-thirds of the ethical entrepreneurs are Conservative MPs, perhaps because it is these MPs who are closer to people and institutions of power, perhaps because the 1980s saw the sickening development of "unfettered self-interest". Half of the ethical entrepreneurs had nine or more years' experience in Parliament. In Parliament long service breeds cynicism. Even so, the thought of the existence in Parliament of over 200 MPs who cannot tell the difference between right and wrong may disturb some.

Ethical muddlers on the other hand do have a conscience, but one which turns morality on its head. They condemn questionable acts which would benefit their constituents but condone acts which would benefit themselves directly. Younger muddlers look at older MPs who are involved in questionable acts and see this as a good enough reason to follow suit. Belonging to all parties, they are a bit to the right of centre in the ideological spectrum of their respective parties.

The ethical servants act in a way which is closer to what the man on the Clapham omnibus would consider acceptable conduct. Moderate in their respective political parties, they frown on questionable activities which benefit themselves but are prepared to go over the top and carry out questionable acts on behalf of their constituents. Perhaps the ethical servants can afford to be self-sacrificing because three-quarters of them have another occupation besides being an MP. They are part-timers – lawyers, businessmen, consultants, journalists.

As you would expect the ethical puritans, a fair number of whom must be lying, are against all questionable acts, whether they are intended to benefit themselves or their constituents. Two-thirds of them are Labour MPs; the rest are Conservative wets or on the left wing of the Lib-Dems.

In normal circumstances, and assuming you do not want to look odd, you would be well advised to become an ethical entrepreneur. It is the only stance that brings peace of mind. But should you enter Parliament at a time when sleaze is uppermost in people's minds and Parliament is going through one of its periodic fits of morality, it might be better to pretend that you are an ethical servant. On no account claim to be an ethical puritan. Nobody will believe you.

The Right to Lie

It is a truism for which we are indebted to Swift that all politicians ultimately die of swallowing their own lies. And perhaps H. L. Mencken, the political commentator, was right when he argued that there are some politicians who, if their constituents were cannibals, would promise them missionaries for dinner. At best there are in Parliament today too many MPs who see their trade as a way of getting on in the world and who, in the pursuit of that, realise that the truth can often be an unpalatable impediment to progress. At worst there are those who comfortably fit the description with which Harry S. Truman, the former President of the United States, summed up another former President of the United States when he said: "Richard Nixon is a no-good lying bastard. He can lie out of both sides of his mouth at the same time, and if ever he caught himself telling the truth, he'd lie just to keep his hand in".

Nixon, as Truman recognised, had real class. The similarity in approach between that of the President of the United States (George Bush) – "Watch my lips. No new taxes" – and of the British Prime Minister (John Major) – "I have made it clear, we have no plans and no need to extend the scope of VAT" – is all too obvious. In Major's case the lie paid off; in Bush's case it failed. In time, of course, Major and Bush will be regarded as elder statesmen and all their misdeeds will be forgotten. When they die they will, like Richard M. Nixon, become paragons of virtue.

Every time you listen to someone else speaking, remember that all politicians lie and Ministers lie the most. Recently a whole new lexicon of lying has defined the political system. Civil servants lie to Ministers, Ministers lie to Parliament and MPs lie to their constituents, and not only at the time of General Elections. Today we have lying by omission, lying through innuendo, white lying, less than accidental lying, lying by telling half-truths, lying to dig oneself out of a hole, lying through the teeth

and, worse, lying caught-in-the-act.

In these categories Parliament has been told whoppers about the development of offensive chemical weapons ostensibly abolished four decades ago, which even today put in jeopardy the Convention to Abolish Biological and Chemical Weapons; the deceit of Suez; the use of plutonium at Sellafield for military purposes; British involvement, still not admitted today, in spy planes over Russia, which if known at the time could have put the whole of Europe in jeopardy; and sanctions-busting in Rhodesia, where civil servants and the Prime Minister were parties to the lies.

But lying today extends well beyond military matters. Lying in government is now so institutionalised that Ministers and their advisers have developed whole new theories of the right to lie.

The top adviser to the Prime Minister is the Cabinet Secretary, a person whom some say is more powerful than his boss. The recent revelations that Prime Ministers and Cabinet Secretaries conspire to lie must be seen as a vindication of lying as an essential, necessary and integral part of modern politics. So you should not be surprised to learn that the theory of the right to lie in politics has its genesis in the acts and sayings of two Cabinet Secretaries – Lord Armstrong who had the job from 1977 to 1989, and Sir Robin Butler, the current Cabinet Secretary.

In 1987 when a former counter-intelligence MI5 officer called Peter Wright decided to publish a book – *Spycatcher* – about treachery within MI5 and a plot to remove Harold Wilson as Prime Minister in 1974-76 which involved MI5 officers unlawfully bugging and burgling their way round London, Lord Armstrong, the Cabinet Secretary, acting under the orders of Prime Minister Margaret Thatcher, masterminded an attempt to prevent publication of the book in Australia and information about its contents in Britain. He travelled personally to Australia to give evidence in Court, following on his affidavit which said that publication would cause "unquantifiable damage" and would endanger the lives of intelligence officers and their families. Forget for the

MI5 and the kangaroo court: Peter Wright, author of "Spycatcher"

moment that a man as super-intelligent as Lord Armstrong would have known that he was deceiving the Court by swearing to such nonsense. More to the point, during his evidence Lord Armstrong was caught lying.

However, with the consummate skill of a mandarin with a silky mind he preferred to say that he had been "economical with the truth". Subsequently, when asked (by the author) at a meeting of the Middle Temple Historical Society in London if the integrity of the constitution or of his office was helped by his travelling 12,000 miles around the world to lie in a foreign court, he replied: "I was only economical with the truth once". It was as though a man on a double murder charge asked to be let off on the grounds that he had only severed the head of one of the victims.

On 9 February 1994 Sir Robin Butler, the Cabinet Secretary who advises John Major, went a stage further when he gave evidence to the Scott Inquiry into the role of arms to Iraq. At the inquiry, which was looking into allegations that Ministers and civil servants had lied to MPs, broken their own guidelines and had been prepared to let innocent people go to gaol, Sir Robin developed a whole new theory to justify lying. At times his evidence was so full of sophistry and casuistry as to be hilarious. Sir Robin does not like the use of the words "lie" and "lying", as he made clear to the Select Committee on the Treasury and Civil Service when questioned about his evidence. He prefers to say that statements can be made by Ministers which are "false" or "misleading" or are "half-truths" that mislead.

Answering questions (from the author) at the Select Committee hearing, Sir Robin first gave examples of situations where it was appropriate for Ministers to lie to Parliament. Sir Robin added: "any first year student of moral philosophy will be able to tell you that there are very rare occasions ..... when a greater wrong is done by not lying than by lying". The problem with this approach is that it enables Ministers to lie to MPs on an arbitrary basis, providing that Ministers can claim to be acting for some higher and possibly, by necessity, secret, good. Certainly Sir Robin's evidence

John Major gives an incomplete answer about the IRA

stunned the Committee and the public.

Of course top politicians and their advisers wriggle and squirm when they seek to justify lying, as did the Prime Minister, John Major, when he told the House of Commons that he was not negotiating with the IRA and that to do so would make him feel sick, precisely at a time when secret negotiations with the IRA were taking place. Before the Scott Inquiry Sir Robin referred to this lie as "an incomplete answer" and "an answer which, in itself, was true, was not the full situation, it was half an answer, if you like but it was an accurate answer, and went to the point of what people were concerned about". Lord Justice Scott made it clear that he was not impressed with this agonising logic-chopping which could only have come from a linguistic Oxford philosopher who lives in another world from the rest of us.

Sir Robin Butler's views on the right to lie in principle cause him and MPs immense difficulty when he is questioned about the lies of individual Ministers. Sir Robin then immediately leaps to the defence of Ministers, thus taking up a position which some see as unseemly for the principal guardian of our constitution. In defending the indefensible some of Sir Robin's explanations border on the incredible. Giving evidence to Lord Justice Scott's inquiry,

Sir Robin told his Lordship that another senior civil servant had "misled himself" when he told a Commons Select Committee in 1992 that the guidelines on the sale of arms to Iraq had been changed four years earlier. When it was pointed out to Sir Robin that the civil servant in question had obtained his evidence from no less than three Departments – the Foreign Office, the Department of Trade and Industry and the Ministry of Defence, and he was asked sarcastically if this were a case of all three Departments having misled themselves, Sir Robin replied, without a hint of irony, "I can imagine it was. This was all happening below my eyesight level".

In March 1994 the Minister for Open Government William Waldegrave MP, born into the upper classes, nonplussed Parliament when, at another Select Committee hearing in answer to questions (from the author and from Quentin Davies MP), he adumbrated the right of Ministers to lie in the national interest, and like a don in an Oxford Common Room said, wrongly, that the House of Commons had always accepted that this right existed.

A once important document called *Questions of Procedures for Ministers* drawn up by the Prime Minister, states that Ministers "have a duty to give Parliament, including its Select Committees, and the public as full infor-

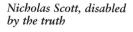

Nicholas Scott, disabled by the truth

mation as possible about the policies, decisions and actions of the Government, and not to deceive or mislead Parliament and the public". But the lying game, about as far removed from the national interest as one could get, continues. Evidence given by civil servants to Lord Justice Scott makes it clear that a number of Ministerial answers to Parliamentary Questions and some evidence to Select Committees were lies. In 1994 a Report by the Foreign Affairs Committee into the Pergau Hydro-Electric Project found that "Ministerial replies to certain questions were literally true, though less open and less informative than the House has a right to expect". This is Sir Robin Butler-speak for lies by any other name.

Since the Profumo affair the House has grown accustomed to Ministerial porkies. In May 1994 Nicholas Scott MP, the Minister for the Disabled, admitted having lied to the House of Commons and his civil servants and his daughter over his part in wrecking a Bill to help the disabled. A terrible lie this, and one which was compounded by a back-bencher, Lady Olga Maitland, who was rebuked by the Speaker. The significance of the case of Nicholas Scott is that he was generally regarded in the House of Commons as one of the good guys. So if the good guys who become Ministers behave like this, what about the bad guys?

Does it matter, you ask. Not at all, providing you accept that politics is simply a means for people like yourself getting on in the world. In another sense, lying enables Ministers and you to get yourselves off hooks. It only matters if you are fastidious and believe that there is some merit in Parliamentary democracy in which Ministers give a true account of their actions to Parliament. Lying destroys the very notion of Ministerial accountability and responsibility to Parliament, and along with them the very concept of Parliamentary democracy itself.

So as you go about your work in Parliament beware of siren sophists. As Mark Twain said on his visit to the West Coast of America: "Never trust a person hereabouts who looks you straight in the eye".

CONDITIONS OF WORK

From the many hard-luck stories that MPs put around you would think that they inhabit a Dickensian workhouse rather than a Royal Palace where the Perpendicular architecture enlivened with Gothic details is grand and in places awe-inspiring. Yet there is something about it that is oppressive, as though it were both calculated and designed to subdue MPs who are potentially radical or subversive.

Westminster, the monastery established in the West of London where Parliament now stands, was the predecessor of the present Westminster Abbey. Edward the Confessor turned it into a Palace. After many changes and vicissitudes, a fire in 1834 saw most of the Palace burned down except for Westminster Hall, the cloisters and the crypt and the Jewel Tower. The present building was designed by Sir Charles Barry and put up between 1840 and 1860. Barry was assisted by Augustus Pugin, an eccentric who carried out the interior decoration, and to whose memory there is a most beautiful Pugin Room for afternoon teas and post-prandial drinks for MPs and their special guests. The completed Palace, purpose-built as a Parliament, contained over 1,000 rooms, 100 staircases and two miles of corridors covering an area of eight acres. So do not feel ashamed if you get lost.

Today there are over twenty drinking-holes in the Palace where alcohol is served. This gives the building something of the character of a licensed Gothic cathedral where monks make merry. Whatever you do, steer clear of hot beverages. In 1987 a researcher almost died after drinking a brew. The authorities, in their inimitable style, generously compensated the researcher so that she kept news of the poisoned chalice to herself.

Except in the debating Chamber of the House of Commons the temperature by tradition is kept high to assist dying old men to stay alive, particularly in the House of Lords.

Accommodation

Stories about bad accommodation or about MPs having no accommodation at all abound. A few years ago Ann Clwyd, who was working in the 'Cloisters', an elongated open-plan corridor with fourteen or so desks where everyone listens in to the conversations of the others, caused a stir when rain started to pour in. She fixed up an umbrella on her desk, put on some wellington boots and invited the press in. Almost in a trice the necessary repairs were carried out and Ms Clwyd was moved.

Some people are very ungrateful. When, along with myself, she was offered a desk in a Portakabin that was literally plonked on the top of the building so that if you stepped out of the door at the end of the Portakabin you would fall vertically to your death, landing on a parapet, she kicked up a fuss again. The Sarjeant at Arms, the administrative boss of the Palace, was told that if we were not moved the press would be summoned again to take pictures of me lying 'dead' on the parapet. We were moved. Meanwhile, not two but three MPs who were less fastidious about the dignity of their offices, were given desks in the Portakabin. Even today quite senior MPs inhabit offices upstairs which are windowless and devoid of fresh air.

However, with the advent of splendid refurbished accommodation at No. 1 Parliament Street and Derby Gate, and the leasing of property at a cost of several million pounds at No. 7 Millbank where MPs and their secretaries have super-new interconnecting offices, the accommodation crisis has eased. One by-product of establishing MPs' offices in Millbank, conveniently close, incidentally, to the new MI5 building, is that MPs are becoming fitter. All the offices, government departments, pubs, and houses around Parliament are linked to the Division Bell which rings and summons MPs to vote. They have eight minutes in which to get into the Division Lobby once the bell starts to ring. From Millbank this means that MPs have to sprint to make it. It

can only be a matter of time before someone's heart gives out. The use of the old Scotland Yard building on the Embankment, the one you see in post-war films, now also provides accommodation for MPs.

Food and Drink

The Palace has so many tea-rooms, rooms for light refreshment, self-service dining rooms, waitress-service dining rooms and bars that to list them all would be tedious. Although the drink and food are not subsidised they are incredibly cheap, presumably because MPs consider themselves to be, in effect, the owners of the Palace, and accordingly they do not charge themselves overheads such as rent, rates, maintenance etc when calculating prices. Beer drinkers amongst the MPs tend to use the Strangers' Bar, or if they want to share a noggin with the press, Annie's Bar, whilst those who prefer G & Ts use the Smoke Room, a cavernous clubby place where Tories who look as though they were born to rule lounge in huge leather armchairs and on sizeable leather settees. Because it is used mainly by Labour MPs the Strangers' Bar is known as the Kremlin. It's here that hard men and even harder women drink studiously.

Monied MPs can and do hire rooms downstairs overlooking the Thames for parties or more expensive dinners. Pressure groups and lobbyists also use these rooms with the help of MPs. Every summer a magnificent awning goes up on the Terrace by the Thames, enabling MPs to feel as much at home as they would be at Henley or Ascot and allowing them to have sumptuous strawberry and cream teas as they watch the boats and little ships pass by.

Lunch on the Terrace or evening drinks there in June truly help to make Parliament London's finest club. Closer to bliss than this do few men or women get. Everything, the architecture, the river and the ambience delights the senses. Is it any wonder that when the powers that be abolished the right of critical parliamentary journalists to use the Terrace the journalists were mortified? Allegations that one MP bonked a guest on the Terrace were not only strenuously denied but resulted in legal action against the vile perpetrators of the story. As an alternative there are walks nearby around St James's Park where you can meet up with your old friends from MI5 and MI6.

More modestly, MPs can entertain guests to lunch and dinner in the Strangers' Dining Room or in the Churchill Room, which used to be called the Harcourt Room. The name was changed in a fit of partisan political pique. Be it noted that the Churchill Room provides more choice and better food with an à-la-carte menu. Often a well-known Welsh harpist entrances the diners with exquisite, melodious sounds.

Car Parking

Tory MP Airey Neave was killed as he drove his car out of the five-storey underground car park in the House of Commons. Soon after that the authorities started making daily checks for bombs and explosives on MPs' cars in an effort to protect them from Irish terrorism. The underground car park is a wonderful asset for MPs, who not only avoid the tedium of looking for empty parking meters in Central London when they go to work but can use it, if they wish, twenty-four hours a day for 365 days a year. If you want to go to a West End theatre or South Bank concert in the evenings or at weekends, a policeman is always on hand to open the gates of New Speaker's Yard so that you can use the car park. Quickly you will realise that it's little perquisites and advantages like this which give the club a feel-good factor. Of course some MPs get greedy. Not content with the free use of a five-storey car park, Ann Clwyd decided it was more convenient to park in the Speaker's Court where traditionally places are reserved for the limousines of Ministers. She tried to turn it into a constitutional row between Parliament and the Executive. But magisterially the Speaker, Betty Boothroyd, gave her a wigging in the Chamber of the House of Commons and we all chuckled. Who on earth could have egged Clwyd on to do this?

Library Services

As an MP you will find yourself exceptionally lucky in having the best library service in the world at your disposal. Indeed you would have to be several sandwiches short of a picnic not to admire and, more importantly, use it. Airy, spacious, comfortable, colourful and a bit grand yet inviting, the Library in the House of Commons is the perfect place in which to work. Overlooking the Thames, it brings the best out of people. Like the London Library, British Museum and the Bodleian Library in Oxford, the House of Commons Library is entitled to a copy of all books published in Britain. Its stock of books, magazines, newspapers and periodicals is huge. Strangely, when an MP wants to borrow a book from another library the inter-library service works like an express train.

Then there is the Research Division of the Library, which is staffed by people with PhDs and awesome brains capable of briefing you succinctly with both sides of the most com-

THE PACKAGE OFFERED TO YOU AS AN MP IN 1995	
INNER LONDON MPS	
Members' Pay	33,189
Members' Office Costs	42,754
Supplementary London Allowance	1,289
	77,232
OTHER MPS	
Members' Pay	33,189
Members' Office Costs	42,754
Supplementary London Allowance	11,661
	87,604

plex arguments on any subject you care to mention, from moral philosophy to the sex life of camels. Last but not least there are the green leather armchairs in which, after the fashion of Sir Winston Churchill, you can take a catnap or in which you can lose yourself in the fantasies of the great mansions advertised in *Country Life*, the elegance of the dresses in *Vogue*, the wit of the *New Yorker* or the brazen tittle-tattle of *Paris Match*.

Pay and Allowances

The prestige of the British Parliament is recognised throughout the world. Presumably that is one of the reasons why MPs are so badly paid. The status of MPs and the veneration in which they are held, even in an increasingly cynical world, is said to compensate in part for their miserably low incomes. Another reason may be that over the years back-bench MPs have ceded much of their power and influence to Ministers, civil servants and others, so they do not deserve a proper salary.

However, one concomitant of not giving them a proper salary, as we shall see, is sleaze and shady financial dealing, which threatens to destroy the one virtue to which Parliament must cling if it is to survive without becoming the object of hatred, ridicule and contempt – respect. Perhaps it is too late for Parliament to regain respect. Perhaps the theology of greed which dominated the 1980s has ruined it for us all – for ever.

The big difference between Inner London

MPs and all the others is that the others get an extra £11,661 called 'Additional Costs Allowances' to help them rent or buy accommodation in London. In the 1980s when house prices were roaring ahead by twenty per cent a year most MPs used this allowance to buy property and were making huge capital gains. Happily, the recession tempered their moves into property speculation.

Members' Office Costs Allowances enable you to hire secretaries and researchers and run offices with rows of computers both in the constituency and at the Palace. For the conscientious MP who needs two full-time secretaries and one full-time researcher the sum is inadequate. However this does not stop stories circulating in the tabloids, which are repeated every time MPs' salaries are raised, that MPs pocket this money for themselves. Most MPs who employ their wives, relatives or loved ones as researchers and secretaries do so on a bona fide basis. The Fees Office has cut out most of the cheating – although one MP still writes to his constituents in long hand.

MPs get quite a generous car mileage allowance, based on the environmentally unfriendly principle that the bigger the gas-guzzler that they drive and the more it pollutes the world, the bigger is the allowance.

Racketeering in the claiming of car allowances used to abound. Four MPs would come down in a car from say Glasgow, Cardiff or the North East and each would claim the full allowance, which for a 400-mile round trip would amount to some £280. A Tory Whip tells the story of one of their number who was called in because he was suspected of cheating. When he protested, it was pointed out that he seemed to have travelled twice around the world and back in his car on parliamentary business in six months. Delightfully, the House settles these matters quietly, and a repayment was made. If, however, you want to spend a few days fishing in Devon and you arrange at the same time to talk to someone in Kingsbridge about some aspect of parliamentary business, then the Fees Office has no option other than to provide you with a first-class return rail ticket.

CAR MILEAGE ALLOWANCE		
Engine ratings	Journeys not exceeding 20,000 miles per annum	Journeys in excess of 20,000 miles per annum
up to 1300 cc	30.5 pence per mile	15.9 pence per mile
1301-2300 cc	46.0 pence per mile	21.1 pence per mile
over 2300 cc	72.2 pence per mile	6.1 pence per mile

For those MPs who do not drive there is an unlimited supply of free first-class rail warrants for travelling between home, the constituency and Westminster. And there's a nice wad of rail warrants for spouses to travel to Westminster too. And one free trip to Europe each year. Unfortunately this generally means Brussels, not Biarritz.

And if you're on holiday in the Bahamas during the recess and Parliament is recalled, don't worry. The House of Commons will pay all your travel expenses, including Club-class airfares to bring you back to Britain, and then return you to the sun-kissed beaches of the Bahamas to rejoin your wife or mistress. Should it be necessary for you to stop off somewhere overnight when the inconvenience occurs, appropriately generous hotel expenses will be forthcoming from the Fees Office.

Ironically, Ministers get a reduced parliamentary salary of £24,985 instead of the £33,189 for a back-bencher. No, it's not altruism on their part, because to this reduced parliamentary salary have to be added the Ministerial salaries shown in the table.

The Prime Minister's package also of course includes the use of two grace and favour houses, one at 10 Downing Street, the other a country mansion at Chequers.

Many people wonder how the pay and allowances of a Member of the European Parliament (MEP) compare with the pay and allowances of an MP or a Minister in Parliament. The answer is in the box below.

The MEP then tops up this handsome sum with £155 a day for attending official meetings within the European Union, plus the cost of overnight accommodation for attending official meetings outside the European Union. So we're talking about an extra £15,000 to £20,000 a year here. The MEP then gets a staggering 57p per kilometre for the first 800 kilometres and 29p for each additional kilometre for travel to attend meetings within the European Union; a return air fare for official meetings outside the European Union; plus up to £2,340 per annum for other travel on official business. With various little scams tossed in, even the least financially aware MEP should be banking £50,000 a year from expenses which he or she does not spend. Become an MEP for ten years and you can retire on your half a mil-

MEP'S PACKAGE

MEP's Pay	33,189
Secretarial Allowances	69,912
Office Costs	25,572
Data Processing Allowance	780
	129,453

MINISTERIAL SALARIES

Prime Minister	57,018
Cabinet Minister	42,834
Minister of State	30,307
Parliamentary Under Secretary of State	23,002

SO THE FULL PACKAGE FOR THE PRIME MINISTER IS:

Ministerial Salary	57,018
Reduced Parliamentary Salary	24,985
Office Costs	42,754
Additional Cost Allowances	11,661
	136,418

lion pounds expenses slush fund. And all for performing the none too arduous task of being an international traveller without portfolio.

Golden Handshakes

When either the electorate or the Great Reaper in the sky tells an MP that his or her time is up, the MP or the executors can claim a winding-up allowance of one-third of the Office Costs Allowance to enable parliamentary and constituency business to be completed. Currently this enables an MP to claim up to £14,251. MPs whose time has come can also claim a Resettlement Grant based on their age and length of service. Thus an MP aged fifty-five to sixty-four who has been in Parliament for fifteen years would get a grant equivalent to a year's salary. An MP under 50 years old who has been a member for under ten years would get a grant equivalent to half a year's salary. Ministers also get severance allowances which amount generally to one-quarter of their annual Ministerial salary.

Best of all, MPs get pensions which can provide them annually, depending on their length of service, with index-linked pensions amounting to up to two-thirds of their salaries when they left Parliament. If an MP dies, his widow gets a pension equivalent to five-eighths of the pension which the deceased MP would have received. An MP's widow, live-in partner or whatever gets a lump sum equivalent to two years' salary, currently therefore some £66,000. There is nothing to stop an MP naming his or her mistress or toy-boy to be the recipient of

this money, and better still there is a proposal to raise the figure to £100,000.

From the outset you should realise of course that no amount of money can compensate an MP for losing his or her seat at an election, or a Minister for being consigned to the oblivion of the back-benches after a Prime Ministerial re-shuffle. There is little satisfaction to be gained from the knowledge that politics almost always ends in death or failure for individuals, only one of whom can get the top job for which they crave and then only for a limited period. As for losing one's seat at an election, that combines unbearable humiliation that sooner or later will express itself in tears, with the personal devastation that comes from rejection, loss of self-esteem, a crisis of identity and a knowledge that life can never be the same again. If you do lose, the world will crash in on you and you'll need something more than a thick skin to cope with the ingratitude of the electorate. Don't bottle your feelings up. There's no shame in being a cry-baby in these circumstances. But if you want to get back into Parliament avoid therapy, however distraught and depressed you feel. Politicians can get away with most things but the public's perception of what is permissible does not yet extend to their seeing a shrink. Psychiatrists are definitely off-limits.

As a defeated Labour MP you'll find it virtually impossible to get another job. But as a Tory you might be able to pretend that you've still got influence through your contacts in government. If you think that life is hard for seamstresses or shoemakers who lose their jobs, imagine how much worse it must be for a Prime Minister. Even the Iron Lady, Margaret Thatcher, was reduced to blubbing when, the victim of treachery, she was forced to stand down. Overnight she became a nobody, an embittered, physically decaying old woman, swallowed up in the isolation of defeat. Where once people had deferred, they now sneered. Where once she was buttressed by every support system a munificent constitution could offer, she suddenly found herself desperate for someone to listen, and so clearly in search of money that she turned into a grub.

The final twitch: Mrs Thatcher about to leave No. 10

EXPECTATIONS OF THE JOB

Helping your Constituents

Life is complicated for your constituents. So they need your help in getting them a Council house, prosecuting their dreadful landlord, overcoming the negligence of their solicitor who has made a mess of that contract to build an extension to their house, regularising their immigration status, extracting a rebate and an apology from their taxman, getting the local Benefits Agency to use its discretion to increase their benefits, and complaining on their behalf to everyone and every organisation whose name begins with one or other of the letters A to Z.

You are the local Ombudsman who redresses everyone's grievances and performs miracles when all else has failed. Of course you will get a lot of letters, but not as many as your colleagues boast about. Most weeks you will not get more than fifty new cases to deal with through your correspondence. Some people will insist on seeing you personally. So you will have to organise what are called 'surgeries', where you meet individuals who want to cry on your shoulder and make you as upset as they are. Tory MPs tend to hold surgeries in halls scattered throughout rural villages in their constituencies.

Most Labour MPs in inner cities hold surgeries once a week, but for some reason which no one can understand a number of Welsh and Scottish MPs, many of whose constituents live in grinding poverty, somehow only manage to hold surgeries every other week. Expect fifteen to twenty people to turn up at your surgery. One-third will have problems that only they can solve themselves; one-third will have problems that you may be able to solve; and the rest will have problems that God Almighty could not solve. The reply to the constituent who complains that strange creatures step out of his TV set and attack him is as follows: "Yes, I can see this is a serious problem. The next time it happens, do two things. First turn the set off, then disconnect it from the electricity. That will kill them." Of course he'll be back again next week. So probably it's advisable not to hold a surgery around the corner from the local mental hospital. The patients will tease you unmercifully.

Calling Ministers to Account

The constitutional textbooks will tell you that this is the traditional and most important role of a back-bench MP. Someone has to see that Ministers behave properly, keep to the rules, account for the expenditure of public money, ensure that Ministers mean what they say and say what they mean – and that's you! It is of course a Herculean and impossible task, best performed by ensuring that you stay a back-bencher for as short a period as possible.

Because you cannot beat Ministers the important thing is to join them. We have seen that there is a problem in calling Ministers to account when there is a culture of lying. The problem is compounded a hundred-fold because of the culture of secrecy that pervades the actions of Ministers and their civil servants. Although governments leak like sieves, the purpose of these leaks is often to provide misinformation rather than accurate information. That is why every government department employs a battery of spin doctors.

Nooks and Crannies

As an MP trying to make your way you may be tempted to argue for more open government. If you were to win the Private Members' Ballot allowing you to introduce a Bill, you might be tempted to bring in a Freedom of Information Bill designed to open up the nooks and crannies of Westminster and Whitehall. But be careful. When you're in government yourself the release of all this information could backfire on you. Give people information and they will want to use it in their own best interest. It's only human nature. Potentially that means debate, discussion, argu-

ment, choosing between options; in other words, trouble, trouble, trouble. Tell people the truth about civil nuclear power and your job as a Minister working on energy resources at the Department of Energy could become a nightmare. Give the green lobby a fraction of the information that they want, and life as a Minister at the Department of the Environment will be unbearable.

In theory, as we'll see later, everything that goes on in Parliament – the debates, oral questions to Ministers, written questions to Ministers, the making of Statements by Ministers who then face an hour's grilling on the floor of the House of Commons, all the stages through which a Bill becomes an Act of Parliament, and the work of Select Committees – enables you to call Ministers to account. But at the end of the day, dispiritingly, you have to realise that there is a hierarchy of knowledge and that as a back-bench MP you are at the bottom of the hierarchy, your position only marginally better than the position of the general public. So far as the government is concerned, the smooth running of Parliament depends on the existence of a large number of ignorant back-bench MPs. Only try to change the system if you are without Ministerial ambition.

Great Debates

Every experienced MP will tell you that most of the great debates which are given a star-billing in advance turn out to be flops. Great speeches are every bit as likely to be extemporary as planned. Passion has a tendency to spill over in the House of Commons when you least expect it. Denis Healey MP may have been right when he said that being attacked by Geoffrey Howe MP was like being savaged by a dead sheep. But never tell that to Margaret Thatcher. When she forced Howe to resign as her Foreign Secretary he stunned the House with his disdainful and elegantly savage attack on her. She never recovered. And who cared if the poison in his speech had been put there by his wife, Elspeth? This was great unexpected drama of a kind that can make Parliament the best theatre in town.

A debate that ends with Labour MPs breaking all the rules and singing the Red Flag and Tory MP Michael Heseltine going over the top and carrying the Mace with him must have something that is great about it. Perhaps these heady debates in the 1970s in crowded Chambers where Tony Benn and Michael Heseltine starred were the last of the great debates. Nothing that happened in the 1980s and 1990s – though John Smith had the makings of a great debater with his incisive wit and flexible mind – matched Wilson and Harold Macmillan fighting it out with their very different styles, or the eloquence of Ian Macleod or Aneurin Bevan.

As a back-bench MP you will probably only get three and possibly four chances to speak in a debate each year, and then not in the great debates. The Speaker usually ensures that yesterday's statesmen, former Cabinet Ministers and long-established placemen are called in the great debates. The phrase "catching the Speaker's eye" refers to the protocol of MPs standing up in debate and looking pleadingly at the Speaker, begging to be called to speak, as it were, in preference to the other MPs, who stand up each time the last MP finishes his or her speech and sits down. For the most part their speeches are as predictable as the iambic pentameter itself. The philosophy behind this approach is simple. As with George Orwell's pigs, in his novel *Animal Farm,* all MPs are equal but some are more equal than others.

Certainly it will pay you dividends to put in some work on the few speeches that you do have to make. A bit of wit, a bit of rhetoric, a bit of flattery towards your own front-bench and a peroration that sounds genuine, and you will quickly find your star rising in the firmament. People who could speak much better than they could think often used to make it to the top in politics. Perhaps with Major and Blair at the helm, neither of whom could be accused of being a brilliant speaker, still less a brilliant thinker, times are changing. Menacingly ordinary and unexceptionally wor-

thy, they aspire to be common.

The Chamber of the House of Commons can sometimes be a cruel and lonely place. It destroyed Neil Kinnock MP when he was Leader of the Labour Party. A brilliant speaker on a public platform, he was never at home in the intimacy of the Chamber, perhaps because before he became Labour's Leader he had never spent much time in it. Worse, MPs quickly get bored by Members who use ten words where one will do. Despite the abundance of lackwits and numbskulls in Parliament, you should always prepare your speech on the basic assumption that there will be at least one person present in the Chamber who, unlike yourself, is a real expert in the subject under discussion and who will know their stuff. The arrogant usually come unstuck, the buskers are quickly exposed, the mediocre soon ignored and the charlatans readily made the object of ridicule.

You must also get used to speaking in an empty Chamber. As a newcomer you will probably get called to speak in a debate between 7 pm and 9 pm when most half-civilised MPs are having a good dinner or drinks, or are attending meetings that mean far more to them than anything you have to say. So there could be twenty or even fewer MPs present to hear the brilliant thoughts which you have polished and burnished so that they will inspire the world. Powerful rhetoric which brings you and everyone else to the verge of tears in such circumstances is difficult.

The rules of debate in the Chamber of the House of Commons are simple. In order to maintain the cut and thrust of debate, an MP is not allowed to read his or her speech. However, daily Ministers can be seen reading from scripts prepared for them by civil servants. Although MPs must speak "standing and uncovered", women MPs are permitted to wear hats while speaking. The only time that male MPs can wear a hat is if they wish to raise a Point of Order when a division has been called. If this happens, then ancient custom turns to farce because an MP can *only* raise a Point of Order during a division if he or she puts on a black top-hat which is kept in reserve by the Sarjeant at Arms and is of the kind worn by magicians and toffs at Ascot. If someone else has the top-hat on and you wish to raise another Point of Order during a division the Speaker will sometimes allow you to go ahead by putting a handkerchief on your head and pretending that it's a top hat. You would be making a mistake to think that all this is nonsense which can be ignored. *Au contraire.* It is revered tradition that must be observed.

When the division eventually does take place MPs can, amazingly, vote in both lobbies, i.e. both for and against the same motion at the same time. This is very handy for those MPs who drunkenly and mistakenly wander into the wrong lobby as it enables them, when their error is pointed out, to be dragged protesting by the Whips into the correct lobby, thus cancelling out their original vote.

During times of war MPs have been worried about the presence of foreign spies listening in to their proceedings in the public gallery. So the practice developed whereby one of their number – the MPs, not the spies – would leap to their feet and cry: "I spy strangers. I spy strangers". Whether or not MPs could recognise members of Hitler's SS or, later, members of the KGB and CIA in the public gallery is a moot point. Never mind, the Speaker would then allow a division to take place so that MPs could vote to clear the gallery and continue the proceedings in secret. MPs still jump up today and cry: "I spy strangers. I spy strangers", but now they do it merely as a time-wasting tactic, knowing that the ensuing division will take some twelve or so minutes. Only members of Her Majesty's Opposition are supposed to waste time in this way. Usually it only happens when the ego of some pompous MP has been bruised and he or she can think of nothing better to do to draw attention to themselves or express a cry for help.

Everything that you say in the Chamber of the House of Commons is said to be reported in Hansard. However, the idea that Hansard is a verbatim report of the proceedings is a myth. The Hansard reporters themselves are often helpful and 'tidy up' incoherent speeches so as to make them readable and give the impression to the general public that MPs talk

grammatically. Back-bench MPs often go up themselves to the Hansard rooms and 'correct' their speeches, while Ministers frequently send their Private Secretaries up to make 'alterations'. The rule is that while alterations and corrections can be made, the substance of the speech cannot be changed. Changes made by MPs can be challenged on the floor of the House as being in breach of this rule and the Speaker may order that the words actually spoken remain as part of the permanent record. Usually it is only Ministers who try to cheat.

In an effort to prevent the debates becoming unruly through MPs interrupting the speeches of Ministers with vulgar comments as they lie back on the green leather benches in the Chamber, the Speaker has ordered that such interruptions should not be recorded in Hansard. Of course that does not stop them being heard on TV or radio. And should the Minister respond in his speech to a witty comment such as "you snivelling little git", made from a sedentary position (this was in fact a remark that the author once made about the Chancellor of Exchequer, Nigel Lawson, when he was, for once, on his feet) then Hansard has no option other than to report the comment in order to make sense of the Minister's response. In these cases Hansard reporters who sit in the gallery send down notes to the MPs asking which one of them bawled out the offending words so that they can be properly attributed.

Some of the procedures in the House of Commons are byzantine. If you wish to be seen on TV asking the Prime Minister a tough question on schools or on the future of the National Lottery then you have to put down a question which says: "To ask the Prime Minister if he will list his official engagements for Thursday 9 November". If you've got the first question to the PM he will reply: "This morning I presided at a meeting of the Cabinet and had meetings with ministerial colleagues and others. In addition to my duties in the House, I shall be having further meetings today". Then you get up and ask the Prime Minister your question on schools or the National Lottery. Why does it have to be done in this silly way? Quite simply, because if you ask the Prime Minister a direct

LEGISLATING FOR THE GOOD LIFE

Everyone says that Britain has too much legislation. Yet as soon as something goes wrong there is never any shortage of members of the public or MPs to call for more. Under these circumstances, and with an ever-present sensation-hungry media to whip up feelings, is it any wonder that from the treatment of dogs to laws on criminal justice much of the legislation passed by Parliament is ill-thought-out, rushed through to suit bigots and zealots and designed to last only until the next outburst of public prejudice calls for the new law to be changed? As weather vanes MPs are brilliant; as climatologists they are useless.

Changing the law or passing new laws in the United Kingdom, is, as you will soon find out, a time-consuming process. Before a Bill presented to Parliament becomes an Act, and therefore enforceable in the Courts, it goes through the following stages in the House of Commons:

1 First Reading This simply means that the Bill is published

2 Second Reading This consists of a debate on the general principles of the Bill followed, if it is contentious, by a vote. This debate usually takes place on the floor of the House of Commons

3 Committee Stage of the Bill A Standing Committee of twenty to thirty MPs, accurately reflecting the composition of the whole House, considers the Bill line by line. Most Committees sit in the mornings, but not the Finance Committee which considers legislation arising out of the Budget. The Finance Committee starts at four o'clock in the afternoon, thus giving MPs who are financial specialists time to do a day's work in the City as stockbrokers or merchant bankers or currency speculators before they get down to work on the Committee.

The sittings of the Finance Committee sometimes go on and on all the way through the night, thus allowing the Committee membership to admire the sun rising over the Thames. A gruelling experience which makes for bad legislation. The procedure killed one Labour MP. In an effort to prevent further deaths, the Finance Committee now adjourns every three hours or so during the night for twenty minutes to enable its members to have tea, coffee and bacon sandwiches. Except where Bills propose changes in the constitution, the Committee Stage takes place upstairs in a Committee Room

4 The Report Stage The whole House now considers the Bill as amended by the Committee and may recommend further changes

5 Third Reading After a three-hour debate, a final vote is taken on the Bill in the House of Commons.

After leaving the House of Commons, Bills then go to the House of Lords. The Lords cannot amend or reject Finance Bills. Any amendments passed by the House of Lords need the approval of the Commons. If that is not forthcoming the men and women in ermine usually cave in. If they remain stubborn they can hold up Bills for a year, but by this time you and everyone else would know about it because we would be in the middle of a constitutional crisis.

Basically, you want to get involved in the procedures of as few Bills as possible. A good speech on the Second Reading of the Finance Bill would put you in good stead but as a putative Prime Minister you will probably have to become Chancellor of the Exchequer on the way. A word of advice, though. If you are a Labour MP you should consult with one of your colleagues on the Select Committee on the Treasury, who will be terribly well briefed. On no account trust Labour's front-bench Shadow Chancellor, while if the Economic Secretariat which advises him gives you a statistic, check its accuracy at least three times. Too many Labour MPs have come unstuck in the past in the jungle of economics, pretending, ludicrously, that they understand that dismal science.

Lastly, avoid big Bills like the plague. The Great Education Reform Bill of 1988, called GERBIL, and many of whose provisions have since been dismantled or ignored, tied up MPs in Committee for over 200 hours. Hilary Armstrong, an excruciatingly boring MP, and Paddy Ashdown, even less humorous than a Dalek, were on the Committee. No sane person should be made to suffer such people as these gladly for so long.

question about schools or the National Lottery he can if he wishes, transfer it to the relevant Minister for a reply and, hey presto, your chance of jousting with the big man on the floor of the House is gone. If you're second in the queue and ask the Prime Minister about his official engagements, his ritualistic answer is: "I refer my honourable Friend to the reply I gave some moments ago". Then it's your turn for stardom.

Prime Ministers ignore back-bench MPs from their own party at their peril. Even so, a Prime Minister is a busy person, well-protected by civil servants, secretaries and the like. So they may make excuses and prevent you, as a lowly newcomer, from seeing him in his office in Downing Street. Worry not. Like every other MP, a Prime Minister has to go into the Division Lobby to vote. The two voting lobbies, one for the 'Ayes', one for the 'Noes', consist of long enclosed corridors that run parallel to the debating Chamber itself. Once the Prime Minister is inside and the doors are locked you can touch his arm or, *in extremis,* grab him by the throat and tell him what you think. There's no hiding-place even for the PM in lobbies – unless of course he slips into one of the lavatories that exist for the convenience of MPs during votes.

Politics in Britain is adversarial. People sometimes say that they wish that it could be otherwise. In theory, now that so little separates the two major parties, things could change. Actually there is no chance of that. Conservative and Labour politicians have to believe that they hate each other – how else can they justify their competing claims for power? Besides, the very shape of the Chamber demands confrontational politics.

Two armies face each other, separated by a thin neutral line, nerves stretched and sinews stiffened for battle on a daily basis. The job of the Opposition is to destroy the government. The job of the government is to ignore the Opposition. If the differences between them are small, then they must clearly be exaggerated. If there are no differences, then they must be artificially created. When Tony Blair says that he is going to change all that no one takes him seri-

ously. Indeed he cannot conceivably take himself seriously on this issue. As Leader of the Opposition he needs the oxygen of confrontation, not the sweet reason of compromise.

The House of Commons can never be a place where men in suits and women in skirts search for agreement. The passion, the shouting and the hysteria are here to stay – and let no one fool you when they say that it would be different if there were more women MPs.

Finally, you should keep things in perspective and remember that your purpose in speaking in a debate is not to get anyone to act in a way other than that which they would have done had you not spoken, still less to attempt to change anyone's mind on issues of principle – MPs have closed minds and such ideas are for dreamers and the Oxford Union – but to let those who count know that you exist, that your ambition is undiminished and that once the debate is over you will be in the corridors of power conspiring and manoeuvring to get upwards and on. As in any office or corporation, in the Palace of Conspiracies the corridors are far more important these days than the Chamber itself, more important, even, than the rooms off them. Private words in people's ears delphically accompanied by promises and threats alike are likely to be far more effective than grand public gestures in helping you climb the greasy pole.

Promoting Parliamentary Democracy

As a member of the Mother of Parliaments you have a duty, which you would ignore at your peril, to spread the creed of parliamentary democracy throughout the world. Burdensome though this may be, it behoves you to visit all parts of the globe in pursuit of this end. To lighten the burden other people, sometimes the taxpayer, sometimes overseas governments, pay the bills. At the same time as you are spreading the parliamentary gospel in the tiresome and unremitting heat of Barbados, by the Great Wall of China, at the Watergate Hotel in Washington or in film studios in Hollywood, you can learn a lot from your hosts too and use the invaluable experience that you gain when you return to work in Parliament.

In 1995 the Select Committee on Agriculture, led by Jerry Wiggin MP, went all the way to South Africa to study horticulture or, as one of their members put it, "how to grow cabbages and tomatoes". The return air fare for each MP was £1,700, a staggering figure when you consider that a bucket-shop ticket would have cost some £300. More about Jerry later. Previously the same jaunty Committee had stunned MPs when it went all the way round the world to New Zealand to look at trees, apparently oblivious of the fact that there are several billion trees between Britain and New Zealand which they could have admired at considerably less cost to the taxpayer. On that occasion MPs on the Committee had stop-off-around-the-globe air tickets.

Foreign Visits

Select Committees have come to understand the invaluable nature of these foreign visits. Hardly any of them fail to get at least one trip abroad each year which enlightens their minds and their deliberations. In recent years the MPs on the Select Committee on the Treasury have come to realise that the problems of the British economy can only be understood in a global context and that they have to be well-informed on international monetary relations if their reports are to be respected by their colleagues. So most years they have to go to Washington and New York for high-powered discussions. Visits to Mexico, Houston, Tokyo, Hong Kong, Frankfurt, Paris, Budapest and Berlin have also had to be undertaken.

A Chairman of the Treasury Select Committee, Terence Higgins, one of Parliament's most respected senior members and a former Treasury Minister, became an expert in getting the Committee upgraded from Economy Class, which is all the taxpayer would pay for, to Business Class. Even with Business Class travel and first-class accommodation, living out of a suitcase is not pleasant. On visits abroad you must always be polite to your hosts and do them the favour of having done your homework. You must remain on good terms with British Ambassadors around the world. Two Tory MPs on the Treasury Select Committee, Nicholas Budgen and Anthony Beaumont-Dark, once made the terrible mistake of insulting, by accusing him of "betraying his country", the British Ambassador, Sir Richard Ackland, at a dinner at the Embassy in Washington in the presence of a number of distinguished Americans. Their conduct demeaned our country. The fearful rows which broke out afterwards at the Embassy, amongst members of the Committee and in the Foreign Office back in London still rumble on, whilst the Committee is no longer invited to dinner at the Embassy in Washington.

On becoming an MP, for a nominal payment of a few pounds a year you can and should join the Inter-Parliamentary Union and the Commonwealth Parliamentary Association. These excellent organisations both entertain members of overseas parliaments and organise splendid visits abroad for British MPs. Membership of their Executive Committees is coveted because it is these committees which select who can go on which trip. A crisis arose in 1994 when evidence emerged that the party Whips were usurping the function of these executive committees and were using the offer or lack of an offer to MPs to go on these jaunts in order to bring them into line. In the Parliamentary Labour Party (PLP) the allocation of places for these visits was clearly used to buy votes for unrelated PLP elections. Labour Whips are, it seems, the direct descendants of Machiavelli's Prince, for whom no exercise in dishonour is extreme enough.

If overseas visits by MPs are paid for by foreign governments or private individuals and organisations then they have to be declared in the Register of Members' Interests. Select Committee trips do not have to be declared at all. Clearly, if an MP stands up in the Chamber to challenge Solzhenitsyn's view that Boris Yeltsin's Russia is corrupt, the knowledge that he or she has recently been to Russia at the expense of someone associated with the gov-

Jetset factfinder: Jerry Wiggin investigates South African vegetables

ernment provides a context for that MP's view and puts it in perspective. So the Register, which requires overseas visits to be filed within four weeks of the end of the trip, is important. In 1994 at the height of the sleaze scandals it became clear that a number of honourable MPs had not been declaring such visits. Some forty-seven members took fright and suddenly declared over sixty foreign trips. The declarations that were made out of time came about, of course, as a result of oversight, forgetfulness, the pressure of work on MPs and their assistants, and sheer inadvertence. No one had anything to hide and no one was ashamed to be seen as a globe-trotter or receiver of freebies *extraordinaire*.

Amongst those MPs who travel heroically for Britain, much as MI6 agents, men and women, who to their dislike once had to fuck for Britain with foreign counter-intelligence agents in order to get information, were:

Matthew Banks MP (Conservative)

June 1992	Jakarta – as guest of British Airways
Sept 1992	Dubai – as guest of Emirates Airlines in capacity as member of Conservative Backbench Tourism Committee
May 1993	Lake Como – to attend two-day seminar
June 1993	Oslo – funded by Roads Campaign Council
Sept 1993	Dallas and Atlanta – air tickets funded by British Airways
May 1994	Cadennabia, Italy – paid for by Conrad Adenauer Stiftung
Sept 1994	Caracas and Orinoco Belt, Venezuela – accompanied by wife, paid for by Venezuelan Government and BITOR
Sept 1994	Muscat, Oman – travel costs paid by myself. Two nights accommodation at the Al-Bustan Palace Hotel paid by government of Oman in return for dinner and hospitality provided by me to Omani Ministers at the House of

	Commons in July 1994
Oct 1994	Washington DC, USA – air ticket provided for myself and my wife by British Airways

Robin Corbett MP (Labour)

Sept 1993	Cyprus – paid for by Friends of Cyprus and House of Representatives
Oct 1993	Hong Kong, accompanied by wife – paid for by Hong Kong Government
Nov 1993	France – paid for by West Midlands Passenger Transport Authority
July/Aug1993	St Petersburg, accompanied by wife – for Goodwill Games, paid for by Turner Broadcasting System
Sept 1994	Paris – with All-Party Cable and Satellite Group – paid for by Compagnie Générale des Eaux
Sept/Oct1994	Kashmir – paid for by Indian Government

Bernie Grant MP (Labour)

Nov 1992	Curaçao – paid for by West India Committee
April 1993	Nigeria – paid for by Organisation for African Unity
May 1993	USA – paid for by PACE University, New York
June 1993	Denmark – paid for by Danish anti-racist organisations
Nov1993	Dominica – paid for by Dominica Labour Party
Jan 1994	Anguilla – paid for by Anguilla Democratic Party
Feb 1994	Libya – paid for by Libyan Government
April 1994	Uganda – expenses met by Pan African Congress
July 1994	South Africa – expenses met by British black businessmen and women

Aug 1994	Dublin – expenses met by Time for Peace, Time to Go Campaign
Aug 1994	Libya – expenses met by Libyan Government
Sept 1994	Sudan – expenses met by Libyan Government

Lady Olga Maitland MP (Conservative)

April 1993	Kuwait – as guest of Kuwaiti National Committee for Missing Prisoners of War (KNCMPW)
Sept 1993	South Africa – fact-finding tour arranged by South African Ambassador
April 1994	Kuwait – as guest of KNCMPW with husband and son (husband has received payment for legal advice to the Committee)
July 1994	Hong Kong – with husband, paid for by Hong Kong Government
July 1994	Malta – one night's stay at Phoenix Hotel accompanied by husband, son and a school friend, as guest of Maltese Government
Undated	Dublin – gift of return air ticket from Dr Edward Haughey

Often Ministers have to make overseas visits as part of their Departmental duties and obviously they travel at public expense. Despite the limousines and the massive support that Ministers get from civil servants, even to the extent that they have their thinking done for them, a Minister's lot is a hard one. Therefore should we be surprised that when travelling abroad Ministers can only benefit from having their wives or husbands with them? Loss, even the temporary loss of a loved one, can have catastrophic consequences which unsettle people who work under immense pressure. So the presence of spouses on visits provides equilibrium and removes temptation. But who pays – the Minister or the taxpayer?

The short answer is that if the wives of Ministers want to accompany their husbands on visits abroad they are expected to pay for themselves. For a Minister to seek to have it otherwise is corrupt. However, as so often happens in British public life, there are loopholes, and, as we all know, loopholes exist to be exploited. Give an MP just a whiff of the possibility of personal advantage, and snouts will quickly be found exploring the trough. The loophole in the case of foreign visits is contained in the PM's document *Questions of Procedure for Ministers*. This states that a Minister's spouse when accompanying the Minister on an official visit abroad "may occasionally be paid from public funds, provided it is clearly in the public interest that he or she should accompany the Minister.... the Prime Minister's prior assent should be obtained on each occasion".

Merry Wives

Some of these merry wives of Westminster were not only involved in official programmes but undertook separate engagements on these visits, so the modest financial help that they received from the taxpayer was no less than their due. And who would disagree with the Prime Minister when he asserts that everyone benefits from these arrangements, not just Ministers and their spouses but the nation at large, because politics is all the better for it. Not only that but the rest of the world benefits from the presence of such gracious and experienced wives. Anyway, who amongst us would criticise the power of love?

Ministers apart, you may be wondering what the benefits are of trips abroad nobly undertaken by back-bench MPs who seldom have to file a report afterwards. Although difficult to quantify them, there are basically three answers: firstly, MPs return better-informed about the world's problems; secondly, as they are often able to take their wives with them and thus fan the guttering flames of stagnant marriages in exotic climes, they return empowered and invigorated; and lastly, they can and often do use these trips for a little profitable private business.

TOTTING UP THE COST

In 1994 the Prime Minister insisted that the taxpayer should foot the bills of the former model Sandra Howard, who accompanied the Home Secretary on a visit to the US and Latin America at a combined cost of £8,317; and the bills of Judith Hurd who accompanied the Foreign Secretary on visits to New York and Canada at a cost of £4,030, Russia at a cost of £279, the Far East, Hong Kong and Japan at a cost of £282, Luxembourg and Paris at a cost of £77; and the bill of Cecilia Goodlad, who accompanied FO Minister Alastair Goodlad on a visit to Singapore, Australia, New Zealand and India at a cost of £7,777; and the bill of Arabella Lennox-Boyd who accompanied FO Minister Mark Lennox-Boyd on a visit to Pakistan at a cost of £3,612; and the bill of Linda Heathcote-Amery who accompanied the FO Minister to Ecuador at a cost of £3,974; and the bill of Catherine Baldry who accompanied FO Minister Tony Baldry to Canada at a cost of £2,997; and the bills of Anne Heseltine who accompanied Michael Heseltine, the millionaire President of the Board of Trade, to Australia and Japan at a cost of £12,010 and to South Africa at a cost of £7,900; and the bill of Lady Ferrers who accompanied her husband Earl Ferrers, a DTI Minister, to Singapore, Australia and New Zealand at a cost of £12,037; and the bill of Christine Hamilton who accompanied Neil Hamilton, a DTI Minister, on a visit to Romania at a cost of £2,000; and the bills paid as they all were, ultimately, by the taxpayer, of Carole Taylor who accompanied Ian Taylor, a PUSSY at the DTI, on a visit to Germany at a cost of £726; and the bill of Diane Eggar who accompanied Tim Eggar, a DTI Minister, on a visit to South America at a cost of £11,319. Etc, etc.

A Day in the Life of an MP in Middle England

7.30 am Wake up to the sound of the alarm in the flat at Dolphin Square.

7.40 am Caroline brings me a cup of coffee. Exciting, full of charm, good in bed and everything else that my wife is not, she's now become the problem. The Whips say I'm in line for a Ministerial job but in the current climate mistresses, especially secretaries, are out of order. Apparently we were spotted at it in my office by the security guard in the days before I bought the flat at Dolphin Square, which makes sex handy and easy. Now I'm on file in the Sarjeant at Arms' office, in the Whips' office and at MI5. According to the Whips if I get the job, and it's predicated on saying good-bye to Caroline's body, I'll also go into the Cabinet Secretary's *Precedent Book* which contains details about the personal affairs of existing and former Ministers. Thank God Sir Robin Butler refuses to publish it. The Whip's parting comment to me yesterday evening had been: "One last fuck for the road and that's it. Let me know your decision over breakfast tomorrow".

7.45 am Have summoned up courage to tell Caroline it's over.

7.46 am Caroline, sensing that something's up, takes off her dressing-gown and climbs back into bed, with disastrous effect. Her tits are in my mouth. I can't tell her now.

9.00 am Over at my office in the House of Commons, dictate letters that can't wait to Caroline. Tell her to do the rest herself. I'll sign them later. A leading QC, one of my colleagues at the bar, when asked how often he thought about sex, replied: "If by that you mean penetrative sex, I'd say every half-hour or so". I understand what he means.

9.45 am Breakfast in the tea-room of the Commons with the Whip – sausages, tomato, bacon, beans on toast. Assure him that it's over between me and Caroline. What else could I do? I will end it – hopefully tonight.

10.30 am This could be my last Standing Committee. We're examining the Post Office Privatisation Bill word by word in Committee Room 10 upstairs. All the speaking is done by Opposition MPs. On our side only the Minister speaks. Our instructions as his supporters are to keep our mouths shut. The Minister wants his Bill through as fast as possible, so not even friendly interventions are welcomed. A government Whip is present to throttle any government MP who is moved to break ranks and speak. So we carry on dealing with our mail. Sadly, we're not allowed to bring newspapers into the Committee. Every now and then there's a vote so we can't go anywhere except outside into the corridor where tea-ladies keep us refreshed with coffee and biscuits which are being wheeled around on trolleys. Make a phone call to my stockbroker on one of the telephones in the corridor about buying shares in a company which is represented by a specialist in corporate law which may be about to be taken over. Precisely at 1 pm the Chairman of the Committee terminates the proceedings. We're not making much progress. It's only a matter of time before the Guillotine falls on the Bill.

1.15 pm Pre-arranged quickie with Caroline – back at the flat.

2.15 pm Return two emergency calls to constituents who have left messages on the telephone board in the Members' Lobby. Ask my office to deal with it.

2.26 pm The Speaker's procession makes its way round the building – rather splendid, I think – into the debating Chamber of the House of Commons.

2.30 pm About fifty MPs have come in for prayers led by the Speaker's Chaplain. A very nice man, he. I couldn't bear it if one day a woman got the job. Still, it's bound to happen, especially if the socialists get back in power. After prayers the House fills up for questions to Health Ministers. I manage to catch the Speaker's eye and congratulate Stephen (Dorrell MP) on appointing Admiral Sir Rodney Crampton as Chairman of my local District Health Authority. He's Caroline's father and Treasurer of her local Association.

3.14 pm The Prime Minister enters the Chamber to loud cheers and the waving of Order Papers on our side. I think he does rather well in referring to one Labour MP who asks about sleaze as "an indescribable nerd".

3.30 pm The Prime Minister makes a Statement on the Nolan report into conduct in public life. As I suspected all along, things on the whole are not too bad but could be improved. People getting a bit sloppy, need for clearer guidelines, probity essential for public confidence – that sort of thing. Well done, Prime Minister. You handled it in masterly fashion. As for the battle between you and Tony Blair, it's a statesman versus a schoolboy.

4.45 pm Listen to the opening speeches in the debate on the Second Reading of the Bill to privatise Nuclear Power Stations. Who says we've run out of ideas? Michael [Heseltine] is at the peak of his form, lording it effortlessly over the Opposition in his capacity as Deputy Prime Minister. He really is the Lion King. As I leave, Jack Cunningham is on his feet... I'm not surprised that his own back-benchers refer to him as Alderman Vanity. He's all show and no substance.

6.30 pm Lovely canapés and cocktails at the Chinese Embassy in Portland Place. Button-hole one of the Counsellors and suggest a need for greater understanding between our two countries, especially with the hand-over of Hong Kong just two years away. Feelers about a possible visit are well received. Do I detect a hint of guilt on the part of the representatives of the butchers of Tiananmen Square?

7.45 pm Collared by a Whip on my return to the Commons. "Where the bloody hell have you been? Not fucking her upstairs again. God, how we've gone out of our way to help you. Flawed genius you may be, but from now on it's brain before cock – geddit? Now on your bike and over to Downing Street soonest. I'd cut your balls off but it seems the PM has a soft spot for you".

8.00 pm The Prime Minister is in his study. Too excited to take it all in. His Principal Private Secretary is with him. Hallelujah, he's offering a job at the Foreign Office. Thinks the Foreign Secretary wants me to help him out in the Far East. Couldn't be better. Gives me a warm handshake. Suggests I have a word with the Foreign Secretary in the Lobby at the vote. I'm on air and in overdrive. It's what I've always wanted, what I can do well. The announcement will be delayed until tomorrow. Seems another Minister wants to spend more time with his family.

8.30 pm Ring Margaret and the children. They're overjoyed. Suggest they come down tomorrow for pictures, photo-call, happy families at Westminster, that sort of thing.

8.45 pm Grab a snack in the Dining Room downstairs.

9.15 pm G & Ts in the Smoke Room. Colleagues ask why I'm on such sparkling form and buying drinks as though I was not the most tight-fisted barrister they've ever met. A Whip sniggers. Everyone knows, of course. Nothing is secret in the House of Commons. Gossip, rumour, innuendo and highly classified information spread like wildfire throughout the building in a trice.

10.00 pm Speak to the Foreign Secretary in the 'Aye' Lobby. Go to his room in the Commons for a celebratory drink. Briefing session with the Permanent Secretary at the FO has been arranged – tomorrow 9 am.

Midnight Lovemaking with Caroline is more exquisite than ever. Pretty sure I can contain the problem.

MAKING YOUR WAY

Snakes and Ladders

The parliamentary ladder you must climb if you are a back-bencher supporting the government is:
1. Parliamentary Private Secretary – PPS
2. Junior Minister – eighty positions to fill
    (a) Parliamentary Under Secretary of State – PUSSY
    (b) Minister of State
3. Secretary of State, i.e. Member of the Cabinet – twenty to twenty-two positions to fill
4. Prime Minister
    If you are a back-bench MP in the Opposition, your goal is to get into one of the front-bench teams, then seek election to what technically is called the Parliamentary Committee (eighteen posts to fill), but is more popularly known as the Shadow Cabinet, and finally to become Leader of your party.
    The third route to fame which is open to all is to become Speaker of the House of Commons, but that requires exceptional ability in climbing greasy poles.

PPS

    Parliamentary Private Secretaries are not strictly speaking members of the government. They get no money other than the normal MP's salary for their services, and little recognition. Yet they have to behave as though they were Ministers and do nothing which would put them in conflict with the government. Although Secretaries of State appoint PPSs as personal helpers or advisers, the Prime Minister nevertheless has to approve the appointments. The detractors of PPSs refer to them as baggage-carriers and dogsbodies who attend to the every whim of their Ministers, flatter their Ministers, excuse the mistakes of their Ministers and even suck the toes of their Ministers. A good Secretary of State, however, will give his PPS access to all his papers, including classified documents, discuss Cabinet decisions with him, want him in at all the big Departmental meetings, use him as a sounding-board and expect him to act as a two-way link with back-bench MPs on the government side. As PPS to Tony Benn when Labour was last in government, I found that the job had all the excitement and danger of living on the top of an active volcano.

Junior Ministers

    Ironically, Junior Ministers, though officially part of the government and paid to do the job, miss much of the action that attaches to being a PPS. There are such a lot of them that there would have to be something seriously wrong with you not to become one. Good Secretaries of State have team meetings with Junior Ministers. Junior Ministers, especially PUSSIES, are by tradition expected to carry out all the fag-end jobs in a government Department and to clear the way for the Secretary of State to make the big decisions. Secretaries of State expect them to attend boring conferences on their behalf, hold meetings with awkward sods from which no good can come, and read and sign hundreds of letters.

At the weekends Junior Ministers go home not to roll up their sleeves, not to mow the lawn but to go through batches of papers in Red Boxes until their eyes redden or close with exhaustion. Civil servants fill these Boxes, which look important because they carry the government insignia, as fast as Junior Ministers empty them. The more papers which Junior Ministers initial as having read, the more civil servants can lay responsibility and blame on their political masters when things go wrong. Yet Junior Ministers have to be polite to senior civil servants because Permanent Secretaries in Departments (i.e. the very top people) report on them to the Cabinet Secretary, labelling them as helpful or unhelpful, lazy or hardworking, stupid or very stupid, able or not able to get the Department's views across at meetings with Junior Ministers from other Departments.

Secretaries of State not unnaturally often insist on having political allies or personal friends as Junior Ministers under them. Prime Ministers on the other hand, who have the final say, often want their own spies appointed as Junior Ministers in each government Department, who are expected to report back to them. Harold Wilson and Jim Callaghan did this as Prime Ministers, while Margaret Thatcher usually put someone who was "one of us" in government Departments run by her enemies and potential assassins. John Major, it seems, does not have enough people in the government whom he trusts, or who respect him, to carry out this policy.

As a Junior Minister you'll have access to a car from the car pool, usually a Rover, and be driven to your Department every morning from your home. One good reason for wanting to be promoted to the office of Secretary of State is that you will then get a regular driver who will take you hither and thither in a Jaguar. Be nice to your driver, because as your friend he will be able to use the car to do odd jobs and errands for you and your family, if they are in London with you. Discretion from the driver is assumed as regards your extra-curricular activities, especially if they concern a good lady other than your wife.

So are there any drawbacks to being a Minister? If you don't earn as much as the Chairman of British Gas you can take solace in the fact that you might well become the Chairman of British Gas when you leave office. More ominously, the Prime Minister insists in the *Rules of Procedure for Ministers* that "Ministers will want to order their affairs so that no conflict arises or is thought to arise between their private interests and their public duties". However, the Prime Minister adds that Ministers "should normally make their own decisions on how best to proceed". Whilst Ministers must resign "any directorship they hold when they take up office", happily this does not normally apply to "directorships in private companies in connection with private family estates".

The Prime Minister also understands that "Ministers cannot be expected, on taking up office, to dispose of all the investments they hold". Of course not. In the case of Tim Sainsbury MP, a Minister and the son of a famous grocer who is said to be worth some £700 million, such a suggestion would be as ridiculous as it would be difficult to carry out. If as a Minister you have investments which might give rise to a conflict of interest with your Ministerial duties then you must dispose of them. It's best and possibly easiest to do this by transferring them to your spouse or a member of your family or, if things get tough, to a blind trust, i.e. a discretionary trust under which you are not informed of changes in the investments or in the portfolio. So there are absolutely no drawbacks to becoming a Minister, even if you are rich, providing only that you employ the right financial advisers.

Secretaries of State

Your ambition to be a Secretary of State is entirely honourable. Inside your Department, always assuming you can cope with the 'Yes, Minister' machinations of your civil servants, it is you who will take the big decisions. More important, as a member of the Cabinet you rule Britain, reputedly, along with twenty or so of your colleagues. Suddenly you have a support system, organised by some of the best brains in the country, which is genuinely the envy of politicians around the world. If information is power, you are given so much of it that you are close to being omnipotent. Because a lot of information is given to you in secret you will always have the satisfaction of knowing that however much others may criticise you, they do not know the full story. All Cabinet Ministers are appointed Privy Councillors and swear an oath of secrecy to the Queen. This enables you to put the prefix 'Rt Hon' in front of your name.

Although the Privy Council is for the most part a constitutional fiction (it never meets) designed to give dignity and status to the Monarch, the Privy Councillor's oath which you will take is important because it symbolises the culture of secrecy which lies at the heart of government in Britain. The oath, which dates back centuries before universal suffrage was established, was at first a device to protect the King and his advisers from Parliament; today it is a device to protect the Cabinet from Parliament and the public.

Every Thursday morning you will attend Cabinet meetings in Downing Street. Although the discussions are strictly confidential you will have to develop techniques, contacts and conduits to allow you to put your own spin on

Who's pulling the strings? The Prime Minister is omnipotent to all but the Cabinet Secretary

what has happened. Metaphorically speaking, lunch-time on Thursdays is leaking-time for Cabinet Ministers. The government machine, however, is so clogged up these days that most decisions are not taken by the full Cabinet but by Cabinet sub-committees, each one with four or five Ministers present. Often you will have to send one of your Junior Ministers along. Can they be trusted? That's the question.

Prime Minister

The Prime Minister is omnipotent – well, to all but the Cabinet Secretary. If you do not understand the extent and irresponsible nature of the power of the modern Prime Minister then you have not been paying attention to the way in which Parliament and government work. Any idea, as is claimed in old-fashioned constitutional text-books, that the Prime Minister is first amongst equals in the Cabinet is a million miles from the truth.

These days it is more accurate to liken the Prime Minister to an elected monarch or benign dictator. In the modern world, television has turned Prime Ministers into leaders who daily go into battle against the enemy, the Opposition. Along with the press, TV initially creates an image of infallibility and omniscience on the part of all Prime Ministers. It is as the image fades that the authority of Prime Ministers diminishes. Margaret Thatcher played the role of Monarch, Pope and God for over a decade. It is doubtful if anyone today could survive the pressures and do likewise.

As Prime Minister you will have a number of deadly weapons to help you. The first is the support of the Cabinet Secretary who, if he is named Sir Robin Butler, will do almost anything to support your government however wrong or badly it behaves – even *in extremis* conducting enquiries into the personal lives of your Ministers as they affect their public duties, and inadvertently acquitting the guilty.

Your second deadly weapon is your right to hire and fire Ministers at will. The problem comes when all around you there is carnage because so many of them have been fired or had to resign or, as in the case of Michael Portillo, Peter Lilley and Michael Howard, are

Cabinet colleagues whom you would describe as "bastards".

As Prime Minister you will find that your power over patronage is awesome. That means lots of people will be beholden to you. In a crisis this gives you renewed strength to carry on. It's best therefore when handing out Life Peerages, Knighthoods and other honours, to appoint those who will be of use either to you or your party, or preferably both. The same goes when you appoint people to run outside bodies such as the Arts Council, the National Rivers Authority, members of NHS Trusts and so on. And of course when you set up Royal Commissions and impartial enquiries you will want a majority of your people on board.

Whether or not you survive in comfort as Prime Minister will depend on how much you are prepared to remain true to the doctrines of Niccolo Machiavelli, the celebrated Florentine civil servant, statesman and political theorist who set out his views in *The Prince*, first published in 1513. The need is to be strong and ruthless, to generate a certain amount of fear and to become a master of the arts of political deceit and intrigue. Better than any theorist before or since, Machiavelli understood the value for a Monarch or Prime Minister in diverting attention from civil strife and discontent at home by going to war.

A war against a much weaker nation, carrying with it the virtual certainty of success, is the best bet, as Prime Minister Margaret Thatcher realised when she took on Argentina to defend an island chain or group called the Falklands which were for the most part inhabited, according to one of their own leading figures, "by a bunch of sheep-shaggers, drunks and whingers". In her treatment of her Cabinet colleagues Margaret Thatcher also seems to have been influenced by Machiavelli's view, set out in 1514 in *Discourses on The First Ten Books of Livy*: "But we must assume, as a general rule, that it never or rarely happens that a republic or monarchy is well constituted, or its institutions entirely reformed, unless it is done by one individual". Whether the sheer ordinariness of John Major and Tony Blair will ever be able to live up to this rule is questionable.

Not that one should be dismissive of John Major. He tried the ultimate Machiavellian manoeuvre. Unable to tolerate any longer the poisoned barbs of the "bastards" in his Cabinet or the insidious sniping of the loonies on his back-benches, he sought the approval of the public by arranging to assassinate himself. The assassination attempt failed – but he's still doomed. Nice one, John. You'll certainly be remembered in the history books.

How to Play

In the age of mediocrity where the writs of John Major and Tony Blair run, MPs who wish to get on must aspire to be ordinary. Above all else, top politicians hate anyone trying to upstage them, grabbing too much of the limelight or achieving glory which should rightly be theirs. So be ordinary, be modest, act without emphasis, speak without rhetoric, leave the thinking to others and avoid any danger of being supposed an intellectual. As a pragmatic party, the Tories have rarely found the space for intellectuals. Indeed, in the nineteenth century they were referred to as "the stupid party".

From time to time, however, they do call upon intellectuals to re-interpret their ideology in a new light. That is not, however, your job as an MP. Leave that to the boffins of Conservative Central Office. In the Labour Party the word intellectual is a term of abuse, connoting a species of being for whom work by hand has always been a mystery and by brain an impediment to be pitied. In post-thinking managerial politics, party leaders would prefer you to be reliable rather than brilliant. Unpredictability is something they cannot stand. So be good but not too good.

One Step Behind

Whilst there will always be bad behaviour in the Chamber of the House of Commons, you should play no part in it. Always stay one step behind: never lead. If you want to climb the greasy pole it will not help if the Speaker is having quiet words in the ear of your Chief Whip suggesting that your behaviour is not all it might be. In the political history books bad behaviour, combined as it usually is with principle, passion, commitment and theatre, carries with it a certain legendary glamour. Eschew such excitements. You are here not to change the world heroically like some village Hampden but to get on in it.

If you do behave badly then you are liable to be 'named' by the Speaker, which means that after a vote which invariably goes in favour of the Speaker you will be ordered to

INTERESTING PARLIAMENTARY HOOLIGANS		
DATE	MP	OFFENCE
12 Nov 1984	Dennis Skinner	Calling David Owen MP "a pompous sod"
11 Nov 1985	Brian Sedgemore	Accusing Nigel Lawson, Chancellor of the Exchequer, of "perverting the course of justice" in relation to his handling of the Johnson Matthey Bank collapse
24 Nov 1987	Dafydd Wigley	Bad behaviour
25 Jan 1988	Ken Livingstone	Accusing the Attorney-General of being "an accomplice to murder"
15 March 1988	Alex Salmond	Refusing to come to order
22 July 1988	Tam Dalyell	Describing Margaret Thatcher as a "habitual liar to Parliament"
13 Feb 1989	Dale Campbell-Savours	Alleging certain MPs were a security risk
7 March 1990	John Browne	Failure to disclose interests on Register of Members' Interests
2 July 1992	Dennis Skinner	Calling John Gummer MP "this little squirt of a Minister"
29 Nov 1993	Rev Ian Paisley	Accusing John Major of "falsehoods"
3 March 1994	Dale Campbell-Savours	Accusing Alan Duncan MP of having "ripped off" the ratepayers of Westminster over the purchase of a Council house
26 Jan 1995	Dale Campbell-Savours	Accusing Lord Archer of "illegal activities" and "insider dealing in the shares of Anglia TV"

withdraw from the Chamber and will find yourself suspended, possibly for the day, or more likely for five or twenty days. The practice of 'naming' was made a Standing Order in 1880 when Irish MPs were hell-bent on disrupting Parliament in pursuit of Home Rule. In 1881 the Speaker named twenty-eight Irish delinquents en bloc, and by a vote of the House of 410 to six they were ordered to withdraw. Each refused to go until the Sarjeant at Arms, sword at the ready and with a bunch of heavies beside him, compelled them to leave. Today most of these heavies, nominally called messengers, would be ex-SAS. Woe betide anyone who defies the Sarjeant at Arms.

None of the MPs involved in the brawl in 1893 when the House was considering the Home Rule Bill went on to achieve high office. Chamberlain started the trouble by taunting the supporters of Gladstone, the Prime Minister, and accusing them of being toadies. He concluded that for them Gladstone's voice was "always the voice of a God. Never since the time of Herod has there been such slavish adulation". At this all hell was let loose. "Judas", cried P. O'Connor MP. One of Gladstone's supporters called Logan crossed the floor and sat in the seat of the Leader of the Opposition, only to find himself manhandled by Unionist MPs. Colonel Sanderson, an Irish Unionist MP, smashed his fist into the face of Michael Austin MP, a Nationalist, whereupon another Nationalist clocked Colonel Sanderson one. As more and more MPs pitched in, some eager for the fray, others naively believing they could restore order, a brawl that would probably have got an X-Certificate had it taken place in a Hollywood film, broke out. Mr Gladstone, so Michael MacDonagh tells us, "not only averted his gaze, but with a perturbed expression of face reclined on his side along the Treasury bench, so that the Table might more effectively hide the horrid business from his view".

Since 1945 fifty-four ruffians have been given their marching orders by the Speaker for bad conduct or using unparliamentary language. In most cases it is not making the remark that results in suspension but the refusal to withdraw the remark. The truth of the remark is no defence since all MPs, despite overwhelming evidence to the contrary, are deemed to be Honourable in the eyes of the Speaker.

No doubt Dale Campbell-Savours MP and Dennis Skinner would bitterly resent being referred to as unrepentant recidivists and serial parliamentary criminals because they are two of the very few MPs who can genuinely claim to take the high moral ground. But that's how it is in Parliament: the good guys lose out and the nasty survive with no more than a grossly insincere apology.

However talented, parliamentary hooligans do not get on or go up the Ministerial ladder. Overwhelmingly, those suspended by Speakers since the war have been Labour MPs, although as everyone in Parliament knows, the best hooligans are Tories trained at public schools. The obvious inference that Speakers, even Labour Speakers, are biased against Labour MPs, is the one that no one can draw since such an inference would itself be a contempt of Parliament, rendering whoever drew it liable to punishment.

Ministerial Misconduct

If as a Minister you want to make it to the top the rule is that you should do nothing in your private life which reflects adversely on your public duties. Generally speaking, if as a Minister you are caught out publicly in any of the following your political career will come crashing to the ground:

1. immoral behaviour, including fornication and bearing false witness
2. the commission of criminal acts and
3. acts which though not illegal are adjudged by your colleagues in Parliament and the public to be corrupt.

So you should read, learn and inwardly digest the lessons of the cases overleaf, which involved Ministers who were forced to resign because their conduct was deemed unacceptable.

There are a number of positive strategies for you to consider. Some may suit your bent; others will not. Without being flashy or flamboyant you can create an identity for yourself. One way of doing this is to turn up regularly for Oral Questions. Be careful, however, if you are an Opposition MP because Ministers always have the advantage in what is basically a stylised minuet. Once you put down your question two weeks before it is due for answer they will turn it over to bright young things in their Department to draft a reply.

You think you can trip the Minister up with your supplementary question on the day but you're wrong. The bright young things at the Department anticipate all the possible supplementary questions and draft answers for these too. Effectively, the sting in your supplementary question has been taken out of it before you've asked it, and maybe before you've even thought of it. If you can't think of what PQs to put down, your front-bench will provide you with them. Civil servants too are happy to get Ministers to arrange for friendly MPs to plant questions. A good supplementary question with a bit of tang in it may even be reported on the early evening news.

But if you have a telegenic face and an inquisitorial mind, then a spell on a Select Committee is the place for you to make a name.

Dennis Skinner, parliamentary hooligan or defender of the moral high ground?

ROLL OF DISHONOUR: MINISTERS FORCED TO RESIGN BECAUSE OF UNACCEPTABLE CONDUCT	
1947	H Dalton (Budget leak)
1948	J Belcher (minor bribery, Board of Trade)
1958	I Harvey (personal scandal)
1962	T Galbraith (Vassall security scandal – exonerated)
1963	J Profumo (lying to the House)
1972	R Maudling (Poulson scandal)
1973	Lord Lambton (personal scandal)
1973	Earl Jellicoe (personal scandal)
1974	Lord Brayley (former business interests)
1983	C Parkinson (personal scandal)
1992	D Mellor (acceptance of hospitality)
1993	M Mates (links with Asil Nadir)
1994	T Yeo (personal scandal)
1994	Earl of Caithness (personal scandal)
1994	M Brown (personal scandal)
1994	T Smith (past non-disclosure of interests)
1994	N Hamilton (past non-disclosure of interests)
1995	A Stewart (grabbing a pickaxe in self-defence)
1995	R Hughes (personal scandal)

Source: Prof David Butler, Nuffield College, Oxford

The work of every government Department is now scrutinised by a Select Committee which meets once or twice a week. Each Committee has eleven to thirteen MPs on it. Although back-bench MPs on the government side have a majority, increasingly Select Committees are expected to criticise the government, not praise it. The TV cameras which are often present love to see a Minister being grilled by an MP from his own party.

Do not go ape, however, for the purpose of transient glory. Heed the lesson of Nicholas Winterton MP, the Chairman of the Select Committee on Health, who attacked his own government so much that it turned nasty and secured his demise as Chairman. If you're in Opposition the position is different of course, and anything that you can do to make the Minister's life miserable will stand you in good stead with the punters and hopefully with some of your colleagues.

If you're a Tory with a flat or house near Parliament be generous but circumspect with your entertainment. If ideology does perchance bug you, invite like-minded people along to smaller gatherings and more intimate parties.

If you're a Labour MP wanting to get into the Shadow Cabinet, it used to be important for you to be a member of a sect like the Campaign Group (serious left) or the Tribune Group (latterly known as the great betrayers). Now you have to claim that you are a moderniser (desire for office at all costs). Although it is a good idea to talk to your colleagues (i.e. those that will elect you to the Shadow Cabinet) and buy them cups of coffee, the real professionals buy the floating voters expensive meals in St James's. They appoint managers to do dirty deals on their behalf. They lie about their influence in finding back-benchers jobs. They get the Whips to fix up the doubters with foreign trips. And they go along with ballot-rigging when voting takes place.

Alice Mahon MP, elected to scrutinise the counting of the votes in the Shadow Cabinet elections, discovered the scam. The ballot boxes were opened by a Whip the night before the voting officially ended. A preliminary count was made, thus enabling one of the Whips, who had a fistful of empty ballot papers handed to him by sleazy MPs, to vote in such a way as to ruin the chances of some MPs who would otherwise have been elected and ensure that other MPs who would not have made it, did so. The method of voting had to be changed when Mahon spilt the beans.

Bizarre voting still takes place, however, in Shadow Cabinet elections. Under Labour's Assisted Places Scheme each MP has to use four of his eighteen votes on women candidates if the ballot paper is to be valid. Some of the men resent this. In one election, one male MP cast only five of his eighteen votes – one for Ron Davies MP, the other four for no-hoper women candidates. In the same election two other male MPs cast only six votes – one for Tom Clarke MP, one for David Clark MP, plus four for no-hoper women candidates. In the 1994 Shadow Cabinet elections a bloc of MPs cast one of their votes for women for Harriet Harman (who had a chance of being elected) and the other three for women candidates who had no hope of being elected.

Clearly there is a lot of skulduggery going on. If you want to get on you must become part of it. Against this background, you will not be surprised to learn that few Shadow Cabinet members cast any of their votes for other existing Shadow Cabinet members, lest they should prejudice their chances of staying in the Shadow Cabinet. Not to put too fine a point on it, behind the frozen smiles they have scant regard for each other.

One Last Push

Once you've become firmly established there is the question of what to do in the last big push to become Prime Minister or Leader of the Opposition. In times gone by, if you wanted to become Labour's Prime Minister or just the Leader of the Labour Party the process was simple. You started out as a left-wing Labour rebel, resigned on an issue of principle and then claimed to be the conscience of the Labour Party. The comrades, brothers and sisters flocked to your banner and there you were, Harold Wilson Prime Minister, Michael Foot and Neil Kinnock Leaders of the Labour Party.

Once you'd made it you grew up, became a statesman and moved towards the centre ground, or as your former allies saw it, started on the process of betrayal.

Tony Blair has done it differently. True, in the early 1980s he pretended to be on the left, supporting CND and Tony Benn for Deputy Leader of the Labour Party. But as Margaret Thatcher cut the ground from under Labour, Blair became the invisible man so far as ideology and policies were concerned. He joined the Tribune Group of MPs and made his way in the Shadow Cabinet on the Tribune Group slate, but never attended Tribune Group meetings. A sponsored member of the TGWU, he rarely turned up at their meetings. And he avoided turning up in the tea-room to talk to colleagues. Bizarrely, he made no contribution to discussions in the Shadow Cabinet, except as regards his own brief. If he was developing a modernising philosophy he forgot to tell anyone about it. However, his strategy had one great virtue. He never made any enemies.

John Major seems to have prospered in much the same way. You can search in Hansard and elsewhere for big speeches on political issues from Major before he became Prime Minister, but you will find none. Like Blair, he was another political philosopher who had nothing to say. Now civil servants search for Big Ideas for Major and young men who have just started to shave advise Blair. Clearly in future if you want to get to the top you should, after signalling your intent, keep your trap shut and your thoughts to yourself. The new golden rule for political advancement is "Make no enemies". Experience shows that one enemy will cause you more trouble than any good which ten supporters can do for you.

Despised Breed

Although Whips are salaried members of the government they are a despised breed. Some say that being offered a place in the Whips' office is akin to being handed a poisoned chalice. Perhaps it is the curious disciplinary powers and the keeping of personal files on MPs, contents of which are used from time to time to keep them in line through blackmail, that dis-

concerts a lot of MPs. Tory Whips write up the sexual and financial peccadilloes of their colleagues in a 'Dirt Book'. Usually they know the names of the mistresses of Tory MPs, whether the MPs are into violent sex or are promiscuous or gay, whether they have sticky fingers, their past affiliations, shady acquaintances, etc, etc. It will all be put on the record together with gossip, rumour and innuendo, much of which will be untrue.

In this latter regard, the information which Tory Whips have is a lot like that contained in the files of MI5 – interesting but speculative. If Tory MPs threaten to move out of line, behave unreasonably towards the government or, worse, vote against it, Tory Whips are masters at subtly trading off the continued secrecy of the information in their possession against the expectation of good behaviour in the future. Of course there's a lot of bluff about what the Whips do and do not know and what they will and will not do. But for the aberrant, naughty MP defying the Whips is a risky business. Tory Whips are a bit like prefects at a public school; Labour Whips like bolshy incompetent managers on the shop floor. The Chief Whip is important because he is a member of the Cabinet and invariably on intimate terms with the Prime Minister.

Each Friday as an MP you will receive by special post a 'Whip', a document in which the business of the House of Commons for the following week is set out and underlined in black once, twice or three times. In the old days governments or Oppositions claimed that the 'Whip' was no more than an order to attend Parliament; nowadays everyone accepts that it is an instruction to vote with the party. If the business is underlined once that means that the Whips do not mind what you do so long as you do not vote against the party. Two lines means that you must be present and vote with the party, unless the Whips on both sides agree to your 'pairing' off with a member of the other party so that the absence of your 'pair' and yourself will not affect the result of the divisions. Three lines means that come hell or high water you must be present and vote with the party, even if it involves coming down to London from the Outer Hebrides in an ambulance on a drip-feed. Obviously this shortens the lives of MPs who are seriously ill.

Eight Traitors

The way in which the 'Whip' operates as an instruction to vote with the party was beautifully illustrated in 1994 when eight Tory MPs defied a three-line whip and refused to vote with the government over the issue of the budget of the European Union. The eight traitors were Teresa Gorman, Nick Budgen, Richard Shepherd, Tony Marlow, Michael Carttiss, Sir Teddy Taylor, Christopher Gill and John Williams. After the vote the Chief Whip wrote to them and told them that the 'Whip' was being withdrawn, i.e. they were being excommunicated from the Conservative Party in Parliament and could no longer attend its meetings or discussions or receive its documents and papers or avail themselves of the help and succour which the Whips' office normally provides.

One of their colleagues, Terry Dicks, referred, with characteristic grace, to those who had lost the Whip as "parasites" and "pimples on the body politic". He described a friend of the rebels as a two-faced sanctimonious hypocrite. Temporarily the government became a

minority government. Because of possible repercussions on the make-up of Standing Committees and Select Committees, the Whip was later restored to the rebels in the hope that, chastened by being out in the cold for a while, they would behave like good boys and girls in the future. The MPs for their part were glad to have the Whip back, partly because without it they could not stand as Conservatives at the next General Election, and partly because they did not wish to have their innermost secrets, all of which would have been within the knowledge of the Whips, made public by way of revenge. Not for fifty years had the Conservative Party seen anything like this.

The Whips also convey back-bench opinion to the Leaders of the parties, as well as making representations about back-benchers who look fit for promotion. They also make up, together with the Leader of the House (he is a member of the Cabinet too) and Shadow Leader of the House, the 'usual channels'. The 'usual channels' oil the wheels and arrange the business of the House of Commons. Opposition members of the 'usual channels' are often criticised for being too accommodating to the government. However, the 'usual channels' have to work on the principle that it is mutually desirable that the machinery of government should work and that the government of the day must, in the end, be allowed to get its business through.

Most Whips like to believe they are stern disciplinarians. Greg Knight MP, the government Deputy Chief Whip (1995), is, however, in a class of his own as a bone-breaker and score-settler. When Dale Campbell-Savours and Ann Clwyd, two Labour MPs, went for dinner in the Members' Dining-Room (April 1994) they found the tables full except for the one in the corner traditionally reserved for the government Chief Whip, Richard Ryder MP. Tory MPs looked on agog. Peter Lilley, Secretary of State for Social Security, complained to the Labour MPs, only to be told that they liked the table so much that they intended to use it every evening.

As this was no laughing matter for the Tory Whips Greg Knight was called in. He called Campbell-Savours outside and suggested the following three-point deal: (1) Campbell-Savours and Clwyd should vacate the table by 9.10 pm; (2) the Whips could help Campbell-Savours in his campaign to keep Tory MP Alan Duncan off the Procedure Committee; (3) the Tory Whips would stop blocking Campbell-Savours' election to the Select Committee on Agriculture, providing Campbell-Savours himself stopped wrecking the whole election process. At 9.10 pm precisely Campbell-Savours and Clwyd vacated the table.

On the Nod

A few days later on 19 April Campbell-Savours' nomination for the Agricultural Select Committee went through on the nod. Duncan never got on the Procedure Committee. He seemed unaware that the Chief Whip's gastronomic comfort was more important than his political career. A couple of months later, Tory MP Tim Devlin told his constituents that he had resigned over some issue of principle as PPS to the Attorney-General. Not so, thundered Greg Knight publicly, insisting that Devlin had been sacked for missing votes. So if you're a Tory keep some distance between Greg Knight and yourself.

Tory Whips are usually selected because they are thought to be able MPs who will move up the Ministerial ladder, whereas traditionally the Labour Whips' office has been a repository for incompetent and sometimes venal MPs. Tony Blair was certainly right in 1994 to try to alter this by moving a few moderately able Labour MPs into his Whips' office. His mistake was to take on the whole Parliamentary Labour Party and indeed show his contempt for it by putting the Prince of Darkness, Peter Mandelson MP, into the Opposition Whips' office and allowing him to forge links between that office and the office of Labour's Deputy Leader, John Prescott.

The Prince of Darkness is undoubtedly the most disliked figure in the PLP – as Blair was told in no uncertain terms. Neither the Opposition Whips' office nor Mr Prescott's office were keen to have an unpopular spy in their camps. As for Labour's back-bench MPs,

they keep asking why Blair is in hock to the Prince of Darkness and why he fails to tell the truth about the role of the Prince of Darkness in relation to himself.

So You Want to be Speaker?

Nobody enters politics in order to become Speaker; a few are lucky to be chosen for this venerated post. The Speaker is the symbol of Parliamentary democracy, the guardian of the privileges of the House of Commons, and as the Chairman of debate, the person who prevents our Parliamentary system from grinding to a halt and debates from breaking up in chaos. Mr or Madam Speaker is also the person who is the Chairman of the House of Commons Commission, a body of senior MPs, which unbelievably employs 1,000 permanent staff. The salary, a pittance in view of the responsibilities of the job, is the same as that of a Cabinet Minister. But the job comes with a sumptuous pad, with gorgeous state rooms. The clothes are sexy too – state robes trimmed with gold and buckled shoes.

Ironically, the Speaker does not make speeches. The name stems from the time when the person who held the office had to speak for and on behalf of the House of Commons to the monarchy, the House of Lords and a number of organisations outside Parliament. The origin of the Speakership is to be found in 'The Good Parliament', held in 1376 in the reign of Edward III. It is sometimes argued that parliamentary democracy, which enshrines the notion

The Prince of Darkness: Peter Mandelson keeps his Leader in the know

of free speech on the part of the elected rulers of Britain, owes much to Speaker Lenthall.

On 4 January 1642 King Charles I entered the House of Commons to arrest five members for treason. Speaker Lenthall replied: "May it please Your Majesty, I have neither eyes to see, nor tongue to speak in this place, but as the House is pleased to direct me, whose servant I am here, and I humbly beg Your Majesty's pardon that I cannot give any other answer than this to what Your Majesty is pleased to demand of me". This historic reply established the principle that the Speaker was the servant of the Commons, not of the King.

If you do go for the Speakership you will have to be able to cope with horrific scenes and deal with hundreds of uncontrollable egos. Are you sure that you have the wisdom, perspicacity and brilliance of Speaker Peel when he was called in to quell the riot of 1893 in the Chamber? One who was there wrote: "He was at once dignified and gentle, with a simple yet noble seriousness. Not a hard word had he to say. His voice, in asking for explanations of what had happened was quite caressing .... He expressed the hope that the regrettable incident pass into oblivion .... Like a parent, wise as well as fond, dealing with a fractious child in a brainstorm, he laid a calming hand on the troubled brow of the House and gently soothed it .... Truly, a striking manifestation of the force of personality and tact".

Betty Boothroyd, the object of Tory fantasies

Each day the Speaker leaves her office in procession for the Chamber. A Doorkeeper leads the way, followed by the Sarjeant at Arms carrying the Mace, the Speaker and the Trainbearer, the Speaker's Chaplain and Secretary. As the procession reaches the Central Lobby where the public gather, the cry goes up "Hats off, Strangers", and the visitors remove their hats as a mark of respect. MPs bow as the procession passes.

On 27 April 1992 history was made when the House of Commons elected its 155th Speaker. Even for MPs it was a moving occasion. For only the third time this century the House debated the merits of two nominees, the Rt Hon Peter Brooke and Miss Betty Boothroyd. When Betty Boothroyd got the job she was the first Speaker to be chosen from the Opposition benches this century, and she was the first female Speaker. And the first Speaker, moreover, who had once danced in a chorus line. As far as we know, at any rate. The age of Madam Speaker, superstar, had begun.

In a desperate effort to return barbaric MPs to civilisation and culture Betty Boothroyd has organised evenings of song and music in the State Rooms, in which we hear of a world of love, a world of peace, a world of joy on earth, a world of birds singing to God. Alas, before each of these soirées ends and the lead singer of the English National Opera has finished, the Speaker is called away to do duty in the less rarefied atmosphere of the Chamber of the House of Commons. One is tempted to ask, however much one is at home in this atmosphere, "What on earth is a nice lady like you doing in a palatial dump like this?"

The Tories love Madam Speaker, partly because she is the stern nanny that they have missed since their early days and partly because they can fantasise about her high-kicking powerful legs as a former Tiller Girl. Labour MPs love her because her roots are in the right place and she is one of them. I had my doubts but I was wrong. She has been magnificent – alternately austere, motherly, friendly, an angry sister, a flowery born-actress, a serious politician and tough. But always fair. If you think you can follow that, good luck to you.

LUXURY AT THE TOP: GRACE AND FAVOUR HOMES

10 Downing Street

Few people know that No. 10 Downing Street, which is to become your grace and favour home in London as Prime Minister, was born of venality. For centuries the site of the front of the house belonged to the Abbey of Abingdon, which established a brewery and the Axe and Gate Tavern there. The back of the house, known as the Cockpit, was demolished in 1675, by which time it had become a conglomeration of lodgings and offices. Cockfighting certainly took place there in the reign of James I, the Treasury accounts referring to the cost of "Matt upon the cockpitt being broken and torne with Cockes fighting there".

The man who started building the current houses Nos. 10 and 11 in 1683 was Sir George Downing, a profiteering contractor who was described by Samuel Pepys as a "perfidious rogue" and by Andrew Marvell as "Judas", whilst according to the *Dictionary of National Biography* his reputation was stained by servility, treachery and avarice, which is perhaps what one would expect of someone who had been both a spy-master for Cromwell and a fawning creature of Charles II.

The first Prime Minister to use No. 10 was Sir Robert Walpole in 1735. All Prime Ministers since Balfour have lived there, except for Harold Wilson who only used it for official purposes during his last spell of office from 1974-76. No Prime Minister has ever been given the keys of the front door because night and day there are always flunkeys or policemen present to open and shut it.

As you know, the road from the House of Commons on foot to the inner sanctum of power at No. 10 Downing Street is one of the shortest in the country, yet tricky to negotiate as one leaves the Members' Entrance, crosses New Palace Yard, greeting the policemen on the way through the gate, turns right towards Whitehall, navigates the traffic which ignores the signals at Bridge Street, heads left across the road at the lights towards the Treasury building on the corner of Parliament Square and Great George Street. Then it's right past the Foreign Office, left through the security gates with a cheery greeting from more policemen at the top of the street, right through the main door at No. 10 past, yes, you've guessed it, yet another policeman, and thence across the black and white marble chequered floor and beyond the Chippendale porter chair in the corner of the entrance hallway. Now one pads over gold-coloured carpet along a corridor of frightening stature with portraits of Victorian thespians on one side and high windows on the other, into the ante-room of the Cabinet Room and finally through double doors into the Cabinet Room itself with its coffin-shaped table.

You will sit in one of the twenty-three mahogany chairs, each upholstered with a tan-coloured hide, with your back to the marble fireplace over which hangs a portrait of Sir Robert Walpole, the only picture in the room,

No. 10 Downing Street: Built by a profiteering contractor

placed there to remind members of the Cabinet of the seamless history of modern British politics, unbroken by revolution or lasting civil strife. At meetings of the Cabinet, the Cabinet Secretary will sit at your right hand. The aura of the room, undistinguished and lit by high windows and three brassy electric chandeliers, lies in its history rather than in its design, style or accoutrements. Not even two pairs of classical pillars, supporting extensions to the room, catch the eye. You should know that the picture of Walpole is a fake, the original of which by van Loo has long since disappeared into the Hermitage Museum at St Petersburg.

Much more likely to delight your eye are the Pillared Drawing-room, the largest of the state rooms, the White Drawing-room, the boudoir for your wife, and the Blue Drawing-room where you will receive your guests at formal receptions and dinners prior to entering the State Dining-room, whose chairs were originally in the British Embassy in Brazil. In your private flat at No. 10 the kitchen is not all it might be, so you will need a cook to help your wife out. The dining-room next to the kitchen, however, is fine for entertaining your personal and political friends. "This place seeps into your blood" said Mrs Thatcher. However, the wife of Tony Blair, Cherie Booth, has intimated that the private flat would be too small for her family should her husband become Prime Minister. Some people are never satisfied.

For relaxation, Nos. 10 and 11 share a delightful garden which even Cherie Booth could admire. A large lawn sweeps around the back of the two houses and plants, roots and flowers are laid out pleasantly in rosebeds, with flowering evergreen shrubs against the high brick wall. In the middle of the lawn is a lovely ilex tree. It's a nice place for a relaxing stroll or a photo-call.

Of all the Ministerial residences 10 Downing Street is the one that has most reflected the differing tastes of its occupants. Disraeli smartened the place up, partly at the expense of the Treasury and partly at his own expense, when he moved into No. 10 for the first time in 1877. In addition to filling the main reception room with "silk-covered chairs and sofas, silk curtains and a number of tables and fine rugs", he adorned it with bowls of primroses sent over to him by Queen Victoria. Yet it was at 10 Downing Street that he told us what we all know, namely that good health is to be valued above material things, when he wrote: "When one has got everything in the world one ever wished for, and is prostrate with pain or debility one knows the value of health".

Gladstone installed his grand piano in No. 10, together with his son Herbert Gladstone MP, while he used Nos. 11 and 12 for himself and his wife together with the servants.

As one would expect, the first woman tenant, Margaret Thatcher, made a number of changes and added a touch of femininity. Grand red carpets gave way to softer gold-coloured piles as she tried to give the house a lighter and more airy feel. To this end, she had the brown baize doors replaced by white-painted wood and glass doors in the ante-room to the Cabinet room where her Ministers used to assemble nervously before Cabinet meetings.

Valuable Objects

For her study she grabbed a portrait of the handsome young Nelson and a Zoffany bureau of the Rojoman family from two museums. These were valuable objects which had no place in Downing Street. Then she turned the main bedroom of the private flat at No. 10 into the sitting-room, with "two two-seater settees, covered in floral patterns of red and blue on a cream background". Above one of the sofas she hung a Lowry townscape painting, *Lancashire Fair 1946,* which she borrowed from an art gallery. One is reminded of Queen Mary, something of a royal kleptomaniac. So widely dreaded was her habit of admiring some picture or *objet* and expecting to be offered the expensive trinket forthwith, that owners of the grand houses she visited took to hiding their most precious things before her arrival.

For all but the grandest and crudest amongst us, the use of 10 Downing Street is definitely a perk of the job. A cat, something of a specialist in dealing with rats, comes with the property.

Chequers

You will soon find that Chequers, your new country residence, is one of the seductive arms of government, a fine Tudor mansion bequeathed by Lord Lee of Fareham to the nation. Standing high in the pure air of the Chilterns, it was hoped that the better would be the health of our Prime Ministers and the more surely they would rule, if they used it. One of your predecessors, Lloyd George, was the first Prime Ministerial occupant.

A singular pink-red brick structure whose colours are picked out by the stone-grey gable copings and mullioned windows, it is a building to make you blink the first time you see it. When you invite your Cabinet colleagues down, be sure to explain that the estate of 1250 acres has 900 years of history to its credit and was mentioned in the Domesday Book as belonging to Maigno the Breton. The Stone Hall, the Great Hall overlooking a courtyard, the Long Gallery which houses the Library, treasures and relics, the Great Parlour, the White Parlour, the Cromwell Passage and the forbidding Prison Room, these are names for your freshly appointed Cabinet Ministers to conjure with. Those with imaginative talents will create their own histories out of the mysteries that surround them.

Chequers: Good for the health of Prime Ministers

Two hundred paintings spanning almost four centuries of Western culture and 900 precious objects proclaim that the house is for men and women of influence and power, perhaps even civilised and appreciative of culture. George Brown, one of the Cabinet Ministers in Harold Wilson's government, rather let the side down in this respect, however, getting drunk in the Long Library before dinner.

It was after a splendid Sunday lunch at Chequers in September 1984 at which the Prime Minister, Margaret Thatcher, and her husband Denis had entertained the maverick tycoon 'Tiny' Rowland, the Chief Executive of Lonrho who was described by another former Prime Minister as "the unacceptable face of capitalism", that Edward Du Cann MP, the Chairman of Lonrho who was also present, suggested that a donation to the Conservative Party of £150,000 might help them in their bid to buy Harrods.

Chevening: Geoffrey Howe was stricken with grief when he was forced to leave

Chequers was bequeathed to the nation on condition that there should be no addition or subtraction to the principal features of the house. Prime Minister Edward Heath, however, was allowed to redecorate the place, spending, according to Tony Benn, "half a million pounds" on garish wallpaper, a swimming pool paid for by the US Ambassador, and other such essentials. Today as you drive off in the evening with your loved ones, the headlights of your chauffeur-driven car will pick out the beech trees on Victoria Drive which were presented to the estate by one of your most illustrious predecessors, Sir Winston Churchill, and his dear wife. Happily, at Chequers the sun always shines too, so go there as often as possible.

Chevening

When you are first offered a job in the Cabinet on your way to becoming Prime Minister it is no use accepting any job. There is a pecking order and you must get one of the top Cabinet posts. That means becoming either Foreign Secretary or Chancellor of the Exchequer. That is in part because both of these Cabinet Ministers have grace and favour homes. Chevening, a grand country mansion overlooking a lake, possibly designed by Inigo Jones in the seventeenth century, with pavilions on either side connected to the main three-storey house, is now the permanent rural residence of the Foreign Secretary. Chevening, set in 3,500 acres on the North Downs, breathes such elegance and is in every way so spectacular that even the most prestigious estate agents would be pleased to have it on their books. The floors are laid with marble, the staircase is magnificent beyond dreams and the rooms, adorned with columns and capitals and moulded ceilings, invite you to linger, whilst the most erudite of men would covet the Library. God, you are lucky. Is it any wonder that when Sir Geoffrey Howe was forced out of office by Prime Minister Thatcher he and his wife Elspeth were stricken with grief at the loss of their country home, whose bills were paid by the Foreign Office when they entertained the big nobs of the world?

Bequeathed to the nation by the Stanhope family, Chevening was originally built for the 13th Lord Dacre in 1630. If architectural history gives you a buzz, feast on the fact that your home emerges as a pioneer house of immense importance, and delight in the skilfully resurfaced red brick, with Ionic pilasters and stone dressings. The circular staircase was inserted in 1721 by Nicholas Dubois and runs straight up from the Hall two full storeys, one complete gyration per storey. The dining-room contains the very finest panelling. Each wall is divided into five bays by the fluted Corinthian pilasters with gilt lead capitals. Inset arches span each bay and rise to the deep cornice, with its coupled guilloche brackets. The walls of the Tapestry Room are lined with superb Berlin-Beauvais tapestries. Here the chimney-piece is copied from chimney-pieces by Vanbrugh at Hampton Court.

These are the perfect surroundings for you and a small group of hand-picked advisers to relax and do your long-term inspirational thinking.

11 Downing Street

No. 11, the home and, when not working at the Treasury, the office of the Chancellor of the Exchequer, is another of Sir George Downing's venal buildings. However, there are compensations, including the whiff and allure of power associated with your next-door neighbour, the Prime Minister.

When you move in with your family, take care about letting out your former residence. No one wants you to come a cropper like Norman Lamont MP, the Chancellor of the Exchequer who found that he had let rooms to a Miss Whiplash, and was then further embarrassed when the taxpayer forked out part of the legal bill which he ran up to resolve the eviction problem. It's best too, if as Chancellor of the Exchequer, you are not seen going into No. 11 with a black eye arising from a dangerous liaison. There could be difficulties, too, if you order your wine from Threshers.

Immediately you enter No. 11 you become part of history as your eye is drawn in the entrance hall by the eighteenth century lantern, the fine grandfather clock made in 1815 by Vulliamy and, best of all, magnificent portraits of Gladstone and Disraeli, the latter hanging over the marble fire-place. In the study off the entrance hall are porcelain caricatures of the same two politicians on the mantelpiece. It is here that you will work on the papers from your Red Boxes. It is from here too that you will make your Budget broadcasts. The State Drawing Room will please your wife, as will the lacquered Chinese cabinets in it. But most exciting of all downstairs is the Soane dining-room. On two sides of this room the shallow vaulted ceiling, suspended umbrella-fashion, is detached from the walls, making room for two long *trompe l'oeil* window 'lights'.

Your private apartments are on the first and second floors and extend above the Chief Whip's office in No. 12 Downing Street. In the early 1960s the architect Raymond Erith refashioned it around an elegant square hall. As you go up the staircase to your bedroom, natural light emanates from a large and decorative glass dome in the ceiling, giving it, as the government estate agents so rightly say, a spacious and airy feeling.

On Budget Day you really can feel proud as you stand outside No. 11 with your wife, holding up the famous red Budget box for the cameras. All of a sudden your life has taken a turn for the better.

Dorneywood

The smell of mown grass at Dorneywood, the country residence of the Chancellor of the Exchequer, and the sight of leaves falling from the trees in autumn as you step down into the oval-shaped sunken lawn, leaving behind the bow window of the music room, is an experience not to be missed. Not quite matching the grandeur of Chevening, this pastiche of a house, part Tudor, part Queen Anne, unfortunately situated near Slough in a mere 214 acres, was bequeathed to the nation in 1941 by a businessman, Lord Courtauld-Thompson. As you enter the house, however, you will be immediately seduced by the Rex Whistler decoration of the inner porch, which began prophetically with the idea that Flora and Cupid would visit the house but ended up, after Whistler had taken a scholarship in Italy, with a scene which Botticelli himself might have painted.

Tea in the drawing-room in comfortable armchairs looking up at mezzotints of eighteenth century notables and surrounded by elegant furniture including a beautiful Queen Anne walnut bureau, will leave you with happy memories. An invitation to dinner in a room whose Georgian silver was once despatched to the vaults of a bank after a burglary is not one that your friends are likely to turn down. Although the upkeep of a house of this size could be expensive, you need not worry because the staff, cooks, maid, gardener and cost of mowers, maintenance and the like come out of the income of the original endowment.

You will find that the music room at Dorneywood is simply divine. The bow window at one end is balanced at the other end of the room by an ellipse, at either end of which are odd Victorian blackamoor figures on marble stands, with gold gesso robes and black lacquered faces with hysterically happy eyes. In the middle of the ellipse is the piano, whose pitch and tone are perfect. Beech furniture painted so that it imitates bamboo, Japanese in design, was especially fashionable in the sparsely decorated rooms of the late eighteenth century. On a Sunday morning after a rave-up on a Saturday night this is just the place to relax. So always invite a pianist down to the house.

Aladdin's Cave

If you like art the house is an Aladdin's Cave, and questions will come flooding into your mind about the Chinese fret balustrade on the staircase; the tent of Indian cotton on the first-floor landing; the silk curtains in the dining-room, which though made in France, were sent to China where they were decorated with hand-painted flowers and animals; the seventeenth century Flemish tapestry on a wall in the Library; the comic drawings by Sir John Tenniel, the *Alice in Wonderland* illustrator and *Punch* cartoonist, various strange mechanical objects; and about the problem in deciding which is the more real, the *trompe l'oeil* painting of a cupboard full of china on one side of the fireplace in the music room, or a cupboard containing identical solid objects on the other side.

Almost the only problem concerns the twin beds in the master-bedroom. If you are a sexually active Chancellor or like to sleep with the naked body of your wife up against you, things are frankly difficult. One Minister's wife, Susan Crossland, who wanted her man by her side, solved the problem by re-arranging the mattresses and linen so as to create a surrogate double bed. Buying your own double bed is unfortunately out of the question because of the terms of the endowment deed, which forbid changing any of the furniture. So most of your fucking will have to be done at No. 11 or at the home of your mistress for the time being.

THE LOBBY AND PUBLICITY

A politician is like a terrorist: without the oxygen of publicity he dies. Yet as you've made your way through Parliament you've become acutely conscious of the fact that getting coverage in national newspapers and on radio and TV becomes more and more difficult. That's why those MPs without ambition, and who gave up even before they arrived at the Members' Entrance for the first time, concentrate on cultivating coverage in the local media.

In times gone by, the proceedings of Parliament used to be reported by gallery correspondents in the House of Commons. Today it is not journalists but political commentators who are sent to Westminster to cover political events. Political commentators are a special breed of arrogant, opinionated poseurs who feel born to declaim and who have absolutely no interest in reporting the actual proceedings of Parliament. Some of them concentrate on writing what they see as magisterial political essays as though they are attempting to produce contemporaneous historical analysis.

Supreme Wordsmiths

Others write sketches, often well-structured and mildly amusing, but invariably calculated and designed neither to explain nor to wound. Real satire is taboo. When you've read a sketch by Matthew Parris, himself a former MP, in *The Times* how much more do you know about politics at the end of it? Nothing. And should you ever pick up the *New Statesman*, the *Evening Standard*, *The Guardian* and almost

any other paper or magazine in which Edward Pearce writes, you will be able to lose yourself in the sesquipedalian verbosity of one of Britain's supreme wordsmiths. Beware, however, because it could be said of Edward Pearce that if you were to transplant a principle into his heart he would wake up from the operation elegantly denying the principle. It's all froth and no substance, you see. Once Pearce attacked Dale Campbell-Savours in the *New Statesman* for being a cranky, self-seeking publicist. When Campbell-Savours complained, Pearce retracted, not necessarily because he was wrong but because he wanted to be loved. Better in the minds of most of us that, right or wrong, he had stood his ground.

As for the other parliamentary reporters, most of them are neatly encapsulated by Tony Bevins, himself a political commentator who has worked for the *Mail*, *Times*, *Independent* and *Observer*, when he says, in an as yet unpublished thesis:

If editors live their lives in revolving doors, political reporting is conducted in a circus ring: riding editorial and political tigers, attempting to find sustenance from the candy floss of official briefings, and, with one of the biggest turnovers in the trade, falling into oblivion from the trapeze.

For their part, politicians are so desperate for publicity that they will do almost anything that the media asks of them. Those who run the media know this, and punish MPs mercilessly for being so craven. At one end of the scale, MPs have succumbed to the scandal of the 'sound-bite'. This derives from studies made by media gurus which tell them that the average attention span of members of the public for political argument is less than thirty seconds. So now instead of interviewing MPs for ten minutes, chopping up the interview and putting out a questionable three-minute item, the media asks MPs, including Ministers, to give their stories, which have predestined outcomes, relevance by producing a twenty-five second sound-bite.

Every night MPs can be seen on the news succumbing to this new form of media prostitution. Nowadays it is even possible to characterise MPs by the kind of sound-bites that they produce. Michael Howard, the Home Secretary, is famous for oleaginous sound-bites, Gordon Brown, the Shadow Chancellor, produces self-destruct, switch-off sound-bites, Tony Banks is a rent-a-yob sound-bite expert, Sir Ivan Lawrence QC intones sonorous, law-and-order, vengeance-be-mine sound-bites, whilst John Prescott parses and paraphrases his sentences so much that they are always several words short of an intelligible sound-bite.

Poor Ann Clwyd became the victim of the ultimate sound-bite when TV promised to send a crew to interview her about child labour. Imagine her surprise when a cameraman turned up on his own, gave her the sound equipment to handle herself, and told her to interview herself. "All we want is a sound-bite. Ask yourself any questions you like. We'll take a sentence from it," he said.

At the other end of the scale are the so-called heavyweight programmes, of which *Question Time* is one. These, you might think, are good for politicians because they enable them to speak for themselves. The trouble is that the Whips now brief the chosen elite who appear on this programme so heavily, providing them with sound-bites for every possible question, that what you get on the programme are MPs lying out of both sides of their mouths at the same time. The synthetic public participation in the programme does not help, because

often members of the audiences who are provided by political parties make the lying MPs look like free-thinkers.

Doing the right thing in Parliament so as to appear in a good light on TV is now so important that senior MPs employ their own spin doctors to tell them how to behave, how to answer questions that are not asked and how to avoid sensitive issues without appearing shifty. When Tony Blair became Leader of the Labour Party he was so nervous about how he might appear on TV at Prime Minister's question-time that on the Sunday before his first encounter he went into the darkened Chamber of the House of Commons to practice. With him were three others – the Prince of Darkness, Greville Janner QC who runs a charm school for his colleagues, and Jessica Bawden, Janner's researcher. While Janner told Blair where to put his arms and legs, Jessica sat on the Tory benches to help him with his eyeline, while the Prince of Darkness pondered how to leak the story so as to show himself in the light of a kingmaker.

The Lobby

If the public is often ignorant of the real nature of what is going on in government and in Parliament, much of this is due to the rituals of secrecy and freemasonry which govern the activities of the Parliamentary Lobby, the club whose members have a virtual monopoly in political reporting. Colloquially, Lobby correspondents are referred to as 'the ratpack' because they hunt together and publish poisoned stories fed to them by manipulative governments, often through the lips of the Press Secretaries of Prime Ministers at daily meetings which take place in a room in a turret at the top of the House of Commons.

No notes are kept of these meetings because officially they never take place. Under the rules, Lobby journalists are not allowed to say who gave them their stories. Worse, should any of the stories turn out to be false or misleading, the government can denounce them with impunity even though its representatives were the source of the stories. Rule 8 of the Lobby – Don't Talk About Lobby Meetings Before Or After They Are Held – prevents journalists from answering back. Members of the Lobby who break the sacred rules of the club are excommunicated just as surely as freemasons who split on their fellow masons are discharged in pain and disgrace from their Masonic Lodges.

In no other sphere of journalism do reporters take a pride in publishing stories which can be denied by the very people who supplied them. In no other sphere in journalism do reporters go out of their way not to provide quotes which can be attributed to the individuals responsible for them, and instead puzzle their readers by starting their stories with phrases such as "Sources close to the Prime Minister suggest...", or "Ministers were saying last night...". Which sources? Which Ministers? Surely readers have a right to be told.

Lobby correspondents are given special access to parts of Parliament denied to the public, and meet MPs every day in the Members' Lobby which is adjacent to the Chamber of the House of Commons. The same Lobby rules apply. Nothing said or seen in the Members' Lobby or other parts of Parliament can be quoted or described. Anthony Howard, a senior political analyst and journalist, describes the scene in the Members' Lobby as "almost like Piccadilly before the Wolfenden Report. There stand the Lobby correspondents waiting, soliciting for the politicians to come out. They treat them as if they were clients and, you know, in some ways I think the fact has to be faced that Lobby correspondents do become instruments for a politician's gratification."

James Fenton, a journalist of superior hue, summed it up as follows after his first day in Parliament when he was introduced to an MP in Annie's Bar: "The MP was so drunk that as he reached forward to shake my hand he fell off his bar stool and slumped to the floor. But of course under the rules I never say this". But Fenton went along with the system. Truly Lobby correspondents are the verminous scum of journalism.

The Lobby was formed in 1884 when London was under attack from Irish nationalists. Two outrages at Westminster led to the Members' Lobby being sealed off from the public entrance, and members of the public being denied access to their MPs there. A special list of those House of Commons gallery reporters and political writers who can use the Members' Lobby is now kept by the Sarjeant at Arms.

As Prime Minister you will have to use the system because it will enable you to use the media as an arm of your government. Like your predecessors you will have to strive mightily to influence press, radio and TV as part of your need to influence Parliament and public opinion. Lobby correspondents will help you in your task because they believe, as willing victims of the system, that the manipulation is worth it, in that it enables them to be close to great men of power and get confidential information from them which would otherwise be denied them. Although they cannot print it, it adds to their understanding of the political process, or so they argue.

If Joe Haines, who was Harold Wilson's chief press secretary in Downing Street, is to be believed, your press secretary should be able to use tame journalists from the Lobby. Speaking of one such journalist, Haines said: "He gave the impression he had more contacts than he

did have. But one of them was the Prime Minister and it was quite cynical on our behalf. We knew he could be bought ...... in the old-fashioned sense of giving him a story. You hire the reporter's soul, you don't buy it".

Sometimes things do go horribly wrong in the best clubs. In early 1989 Cabinet Minister Paul Channon MP and five selected Lobby journalists were caught out after a private Garrick lunch on Lobby terms. The Pan-Am jumbo jet had crashed at Lockerbie in Scotland late in 1988 and Channon was anxious to deflect criticism of his Department for its incompetence in dealing with prior warnings about an impending terrorist attack on a passenger flight. According to the five journalists present, Channon told them that he knew who had made and planted the bomb. The journalists, of course, could not mention his name so Robin Oakley of *The Times*, who was present at the lunch, wrote:

... police and security service investigators now know precisely who made and placed the bomb and the whereabouts of the bomber. The results of what Whitehall sources term 'one of the most remarkable feats of criminal detection ever known' are expected to be disclosed next week.

Times 17.3.89

Writing in the *Daily Record*, the *Daily Mirror*'s Scottish sister paper, Julia Langdon, who was present at the lunch too, reported:

Police probing the Lockerbie air disaster have uncovered all the information needed about the bombers... The Government is expecting a full document from the police within weeks. The police KNOW who placed the bomb on Pan Am flight 103 and where the bomber or bombers are now.

Daily Record 17.3.89

Chris Buckland, also present at the lunch, wrote an even harder-hitting story in the *Today* newspaper:

The terrorist who planted the bomb that blast-

ed 270 people to death in the Lockerbie air disaster was under close arrest last night... The dramatic breakthrough came three months after Pan Am flight 103 was blown from the skies over Scotland and it followed what one senior official called 'the most brilliant piece of forensic detective work in history'.".

Today 17.3.89

However, when other journalists on other newspapers checked the story out they discovered that it was totally without foundation. Things now spun out of control. When questioned by other journalists, Channon was forced to reply: "I never said the Lockerbie bombers had been identified, for the very good reason that I didn't know". The *Mirror*, denounced by a Scottish law officer for reckless and irresponsible reporting, then flagrantly breached the Lobby rules and all the precepts of political journalism by spilling the beans about the lunch, when it revealed:

Last Wednesday, Mr Channon told a group of reporters over lunch, off the record, that the Scottish police knew everything about the bombing. That the bomb came from the Middle East. That it was placed aboard the ill-fated jumbo at Frankfurt. That the police knew WHO had planted the bomb. And that they also knew where he or she was ... The Government has manipulated the press and the truth with deliberation and cynicism. It has got away with it before. It calculates it can get away with it again. But all the press isn't in its pocket. When it accuses us of lying then it makes a fatal mistake. Because we know who the real liars are.

Daily Mirror 21.3.89

When asked to justify his action Joe Haines, now of the *Daily Mirror*, replied:

Well, bugger that. If Paul Channon can't keep his colleagues quiet, we are not going to keep quiet about the source of the story. It's one of the things journalists ought to consider – whether a source remains sacrosanct if that source is guilty of lying to you. In my view, that breaks a contract.

Whatever the truth and whether Channon or the journalists were to blame for misleading the public on such a serious issue, this case illustrates perfectly the corrupt nature of the Lobby system. Responsibility for the Lockerbie disaster remains a mystery to this day.

When he was Margaret Thatcher's press secretary, there is no doubt that Bernard Ingham abused his position as a full-time civil servant with a series of damaging criticisms at press briefings about some of her Cabinet colleagues. In 1981 when Norman St John Stevas MP was sacked as Leader of the House of Commons (he used ironically to refer to Thatcher as "the blessed Margaret"), Ingham suggested that Thatcher had sacked him because she could no longer tolerate leaks of inside information. St John Stevas demanded an apology and got it.

Pym's Demise

Then in 1982 Francis Pym MP, Leader of the House of Commons, found himself vilified by Ingham at a Lobby meeting. Pym had made a pessimistic speech, which was described, ironically, in the House of Commons by Thatcher as "excellent". An hour later Ingham recalled the words of the wartime radio character Mona Lott who used to say "It's being so cheerful as keeps me going". It was the beginning of Pym's demise. His successor John Biffen fared no better. In 1986 on London Weekend TV he criticised Thatcher's style and called for more "balanced government". Ingham, ever the pit-bull terrier, bit back at a Lobby briefing, describing Biffen as a "semi-detached" member of the Cabinet and claiming that Biffen was a maverick who said different things from one week to the next. Biffen's days were numbered. Important papers were withheld from him. Thatcher cold-shouldered him. He is today largely forgotten. Ingham's defence, presumably, was that he was only following orders in abusing his position or, in John Biffen's immortal phrase, he was "the sewer rather than the sewage".

On one occasion Ingham forced the Bank of England to raise interest rates after stories in the newspapers said that the government was not prepared to defend the falling pound against the dollar. The reports were based entirely on a Friday afternoon briefing by Ingham to senior journalists.

During the 1980s three newspapers, led by *The Independent*, left the Lobby only to return to it a few years later. They were childishly deprived of aeroplane seats and the like by the Prime Minister's press office for their temerity and integrity. The other Lobby journalists were horrified, their attitude summed up by Chris Moncrieff, a member of the Press Association, who likened *The Independent*, *The Guardian* and *The Scotsman* to joyless virgins who sought to take all the fun out of life. Moncrieff caught the Lobby's priorities perfectly when he wrote:

For myself I have never yet been able to locate a conscience even if I had wanted to struggle with it. If a story is on offer, it seems to me, it doesn't matter how it is imparted so long as it is within the law... Some of our more righteous and high-minded colleagues throw up their hands in horror at the mere thought that the Prime Minister (as she has done) might 'use' the lobby to criticise ministerial colleagues in an unconventional way. Well, for my money, why not? Even if we thought there was anything 'morally' amiss, why should we bother? We are not an arm of government; we are not contrary to common belief, the fourth estate (although some like to pretend they are); nor are we there to serve the public good – nor yet do it ill. We are in the business to write stories to sell newspapers. I think we are part of the entertainment industry at the down-market end. We do it for the money. And if that serves the public good at the end of the day – well, that's a bonus.

The House Magazine 5.6.89

Clearly, Prime Ministers should be grateful for the existence of the likes of Chris Moncrieff who inhabit the Lobby. May you be so lucky!

Bernard Ingham, wily protector of "the blessed Margaret"

HOUSE OF CORRUPTIBLES

How Corrupt is British Politics?

The House of Commons is a House of Corruptibles. As someone who has climbed to the top of the greasy pole, you are better able to testify to this than anyone else. The verdict of the public, said by some to be unduly alarmist but by others to be prescient, is that MPs today are not just corruptible but corrupt.

Every schoolboy, along with Lord Acton, knows that "power tends to corrupt and that absolute power corrupts absolutely. Great men are almost always bad men". In the eighteenth century, financial corruption in politics was widespread. Sir Robert Walpole, Prime Minister for twenty years, as venal a politician as ever there was, used the public purse to embellish his country mansion in Norfolk and was forever on the receiving end of the savage wit and satire of Jonathan Swift and Alexander Pope. In the nineteenth century, voters continued to be bribed in 'Rotten Boroughs' long after the Reform Act of 1832. Rotten Boroughs were parliamentary seats, the most famous of which was Old Sarum, where there were so few electors that they could easily be bribed, often with barrels of beer, by well-heeled candidates. The bribery stopped with the advent of the secret ballot and the passing of the Corrupt Practices Act 1883. But when Dr David Butler tells us that by the First World War electoral corruption had virtually disappeared, never to return, he is surely wrong. As we have already

seen, electoral corruption in marginal seats is not uncommon and the limit on expenses is often an aspiration unfulfilled.

But just how corrupt is politics in Britain today? According to John Major, corruption, out of sight and out of mind, does not exist. In setting up the Nolan Committee to look into standards of public life, he told the House of Commons that standards of integrity and probity in the United Kingdom are very high indeed, and bear comparison with those elsewhere in the world. Even as he spoke, one's mind went back to the time when everyone proclaimed that England had the best football

PERCENTAGE POLL
In an opinion poll commissioned by the *Daily Telegraph* in November 1994:
64% of voters thought that most MPs make a lot of money by using public office improperly
73% thought that the Conservatives "give the impression of being sleazy and disreputable"
87% thought it was not right for an MP to take a free weekend with his or her spouse at the Ritz
89% opposed MPs taking money or gifts in connection with their duties
95% thought that it was wrong for an MP to accept payments for asking questions in Parliament

team in the world, and did so louder than ever on the eve of that match between England and Hungary at Wembley, which Hungary won by six goals to three.

Is it possible that we have been deluding ourselves about political probity? Well, politics in Britain surely cannot be as corrupt as politics in Italy, where sleaze and scandal arising out of the bribery of political parties and politicians are endemic. There has yet, so far as we know, to be a former hooker seated in the House. Before anyone says that it could not happen here, however, we ought to look back to the stance taken by the Labour Government 1974-79, when a row broke out about allegations that BP, a partially-owned British public company, was bribing Italian political parties to get contracts. Along with one of my colleagues, I went along to protest to the Treasury minister, Joel Barnett MP. The note in my diary picks up the story:

Whilst the Government's public stand was that it would not condone bribery by publicly-owned companies, privately it did precisely that. The issue arose over the disclosure of allegations that BP, a partially-owned public company, had been bribing Italian political parties to get contracts. John Prescott MP and I met a Treasury minister, Joel Barnett, in his room in the Commons to discuss the matter. We were told in the nicest possible manner not to be naive, and that of course British companies, including publicly-owned companies, bribed foreigners to get business. They had always done so and would continue to do so. Morality should not be mixed up with trade. 'Don't be so naive, Brian, do you really expect nationalised industries to stay out of the bribery business?'

Moreover, in the 1980s private companies bribed, bribed and bribed again when signing contracts in the Middle East, and did so with the knowledge of Ministers. Batting for Britain Ministers will turn a blind eye to almost anything. So when Dr Butler writes: "By the mid-19th century, a system of public finance was established which, together with the Civil Service ethos, has meant that extraordinarily little taxpayers' money gets misappropriated. By world standards, our national administration has been amazingly pure for a century", it is not clear whether he is agreeing with John Major or lamenting a past which is in danger of disappearing.

In 1994 the powerful All-Party Public Accounts Committee (PAC) issued a stern warning to the government in this regard, in a report entitled *The Proper Conduct of Public Business*, when it said: "In recent years we have seen and reported on a number of serious failures in administrative and financial systems and controls within departments and other public bodies, which have led to money being wasted or otherwise improperly spent. These

---

CRITERIA OF CORRUPTION

In Chapter 9 we listed a number of MPs who had resigned as Ministers for wrong-doing, and were able to pick out three types of wrong-doing:

1 immoral acts by MPs such as fornication and bearing false witness, the biblical words for adultery and lying. Lying on the part of MPs, Ministers and civil servants is a subject that we looked at in Chapter 5. In Chapter 5 we also examined MPs' own attitudes towards ethical questions and discovered that a third of all MPs classified themselves as "ethical entrepreneurs", an expression, which in layman's terms, signifies the inability of such MPs to tell the difference between right and wrong. In the next chapter we consider so-called immoral acts on the part of MPs which involve sex

2 the commission of crimes by MPs and

3 acts on the part of MPs which, though not criminal, are thought by the public and in many cases by MPs themselves to be corrupt. We glimpsed a few of these activities in Chapter 9. In this chapter we examine corrupt conduct, together with allegations of corrupt conduct, with special reference to

    (a) MPs' outside interests

    (b) cash for questions

    (c) lobbying of MPs and lobbying by MPs

    (d) honours for politicians

    (e) appointments to QUANGOs

    (f) payment for honours

    (g) unlawful acts.

Reggie Maudling, destroyed by cowboy builders

while not claiming that vast sums of public money are being misappropriated, nevertheless challenge the thesis of the Prime Minister. The following quotation taken from the *Independent on Sunday* lacks ambiguity: "Most of us have come to believe that many of our institutions have been corrupted by the arrogance, complacency and self-interest of the people inside them.... Story by story, drip by rotting drip, a picture has emerged over the past two years of an ancient debating chamber ruled by antique custom, filled with a modern kind of person (usually male and usually Tory) whose behaviour suggests that the interests of the people who elected them are not always at the forefront of their minds."

More guarded but nevertheless critical, Tony Bevins, the Political Editor of *The Observer*, wrote: "Sacrificial ministerial resignations, John Major's synthetic tantrums, and the Cabinet Secretary's oil-slick impersonation of Inspector Clouseau are no substitute for answers to allegations of impropriety at the heart of government."

Reginald Maudling MP, John Cordle MP, Albert Roberts MP and a Pot of Gold

In 1965 Reginald Maudling, a former Chancellor of the Exchequer, lost his battle to become Leader of the Conservative Party. Casting aside his disappointment, he decided to combine politics with the good life. Directorships flew his way, and soon he found himself the owner of a country house and a nice Regency pad in Belgravia. Many of his new-found business contacts were fine establishment figures, but he wanted more and decided to go not for broke but for gold.

This led him to associate with three businessmen whose activities were always dubious – John Poulson, Jerry Hoffman and Eric Miller. Before he knew it, he did a deal which he would later regret with Eric Miller, which effectively gave him years of salary in advance, without any tax loss. Soon he was promoting the schemes of John Poulson, a property developer

failings represent a departure from the standards of public conduct which have mainly been established during the past 140 years. This was the period following the publication of the Northcote and Trevelyan Report which condemned the nepotism, the incompetence and other defects of the Civil Service and brought about fundamental change. It is from that period that we acquired the principles and the standards which have come to be copied by some countries and admired by many more. It is our task to retain those standards."

In summarising twenty-six of its earlier reports it concluded: "Almost every case we have examined involved breaches of existing rules or guidance". Typical of the kind of issue worrying the PAC was that of inadequate financial controls at the Foreign Office, where it reported: "The Department's accounting arrangements were open to strong criticism, and inadequate controls created a climate which was conducive to fraud and theft and may have heightened the risk of irregularities remaining undetected".

A number of political commentators,

with the largest architectural practice in Europe.

As well as talking to sheikhs on Poulson's behalf, Maudling as an MP persuaded the Maltese Government to give Poulson a hospital contract, where British public money was involved, on the island of Gozo. The deal this time was that Maudling should buy shares later in a Poulson company fronted by two other MPs, John Cordle and Albert Roberts. In the meantime the company employed Maudling's son and gave substantial donations to his wife's favourite charity. All the time, Maudling was unaware of Poulson's political freemasonry and corruption. Then Poulson's solicitors dragged poor Reggie further down by getting him involved financially in a huge international property scam run by Jerry Hoffman's company, the Board of the Real Estate Fund of America (REFA). Back in Ministerial office in 1970, Maudling resigned from both REFA and Eric Miller's company Peachey.

Unfortunately for Maudling, Poulson hopelessly over-extended himself and filed for bankruptcy in 1972. The nightmare scenario that unfolded left Maudling friendless, disgraced and ruined. The Metropolitan Fraud Squad were called in when the bankruptcy hearings revealed that rewards to politicians and public figures may have involved fraud and corruption.

When Maudling resigned as Home Secretary, solely, he insisted, because the Home Secretary is responsible for the Metropolitan Police, few doubted that his attempts to realise a "little pot of gold" for his old age had backfired. A damning article in *The Observer* forced the new Labour government of 1974 to set up a Select Committee to investigate the relationship between Poulson and the three MPs Maudling, Cordle and Roberts.

The Committee concluded that Cordle had committed a "contempt" in advocating Poulson's cause in Parliament in return for money. Cordle resigned as an MP. Roberts and Maudling were rebuked for not declaring their interests in Poulson's company, and Maudling was further rebuked for being less than frank in his resignation letter of 1972. Roberts insisted he had only "transgressed in the shallow

waters" while Maudling, still referred to as an honourable man by former Prime Minister, Edward Heath, insisted that he had done nothing wrong. After a debate in the House of Commons, MPs merely noted the report of the Committee and took no action. Poulson went to jail.

Harold Wilson MP and the Slag Heap

In 1974 the Prime Minister, Harold Wilson, found himself savagely attacked over what became known as the Slap Heap Affair, which concerned a number of deals over a slag heap and quarry near Wigan. The quarry was owned by Tony Field, a graduate geologist who was a golf companion of Wilson, and his office manager in 1971. Wilson's political office was run by Marcia Williams, now Lady Falkender, who seemed to be almost the only person that Wilson trusted during his frequent bouts of paranoia. Marcia's father helped Wilson buy a house, and her elder sister worked as a secre-

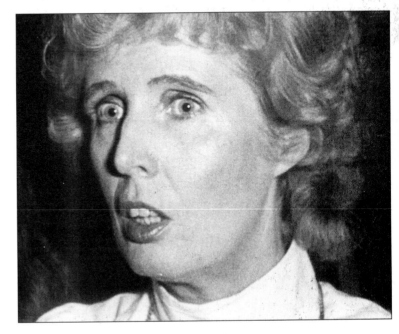

Marcia Williams, Wilson's right-hand woman

tary at No. 10. Field was her brother. In 1973 Field offered some of the land to Ronald Millhench, an insurance broker, in an effort to pay back a public sector loan which had helped him purchase the original site.

Millhench ruthlessly used the 'Wilson connection' in his efforts to re-sell the land. When the matter broke publicly, this led to base claims that Marcia was investing money in speculative land deals on behalf of the Prime Minister. Field wrote a letter on a piece of Downing Street notepaper. A forged letter suggesting Wilson's involvement turned up. But most damaging of all for Wilson was his answer to a Tory MP in the House of Commons: "my honourable friends from Durham know the difference between property speculation and land reclamation.... This is no laughing matter". The eerie silence on the Labour benches certainly spoke eloquently to this latter point. While Wilson had absolutely no connection with any of the slag heap deals, his mistake was to seek to justify the private activities of his staff.

In the end, he and Marcia Williams issued writs which they did not pursue, whilst he sounded just a little hysterical when he suggested that the aim of the press was to spread allegations "however vague, however hidden, of corruption at worst, dubious standards at best".

John Stonehouse MP and the Psychiatric Suicide

John Stonehouse, a working-class lad with serious ambitions to be Prime Minister, became Minister of Technology and then Postmaster-General in the Labour Government 1966-70. Quite the nicest thing ever said about him came from one of his colleagues, Richard Crossman, who wrote that Stonehouse was "a kind of dangerous crook, overwhelmingly ambitious but above all untrustworthy". Between 1970 and 1974, when the Conservatives were in power, Stonehouse set up a number of companies which collapsed, including one called

Partners in crime: John Stonehouse and Sheila Buckley

Connoisseurs of Claret Ltd. In 1971 he set up a British Bangladeshi Trust, which was financed with mirrors and by fraudulently recycling loans and his own money over and over again.

In 1974 as fraud investigators closed in, Stonehouse merged the British Bangladeshi Trust into a new company called the London Capital Group. Amazingly, just as he did so the Czech spy Josef Frolik, who had defected, published a book alleging that Stonehouse was one of his contacts. Then when a final big Nigerian deal collapsed, Stonehouse decided to opt out and faked a psychiatric suicide. Leaving the Fontainbleu Hotel in his shorts, he disappeared off the coast of Miami like a latter-day Sergeant Troy. A couple of months later he was arrested in Australia. In 1976 he was sentenced to seven years' imprisonment after being found guilty at the Old Bailey of forgery, false pretences, theft and fraud. His girlfriend and former secretary Sheila Buckley was given a two-year suspended sentence.

From prison Stonehouse, probably the first Postmaster-General to sew the mail bags, resigned from the Privy Council and then suffered a heart attack. Gallant to the last, he said of his secretary's actions: "It is not a crime when a pretty girl falls in love with a married man".

Fergus Montgomery MP and the Pills

The case of Fergus Montgomery MP, charged with shoplifting, found guilty and acquitted on appeal, is truly a warning to those other MPs who are under pressure from the burdens of work not to seek to find salvation in drugs. The political world was stunned when Montgomery, a former PPS to Prime Minister Margaret Thatcher, was found guilty on 20 September 1977 at Horseferry Magistrates' Court of stealing two books at the Army and Navy Stores in Victoria Street, SW1 – a biography by Lord Selwyn-Lloyd and *Spend, Spend, Spend* by Viv Richardson, a football pools winner. The books were put in a zip bag. Montgomery said he remembered buying a

third book but could not remember putting the other two into his holdall.

At Rochester Road police station he said "It is all true" after a detective had described the theft. At the Magistrates' Court Montgomery said that when accused of stealing the books outside the store he did not know what they were talking about. The previous evening he had drunk three or four whiskies and later took a Mogadon tablet to help him sleep. That morning he had taken a double dose of slimming tablets after having only coffee for breakfast.

Asked by the prosecution what his mental state was when he was stopped outside the store, he replied: "I suppose my recollection is that I felt at peace with the world; warm and comfortable with no signs of stress". At his appeal against conviction and a fine of £60 and £70 costs, Judge West Russell, sitting at the Inner London Crown Court, said that he and his colleagues were not satisfied that Montgomery was dishonestly motivated at the time he took the books. Montgomery was later knighted, and is currently Chairman of the important Committee of Selection which recommends the appointment of MPs to the various committees.

Jonathan Aitken MP and His Brother

Jonathan Aitken, a member of the Beaverbrook dynasty, exudes the effortless imagined superiority of his class. Amiable across party lines and a godfather to the son of Diane Abbott MP, he looks so terribly innocent. In reality, of course, like most wealthy people Jonathan has a mind ringed with steel. In the early 1980s he and his brother Timothy bought into TV-am through a company called Beaverbrook Investments. Tim became Chairman and Jonathan a director.

The Aitken family, however, were far from being the majority shareholders in Beaverbrook Investments. 49.3 per cent of the company was owned by another company called Al Bilad, a company controlled by

Saudis. Their ownership was operated through Aitken Telecommunications Holdings. Effectively, £2.1 million which people thought came from the Aitkens came from a Saudi investor. Jonathan did the deal with the Saudis which became known as the 'disputed agreements'. His fellow directors in Beaverbrook Investments say they had no knowledge of the Saudi agreement until a legal row broke out in 1986 in Curaçao. Jonathan's brother Timothy swears he was unaware of the agreement for five years.

The matter was important because IBA rules prevented non-European Community res-

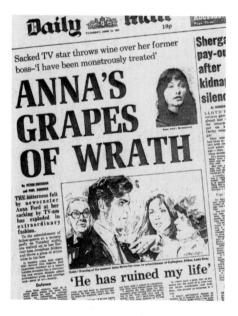

idents from owning more than one per cent of TV-am. It seems clear that not only was this rule broken, but also that when the company went public in 1986 potential shareholders were not told of this breach of the regulations. Whether or not civil or criminal offences were committed through the breach of this regulation, the IBA was certainly seriously misled. A more difficult issue upon which to make a judgement was the provisions in the Broadcasting Act 1981 which banned non-

European Community nationals from controlling TV-am and other TV stations. Jonathan says that the Saudi funding was always under the control of himself and his brother Timothy and that the Saudis had non-voting shares. Timothy says that that is impossible because of his ignorance of the 'disputed agreements' for five years. In 1988 Jonathan was forced to resign as a director of TV-am.

He has only ever admitted to "an error of judgement". No doubt his most lasting memory of his time with TV-am will be the glass of wine that Anna Ford threw over him at a party when Aitken decided that she and the other four amongst the 'Famous Five' who founded TV-am – David Frost, Angela Rippon, Michael Parkinson and Robert Kee – should leave the company.

Aitken and the Arms Merchants

In 1995 Jonathan Aitken's colourful past as a director of a company which traded in arms caught up with him. The company, British Manufacturer and Research Company (BMARC), broke his own government's arms embargo by supplying naval guns to Iran which were ostensibly going to Singapore. The chairman of Astra Holdings, the parent company of BMARC, alleged that Aitken knew about the deal and the ultimate destination of the guns.

Aitken denied all knowledge of the illegal contract, which was code-named 'Project Lisi', and insisted that if he had known about it he would not have countenanced it. Insults were exchanged between the parties. Aitken, paid £10,000 a year to attend board meetings, was a director from September 1988 to June 1990; the contract ran from 1986 to 1989. Company directors are obliged to exercise 'due diligence', and in the minds of the Courts ignorance on the part of directors is not necessarily a defence when it can be proved that a company has acted unlawfully. Aitken's problem, however, was not with the Courts but with his political future. When the story broke he was in the Cabinet as Chief Secretary to the Treasury. What would his peers in the House of

Commons or the general public make of the two facts that could not be denied – the law had been broken and he had been a director at the time?

Perhaps as you'd expect, while partisan Tory MPs cheered him to the echo, partisan Labour MPs demanded his resignation. As for the public, some of them undoubtedly thought that this astute politician and one-time smart journalist had, in his ignorance, let his government and our country down. Ironically, it was Aitken himself who long ago had written chillingly and prophetically: "The shame of the arms merchants will ring down the centuries of history". This ringing declaration sat uneasily beside the disclosure that Aitken had become an unpaid director of another arms company, Future Management Services. Subsequently, when Aitken faced further criticisms about his business interests from *The Guardian* and Granada TV he issued writs.

Then with every pore oozing venom and with his rich, well-oiled, beautiful body shaking with anger, he called a press conference and used the occasion to launch a crusade against "the cancer of bent and twisted journalism with the simple sword of truth and the trusty shield of fair play". Tory MPs were ecstatic that one of their number was fighting back against the great Satans of TV and the press. In the space of a couple of weeks he had heroically decided to take on the BBC, Granada TV, *The Guardian* and *The Independent*. Usually when a person in authority issues writs it has the effect of stopping further criticisms for fear of further writs. In this case, however, *The Guardian* and *Independent* continued to write critical stories about Aitken, mainly in relationship to his Arab friends and his and their interests in various companies.

If Alan Clark, one of Aitken's colleagues, is to be believed then Aitken's "trusty shield of fair play" was nowhere to be seen in 1990. In his published *Diaries* Clark records that on 5 April 1990 he and Aitken decided to take their "revenge" on their Tory colleague Michael Mates MP. They agreed that Aitken should contact Labour MP Tam Dalyell and prime him with a question, which might ruin Mates'

Treasury minister issues writ against Guardian in bid to save political career

Aitken sues over Saudi claims

Editor stands by story

Jonathan Aitken with his simple sword and trusty shield

career, about a company "who pay Mates". Clark went on to describe Aitken as "my old friend and standby for many a dirty trick". Perhaps it does not matter any longer. Much of the glitter went out of Aitken's heroic campaign in search of the truth when in the interests of the government and the country he resigned from the Cabinet so as to give himself more time to clear his name.

Keith Best MP and BT Shares

A barrister with the world at his feet, Keith Best MP decided to go for the quick, illegitimate buck because he thought he could get away with it. In 1984 when BT was about to be privatised it was a racing certainty that the shares would show a huge profit after the first twenty-four hours of trading. Indeed, they had been deliberately underpriced to ensure that this would be the case. This was, after all, in the era when money fell out of the sky and loadsa-money louts staggered around the City weighed down by their bulging wallets. Best decided to cash in, applying for more than the permissible number of shares, using false names and a variety of addresses. In 1987 he was jailed for four months, a sentence reduced on appeal to a fine of £4,500, for making fraudulent share applications. In disgrace and feeling sorry for himself, he resigned as an MP and was suspended as a barrister until 1990. Not that any of this did him lasting harm. He is now a Director of the Immigrant Appeals Advisory Service, a

Jim Callaghan and the funny money bank

judicial body funded by the Home Office. Who amongst us would deny that he was well qualified for the job?

Jim Callaghan MP and the Man from BCCI

The Bank of Credit and Commerce International (BCCI) collapsed in 1991 owing some £10 billion around the world as a result of corruption, fraud, money-laundering and arms dealing. It was the greatest banking scandal in history. The fraud had started long before former Prime Minister Jim Callaghan accepted a payment of £12,500 from the disgraced founder of the bank, Agha Hasa Abedi, in October 1986. Indeed the author of this book had personally told the Governor of the Bank of England before that date that BCCI was up to its ears in corruption. BCCI drew the money for Callaghan from a slush fund, using the Sundry Debtors Expense Account. Callaghan failed to register his interest in the Register of Members' Interests as he was obliged to do. No one suggests that Callaghan had any idea that BCCI was a financial cesspit at the time that he accepted the gift. Nor was he aware that Abedi had misrepresented his relationship with the bank, in stating in an internal document "Mr James Callaghan has joined us as an adviser".

In 1994 when these facts emerged in the *Mail on Sunday* Callaghan described his failure to register his gift as "a technical lapse" because he was winding down his business as an MP. The money, he said, was to pay for a secretary for his Third World affairs when he left the House of Commons. It is surely sad that Callaghan continued to be duped by Abedi. In April 1990, before the collapse of BCCI but after the arrest of some of its officials in the USA, Callaghan described those at the top of the bank in a speech in the House of Lords as "people of the highest integrity and probity".

A pity, therefore, that as a former Chancellor of the Exchequer he did not make a few discreet enquiries in the City or have a word on the phone with the Governor of the Bank of England about the integrity and probity of the mega-crooks who ran BCCI. Since the collapse of BCCI the Select Committee of the Treasury, of which the author is a member, has produced a damning report showing how from first to last the bank was a vehicle for deception.

When today Callaghan still describes Abedi as "a very remarkable man, a very generous man", it should be noted that it was with other people's money that he was generous. In his absence Abedi was sentenced to eight years' imprisonment in Abu Dhabi where many of the shareholders who were duped are based.

Harry Greenaway MP Tries to By-Pass the Courts

In 1991 Harry Greenaway MP, a former teacher, was committed for trial at the Bow Street Magistrates' Court on seven charges of corruptly accepting gifts between 1984 and 1988 in return for using his parliamentary influence to help gain British Rail contracts for the Plaisser Railway Machinery Company, an Austrian manufacturer. He was alleged to have accepted bribes and tried to influence the appointment of the Chairman of the British Railways Board. A hard-line law-and-order MP in favour of capital punishment, Greenaway caused eyebrows to be raised when his QC argued that he should be tried by his fellow MPs, a sizeable majority of whom were, like him, Conservative right-wingers. His QC invoked the Bill of Rights to argue that the Courts had no right to try the bribery allegations against his client, saying: "In principle, MPs are subject to the ordinary criminal law. But in my submission in their parliamentary capacity MPs are only answerable to Parliament".

Mr Justice Buckley rejected the submission on the grounds that those who drew up the Bill of Rights did not intend to preclude the prosecution in the Courts of an MP accused of corruption. No one was ever told what Greenaway hoped to gain from avoiding a trial by a jury of twelve good men and women true and instead appearing before the Committee of Privileges and possibly the House of Commons itself. Cynics argued that the answer was obvious – if the charges were proven, then the evidence of the way in which MPs had approached these matters in the past suggested that they would deal with the case much more leniently than the Courts. In the event, it all became academic when the charges against him which were due to be heard at the Old Bailey were dropped by the Crown Prosecution Service.

The decision to drop the charges was taken by the Director of Public Prosecutions, Barbara Mills, who concluded that there was no longer "a realistic prospect of conviction" following on the collapse of a related trial involving the Plaisser company. Greenaway, who had always denied the allegations, said "I always knew I would be vindicated". What a pity! It would have been fun to have had a full-scale trial of an MP in Westminster Hall and to have been one of the jurors.

Michael Mates MP and the Watch

Michael Mates, better known as Colonel Mates, was a Northern Ireland Minister from 1992-93. A man of impeccable bearing and excruciating naivety, he stunned MPs when it emerged that he had lobbied the Attorney-General on behalf of Asil Nadir, who was facing serious criminal charges in connection with the failed Polly Peck empire. Acting like a driven man in defence of Nadir and behaving more like a civil liberties crank than a person steeped in the law-and-order tradition, he was forced to resign as a Minister. So confident was he of the innocence of Nadir that he gave him a watch inscribed "Don't let the buggers get you down".

Subsequently, Nadir jumped his £3.5 million bail and fled to Cyprus. The Prime Minister and the Attorney-General accepted Mates' insistent claim that he had behaved properly at all times. Some MPs, however, were not slow to point out the irony that while Mates is one of those MPs who proclaims the virtues of British justice, the fugitive Nadir seemed to spend most of his time in Cyprus hurling abuse at it. Others thought that his resignation speech, which amounted to little more than a clumsy defence of Nadir, was flagrantly in breach of the sub judice rule normally operated by Parliament, an irresponsible abuse of the right of MPs to make personal statements on these occasions which cannot be challenged, and a crude attempt to bully Madam Speaker.

Mother's Ruin

The charge against Mark Thatcher was that on a number of occasions he made money on the back of Mumsy and in the process abused the Prime Minister's influence as well as the office of the Prime Minister. The charge against the Prime Minister was that she was indifferent as to whether or not this had happened, preferring instead to point out that she herself had always behaved with the utmost propriety in batting for Britain in order to gain contracts overseas.

Mark Thatcher's denials have on occasion been more oblique than one would have wished. After the row over the Oman scandal which involved himself and his mother and which led to his voluntary exile from the Kingdom to save the Prime Minister from further embarrassment Mark Thatcher, a master of the understatement, commented: "Only a fool, and I am not one, would claim there to be no advantages in having the name Thatcher. I now know some of the disadvantages".

The scandal broke in 1984 when it was revealed that Mark Thatcher was acting as a consultant to the British civil engineering firm, Cementation International, a subsidiary of Trafalgar House. In 1981 after the Sultan of Oman had announced his intention to put out to tender a plan to build a university to firms "renowned for their experience in building universities", the Prime Minister Margaret Thatcher visited Oman. With her in the official party were her daughter and husband.

Mark arrived two days later. Batting for Britain, Margaret Thatcher pressed for the contract to go to a British firm. In September 1981 Cementation won the £230,000,000 contract without tendering and by direct negotiations. In 1984 the political world was rocked when it was revealed that Mark Thatcher had been

Mummy's boy: Mark Thatcher in his playsuit

working for Monteagle Marketing in Oman and that a commission was to be paid into its account. The business of the firm, said an employee, was "catering", by which he meant that "somebody who knows somebody can put somebody in touch with somebody else".

An examination of the account of Monteagle Marketing revealed that not only was Mark's name in the company account but so was that of his father, Denis Thatcher. The Prime Minister complained that this information had been obtained through impersonation and deception. This raised the question of whether the Prime Minister was in breach of her own guidelines to Ministers, which say that they must act in such a way as to ensure that "no conflict arises, or appears to arise, between their private interest and public duties".

The Prime Minister responded that her son's activities were a private matter. Two complaints were made to the Select Committee on Members' Interests, one by the author, that the Prime Minister had not declared a 'family' interest in the Register in relation to the contract, but the Committee ruled that as there was no financial benefit to her personally she had not breached any rule or convention. A number of MPs believe that 'family' interests should in future be declared in the Register of Interests.

It was also alleged that in 1984-86 Mark Thatcher was part of a team of middlemen who brokered a multi-billion pound deal to supply arms to Saudi Arabia. The Prime Minister played an active part in securing what became known as the Al Yamamah deal when she visited Riyadh, the Saudi capital, in April 1985, and met King Fahed. It was said that the Prime Minister's role "cannot be overstated". Mark Thatcher was implicated in tape-recordings which referred to his influence with his mother, but this may have been an example of Middle East arms dealers believing wrongly that the Prime Minister would act like a Saudi Prince towards a son in a similar situation.

Suggestions by the *Sunday Times* in 1994 that Mark Thatcher made £12 million out of the deal were dealt with contemptuously by him, when he declared that he was a poor man worth only £5 million. Many might think that as a person who failed his accountancy exams three times he had done quite well for himself. His other response, "I haven't even sold a penknife", begged the question of whether or not he helped to fix a deal. Baroness Thatcher insisted that she had acted properly at all times.

Robert Maxwell – MP and Megalomaniac

When Robert Maxwell, MP for Buckingham from 1964-70, died after disappearing over-board from the *Lady Ghislaine* in 1991, both the Prime Minister and Leader of the Opposition in this country paid him glowing tributes, while in Israel he was given something approaching a state funeral and buried on holy ground. Yet he will be remembered as a mega-crook who stole a staggering £460 million from the pension funds of his own workers, who died leaving £3 billion of accrued debt, who was once deemed unfit to exercise proper stew-ardship of a publicly-owned company, who swindled the House of Commons Catering Committee, who had extraordinary links with the KGB, and who overbid for the publisher Macmillan and the *New York Daily News* in the United States.

　　Just what is it about the established elites of the world and MPs who cannot recognise a person rotten to the core and devoid of heart and feeling as he stares them in the face? Just what was it that attracted to his side men of such talent as Peter Jay, a former British Ambassador to the USA and a man who once accepted the accolade of being one of the world's top 200 people? Why did he dance to Maxwell's tune? And how did Lord Donoghue, who once worked as a top adviser to a Prime Minister, put his trust in such a man for so long before eventually resigning from two of Maxwell's companies? Even Maxwell's widow Betty says that her husband had been a mega-lomaniac in the last ten years before his death. I met him on a number of occasions as a civil servant and as an MP of a constituency in which he had a factory, and found him at all times to be contemptible. On one occasion I

begged him to consider giving the jobs back to a number of workers whom he had sacked. Showing the quality of mercy for which he was renowned, he held up his palm and said: "Brian, green grass will grow on my hand before I give them their jobs back". In addition to having been an MP, Maxwell stayed close to politicians all his life in countries around the world. His message to the rest of us was that he knew where power lay and how easy it was to dupe those who wielded it.

Sheik, rattle and roll: The power elite danced to Maxwell's tune

Michael Howard QC MP and the 'Egyptian Grocers'

The Fayed brothers, the owners of Harrods, may not be conveniently respectable people but that surely is no reason for English snobs and racists to refer to them, as the *Spectator* has done, as "Egyptian grocers". In 1988 two Inspectors prepared a report for the Department of Trade and Industry into the acquisition by the brothers of the House of Fraser. Harrods is a part of that shopping empire. The Inspectors concluded that: "The Fayeds dishonestly misrepresented their origins, their wealth, their business interests and resources", and went on to say: "We received evidence from the Fayeds, under solemn affirmation and in written memoranda, which was false and which the Fayeds knew to be false".

Subsequently the brothers applied to the Home Office for British citizenship. Under Home Office guidelines two matters in this situation have to be taken into account – length of residence and character. In the light of the Inspectors' report no Home Secretary exercising his discretion properly could have been expected to say that the Fayeds passed the character test. Perhaps not surprisingly, therefore, civil servants at the Home Office recommended that their application for citizenship be refused. So too did the Junior Minister responsible for citizenship at the Home Office, Charles Wardle MP. However, there had been lobbying on behalf of the Fayeds from important people, including MPs, and under the guidelines when this happens the matter is referred to the Home Secretary.

In this case, Michael Howard QC MP was the Home Secretary. Clearly, all he had to do was initial the papers and agree with the proposal to refuse the application by the brothers for citizenship. Michael Howard was, after all, the Minister who set up the DTI enquiry which mangled the character of the Fayeds. But Howard refused to do this and asked the Department and Wardle to think again. Why? What was his problem? In a press release Howard says that the decision was for Wardle to take. But Wardle was adamant that the application should be refused and that the Fayeds could not possibly pass the character test. Civil servants at the Home Office, backed by a furious Wardle, have disputed Howard's version of events. They say that Howard simply refused to accept their recommendation. Certainly, when the author was a civil servant no Minister of any political party would have given the application of the Fayed brothers a second glance. How can a government of integrity and serious intent pass a vote of confidence in the character of two brothers which has been the subject of a successful vote of no-confidence by the same government?

Jeffrey Archer – Money Matters

Jeffrey Archer, an MP from 1969 to 1974, was almost the perfect politician. Rather than deny the mythology of his heroic background he soaked up admiration that was not due to him. He was not born in Somerset; he never went to Wellington College, the famous school with the military background; he never studied at Oxford University, and he never ran for Britain in the Olympics – yet people in their confusion thought he did all of these things.

He had a wife, described by a judge as "fragrant, radiant and elegant", who was twice as intelligent as he. He made money, lost money in a fraudulent company and made it again until today he is a millionaire and Peer of the Realm with nothing to his credit other than the authorship of best-selling books whose prose groans. Like so many politicians who ooze charm and promote themselves beyond their ability, he is treated with suspicion. Why? Perhaps the answers lie in two tales.

One concerns Monica Coghlan, a prostitute who claimed in 1987 that Archer had paid her £70 for her services. Archer denied that he had ever met her, and a jury awarded him £500,000 damages after accepting his account. However, his reputation suffered from his admission that he gave Monica Coghlan £2,000 to help pay for a holiday in Tunisia. By 1994 it seemed that Archer had totally rehabilitated himself, and was on the verge of being appointed Chairman of the Conservative Party.

Alas, the earth fell in for him when he found himself the subject of a Department of Trade and Industry enquiry into 'insider dealing', which is a criminal offence. His wife was a non-executive director of Anglia TV, a company which became the subject of a take-over bid by a company called MAI.

Despite an initial denial – "I did not buy any shares" – it transpired that Archer placed orders for 50,000 shares in Anglia TV in the name of Broosk Saib days before the take-over bid was made public. The price of the shares rose and they were sold for a profit of £80,000. The profit went to Saib. Archer later apologised and admitted to a "grave error" and said that his "deepest regret" was the embarrassment caused to his wife. His poor judgement and reckless behaviour seemed finally to have put an end to his political career. The DTI never published the results of its enquiry. Archer's wife insisted throughout that she had never discussed the take-over with her husband. So there remains a riddle, thus proving that fact is even stranger than the fiction in Archer's books.

MPs and Outside Interests

Before 1911 MPs had to have outside interests if they were to support themselves because they were not paid an official salary. Right up to the publication of the Boyle Report in 1971 which recognised that being an MP was a full-time job, a lot of MPs took the view that membership was part-time.

This encouraged the view that the House of Commons was a privilege best suited to the interests of the better-off or well-connected. However, once MPs were paid what was thought to be a proper salary, the demands for a register of their outside interests grew. Yet even in 1971 after the publication of the Strauss Report which examined the subject, the government took the view that it was better to rely on the general good sense of Members rather than on formalised rules. Even at this time, it should be noted, there was a tenuous custom

for MPs to declare interests in debate.

When a compulsory register was finally set up in 1974 it was only after a parliamentary battle. No less than 168 MPs, anxious that there should be no prying into what they considered to be their private affairs, voted against the motion which was passed. Inevitably, most of the 168 were Conservatives because they had

The Archers: An everyday story of accumulated wealth

more interests to declare. At the same time the custom of declaring interests during debate became a rule.

Today MPs have to list their interests in a Register which is kept by a Registrar. A Select Committee on Members' Interests oversees the Register, examines complaints that certain MPs have failed to declare their interests, and from time to time recommends changes in the Register which have to be approved by the whole House of Commons. MPs list their interests under ten categories – paid directorships, paid outside employment, the names of clients for whom MPs provide services in relation to their parliamentary duties, sponsorship money, gifts worth £125 or more to the MP or spouse, overseas visits, overseas benefits, shareholdings over £25,000 or one per cent of the issued share capital, and other interests which the MP considers relevant. A lot of overseas visits do not have to be declared, including those organised by the Commonwealth Parliamentary Association, the Inter-Parliamentary Union and the British-American Parliamentary Group.

In 1976 the Royal Commission on Standards of Conduct in Public Life recommended that such attempts should be brought within the criminal law, but twenty years on nothing has been done.

The main motive of the House of Commons in establishing the Register was to reassure the public in the aftermath of the Poulson affair that the House of Commons was not corrupt. Many MPs, however, have assumed that any interest if declared can be justified. However, since there are often conflicts of interests such a stance is manifestly absurd.

CRIMES AND MISDEMEANOURS

Erskine May, the bible of procedure in the House of Commons, sets out a number of interests which are not allowable, including the advocacy of a cause for payment and entering into a contract which would limit an MP's complete independence and freedom of action in Parliament. A resolution of May 2nd 1695 forbids attempts to bribe MPs as follows:

That the offer of money, or other advantage, to a Member of Parliament for the promoting of any matter whatsoever depending or to be contracted in Parliament is a high crime and misdemeanour.

Some of the interests which MPs have, clearly have brought Parliament into disrepute. MPs who register consultancies and similar positions can and do misuse their positions on the floor of the House, arguing not for their constituents or in the national interest, but for their clients. The potential problems can be illustrated quite simply. The Police Federation gives two MPs, Michael Shersby (Conservative) and Mike O'Brien (Labour) thousands of pounds to act as their Parliamentary advisers. Mike O'Brien, who uses the money to employ a researcher from the Police Federation, came off the Home Affairs Select Committee because of possible conflicts of interest. But his difficulties do not end there. The Police Federation quite often puts forward illiberal proposals which may be anathema to the citizenry at large or to the constituents of the two MPs. Support from the Police Federation for ID cards could be a case in point in the future.

Clearly, the rest of us expect O'Brien and Shersby not to act as echoes for the Police Federation but to exercise their judgement fearlessly. Fortunately they are both honourable people so we can trust them. But when we get to commercial interests we may well find MPs who are less than honourable.

Sometimes the sheer volume of interests declared by MPs gives food for thought. An *Observer* survey of all 240-plus back-bench MPs on the government side in 1994 showed that 153 of them had picked up 150 directorships and 435 consultancies entirely unconnected with their previous expertise since they entered Parliament. Whichever scientist it was who discovered that time is finite may be congratulated for posing a question mark over MPs whose outside interests pile up exponentially.

Of course some MPs have staggering abilities and can fit far more into a day than others. So their incomes from outside interests may be massively in excess of their parliamentary salaries. David Mellor MP, finding himself under attack in 1994 told TV viewers, and there is no reason to disbelieve him, that he worked his socks off for his constituents. Yet watching him on TV and listening to his radio programmes, reading his articles and studying his 1994 declaration of interests, set out overleaf, it's clear that part of his time is spent working his socks off for his wallet.

Naturally one feels jealous when one reads that Mellor's income from these outside interests may be six times his parliamentary salary. One also envies his stamina.

Congratulations are due too to Patrick Nicholls MP, who as an adviser to nine bodies as set out below, clearly works hard at keeping himself up-to-date in order to bring insights from the real world to his work in Parliament.

Declared Interests 1994

Bad marks to Gerald Malone MP, whose entry in the Register says simply "NIL". What's wrong with you, Gerry? Can't you recognise a good deal when you see one? Still, Malone, the Minister of Health and married father of three, is not quite as dull as he seems. In 1993 it emerged that he had links with Asil Nadir, the tycoon who fled to Cyprus to avoid prosecution. And although he is on record as saying "The Conservative Party and I stand four-square for those values which are traditional in our society", he admitted in 1995 to having enjoyed watching "naked girls play sex games with whipped cream, champagne and margarita cocktails at a private party at a night club".

Bad marks to the London Beekeepers' Association for giving Tony Banks a chance to stick two fingers up to the Register by declaring an annual gift of twelve jars of honey. However, the MP, now retired, who made the biggest mockery of the Register was Dr Dickson Mabon who in 1981 managed to represent (and register the interests) of the Scotch Whisky Association and the United Kingdom Temperance and General Provident Institution.

In an effort to tighten up the rules in relation to those MPs with interests in Lloyds, the House of Commons accepted a recommendation of the Select Committee on Members' Interests that MPs should declare the individual syndicate to which they belonged in the Register. The following eleven MPs were criti-

cised in the Committee's Report for setting a bad precedent in not carrying out the instructions of the House – former Prime Minister Sir Edward Heath, Sir Ralph Howell, Sir Gerard Vaughan, Sir Jerry Wiggin, Sir Richard Body, David Ashby, Winston Churchill, Michael Colvin, Roger Knapman, Anthony Steen and David Tredinnick.

Not content with issuing only the mildest of rebukes, the Select Committee then in cowardly fashion and using weasel words went on to recommend that the obligation to list syndicates should be swapped for an obligation merely to disclose the categories of business they were underwriting. Apparently the knights and the other lesser mortals objected to attempts, wildly inaccurate as it happens, of one MP to calculate their financial losses or gains by reference to the syndicate numbers. As a former Prime Minister, Edward Heath surely let the side down on putting his own tawdry interests above Parliament. That's how it is these days, though.

Despite the view of some MPs that the Register has become an expression of venality rather than a protection against it, and notwithstanding the defaulters and those who register their interests belatedly, most MPs and outsiders are agreed that MPs should register

**PATRICK NICHOLLS MP
DECLARED INTERESTS 1994**

1 Fast-Track Associates; marketing and public affairs consultancy.

2 Parliamentary Consultant to Hill & Smith Holdings plc, a major industrial company. Parliamentary Adviser to the Federation of Associations of Specialists and Sub-Contractors. Consultant to Waterfront Conference Company Ltd (formerly Port Enterprises Ltd), conference organisers. Parliamentary Consultant to Howard de Walden Estates Ltd, property company. Consultant to the Waterfront Partnership, public affairs consultancy. Parliamentary Consultant to the National Sub-Contractors Council (NSCC). Parliamentary Adviser to Channel Express Ltd. Parliamentary Adviser to the British Shops and Stores Association (BSSA). Partner in Messrs. Dunn & Baker, Solicitors. Parliamentary Adviser to Wells, tailors, London.

their interests. There is merit in the principle. If an MP makes a speech saying that Yeltsin is a person of the very highest integrity and is pursuing economic policies that will bring prosperity to Russia, other MPs are likely to examine the speech critically. If, however, the MP making the speech has declared in the Register that he has been on a two-week fact-finding trip to Russia followed by a week's holiday in the Crimea, all paid for by the Russian government, then MPs are likely to view the speech with a very jaundiced eye. Indeed, some of them might shout out from a sedentary position as the paean of praise to Yeltsin is made: "Mine's a vodka. What's yours?".

Entries in the Register sometimes fail to illuminate what is really going on. For example,

---

RT HON DAVID MELLOR MP
DECLARED INTERESTS 1994

❖ Consultancy with: Racal Tacticom Limited, UK manufacturing company; Shandwick Consultants, public affairs company; Investcorp Bank AC, an investment bank; Middle East Economic Digest, business magazine; Middle East Broadcasting Centre, British-based satellite television company; Abela Holdings (UK) Limited, international catering and hotel keeping; Ernst & Young, Chartered accountants; Chelsfield Plc, a property development company; Short Brothers plc, a high-technology manufacturing company; Vosper Thornycroft, shipbuilders; British Aerospace Plc. In relation to Shandwick I work as a public affairs consultant. In relation to the other consultancies, I work on business development unrelated to my position as a Member of Parliament, I also receive fees from journalism, presenting or participating in radio and television programmes, and from lectures and public speaking. Barrister at law (not practising).

❖ Bartle Bogle and Hegarty (single project for one week in June 1993). I am available to advise certain Shandwick clients from time to time about matters relevant to their businesses. I do not lobby Ministers on their behalf. Shandwick publish a list of their clients. I do not speak on behalf of those clients in the House of Commons or table Questions related to their interests.

❖ My overseas visits are related to the business interests declared in section 2 above, and do not arise out of my membership of the House of Commons.

---

no one would guess from the entry of former Prime Minister Sir Edward Heath about his lectures that payment for some of these has come from the Moonies, and that the Moonies have in consequence used his name in trying to recruit new members. Political leaders from around the world have condemned the Moonies as "evil", partly on account of their history of brainwashing and breaking up families.

Asked if he felt he was helping the cult as they strive to gain respectability or if he felt he was being exploited by Mr Moon, the leader of the Moonies, Sir Edward replied: "No. In no way. In my lectures I tell the audience the full truth about the international situation as I know it.... If you allege that Rev Moon is misleading his audiences, surely it is a good thing that they should hear our point of view, just as Parliament hears mine". This is a pretty straight answer to those who argue that there are some bucks, like those coming from the Moonies, which should be passed up.

But if there is a Register who is to police it? Are MPs fit to police themselves? The public's answer to this is a very definite "No". They are convinced that MPs are now so mired in sleaze that they do not have the will to take firm action against their colleagues who fail to declare their interests or abuse the system in other ways. The public believe that just as self-regulation has failed in the City, so it has failed in Parliament.

An ICM poll taken for *The Guardian* in 1994 showed that only eight per cent of voters believe that regulation of the MPs' Register of Interests and an MPs' Code of Ethics should be left to a House of Commons Committee. Most of those polled thought that the Register should come under the law of the land or be entrusted to an independent committee, headed by a judge, with members from inside and outside Parliament. The public liked the idea, too, of a Code of Ethics for MPs, enshrined in law. Most people also thought that MPs should have either no outside interests or only limited outside interests. Only a third supported allowing MPs unlimited outside interests as long as they are declared.

In the end, of course, it is not so much the existence of the Register or even the rules that count, because MPs will always get round these. No, the real need is for MPs who can tell the difference between right and wrong. It's also evident, if things are to improve, that those in the very highest positions must adopt more rigorous standards.

The observant reader will have noticed that already in this chapter we have looked at cases involving four recent Prime Ministers – Edward Heath (wilful refusal to declare his Lloyds syndicates in the Register), Harold Wilson (defending the private interests of his staff in the Slag Heap affair), Jim Callaghan (failing to declare money paid to him by a banker) and Margaret Thatcher (indifferent to the effect of her son's activities on the office of Prime Minister). If Prime Ministers believe that they are above decency, above morality and above Parliament, then there is nothing that anyone can do.

Remember too, that squeaky-clean Tony Blair who aspires to be Prime Minister was rebuked but not censured for failing to declare in the Register of Members' Interests a trip to Washington by Concorde funded by industry. Of course he had an excuse. They all do. In Blair's case – although he was obviously a member of the Opposition – he thought that he was on Government business. Then there was his failure to register a free weekend with his wife Cherie at the luxury Gleneagles Hotel in 1989, paid for by an oil company. More official business, it seems. Oh dear!!! Plus ça change...

Cash for Questions

For some time rumours were rife in Parliament that MPs were being paid for asking Parliamentary Questions (PQs), arranging meetings with Ministers on behalf of outside organisations, and obtaining adjournment debates. It was said that the going rate for an adjournment debate was £15,000, a meeting with a Minister £5,000 and a PQ £1,000. But there was, in the nature of these things, no evidence.

Then Graham Riddick MP, a former Coca-Cola sales manager, admitted that he had agreed to accept £1,000 for putting down a PQ on behalf of a businessman. Offered £1,000 to table a question to the Secretary of State for Social Security, Riddick agreed, saying: "If it helps industry, I think it is perfectly useful". And profitable, he might have added. Asked how he wanted the £1,000 paid, he replied: "I don't really mind. Why don't you just send it to me? Do you want my home address? You can send it there". At this point the chump who one day could win the 'Upper-Class Twit of the Year' award gave his address.

He put down the PQ and was sent the cheque, but returned it when he smelled a rat and experienced that uncomfortable feeling which overcomes those who are in the process of drowning. It is a measure of how bad things are that even after he had been exposed as an 'MP for hire' he could not see that he had done anything wrong. Without remorse he said: "I have nothing to worry about because I haven't taken your money. I haven't got an interest to declare". Stunned MPs, government Whips and

the Prime Minister took a different view and Riddick, who was PPS to the Secretary of State for Transport, was forced to resign. He also made a sort of apology to the House of Commons.

David Tredinnick MP, a rich and stupid Old Etonian who lost vast sums at Lloyds because of payments relating to Hurricane

Hugo and the Exxon Valdez oil disaster, also agreed to ask the Secretary of State for Health a PQ in return for £1,000. Unaware that his telephone conversation was being recorded, he said of earning money this way: "It's hardly work". When the businessman who asked him to put down the PQ said: "So I'll send you the £1,000 in the post now, then", Tredinnick replied: "Well, that is very kind of you". Later, in what the logicians call *lapsus memoriae* and the rest of us refer to as loss of memory, he told 'The World This Weekend' on BBC Radio 4: "I did not expect to receive a cheque from him. I refused to accept a cheque from him...." Oh, dear! As regards his obligation to declare the payment of the £1,000 in the Register he said,

somewhat confusingly, "I probably will declare the interest, yes. But I don't have to be specific in that, and it's confidential between the two of us". Tredinnick, another PPS (to a Welsh Office Minister), was also forced to resign.

A third MP, Bill Walker, a Scot who sometimes turns up in the Chamber of the House of Commons in a kilt, also agreed to table a question in return for £1,000 about the incidence of the non-existent "Thising" disease, then phoned his contact back and requested that the cheque be made out to his favourite charity. Later he said: "I didn't take any money. I said if he wanted to pay money, he could give it to charity". A fourth MP, John Gorst, a man who knows a bit about consultancies and public relations, refused an offer of £1,000 for putting down a question and said he would ask it for nothing. Later he confirmed: "I would not accept money to table questions". But he did tell the dotty businessman who approached him, possibly to get rid of him, "If you were interested in a sort of longer-term relationship – public relations/public affairs advice – that would be more in my field".

These four MPs have all complained bitterly that they were entrapped in a 'sting' organised by the Insight team of the *Sunday Times*. Whatever Parliament might think, entrapment is not a defence in English Law, whilst most people outside Parliament took the view that the *Sunday Times* had performed a service to the nation by exposing indescribably sleazy conduct on the part of Riddick and Tredinnick, which not only brought the House of Commons into disrepute but made it a laughing stock. The general feeling was perhaps well summed-up by a senior Tory MP who was a Minister of State, who said to the author when the *Sunday Times* first published its explosive information: "I hope you chaps are not going to let these buggers off the hook. They should be made to resign from Parliament".

The Committee of Privileges of the House of Commons took a less robust view. It reprimanded Tredinnick and Riddick and recommended in addition that Tredinnick should be banned from the Commons for a mere twenty sitting days and Riddick for ten sitting days. The two MPs were extremely grateful to the Committee for the leniency, as was Bill Walker, whom the Committee decided had "acted unwisely" but not so unwisely as to merit action against him. The puny penalties imposed by the ancients on the Privilege Committee, which had met in secret, were upheld after a debate on the floor of the House of Commons. Immediately after the debate 156 Tory MPs showed what a desperately sick and sad place the House of Commons had become when they wrote to Riddick's constituency association saying: "Mr Riddick continues to enjoy the confidence of us all".

With MPs asking some 60,000 written questions a year, at £1,000 a question there is £60 million worth of potential business. Perhaps the way forward is for the Fees Office rather than outside bodies to pay MPs £1,000 a question. Such a scheme, rewarding as it would high productivity, would fit the ethos of the age well. It would also mean that without too much difficulty the average MP could top up his or her salary by £100,000 a year. If that happened then all but the most insatiable of MPs could resist outside temptations!

Lobbying

The 'Cash for Questions' scandal quickly spilled over into another scandal concerning lobbyists, who are generally regarded as parasites on the body politic. These people lobby not because they believe that the causes they pursue are in the national interest or because they think they have moral or social merit, or even because they think they are financially sound, but because third parties on whose behalf they act pay them money.

The owner of Harrods, one Mohammed Al-Fayed, sensing that the 'Cash for Questions' issue had touched a raw nerve, accused two Ministers of having accepted £2,000 a question through a lobbying firm, as part of a £50,000 parliamentary lobbying campaign to help him retain Harrods at the height of a dispute between his own firm, the House of Fraser, and his bitter rivals Lonrho, whose campaign was spearheaded by 'Tiny' Rowland. One of the MPs concerned, Tim Smith, a Northern Ireland Minister, was forced to resign, conceding that he had received payments from Mohammed Al-Fayed which he had failed to declare in the Register of Interests. The sums involved were considerable. Neil Hamilton MP denied receiving any payments for putting down questions for Mr Fayed and issued a writ against *The Guardian,* which made the original allegations. The lobbying firm involved, Ian Greer Associates, also issued a writ saying: "These allegations are wholly and totally untrue". Hamilton, the Minister for Business Probity, decided to brazen it out and refused to resign over baseless allegations.

However, he had problems. Leaving aside the 'Cash for Questions' allegation against him, he had no answer to the criticism that he and his wife had spent a free week's holiday at the Ritz Hotel in Paris which was owned by Mr Fayed, and had failed to declare the visit in the Register of Interests. MPs were sickened when they learned that in addition to the bed for the week which cost over £2,000, he and his wife spent a further £2,000 on afternoon teas and extras, all paid for by Mr Fayed, and then had the temerity to complain of the view from the window. Yet when Mr Fayed wrote to him later congratulating him on his appointment as a Minister, he rudely never even acknowledged the letter.

Determined not to be another sacrificial victim of the press and TV, he proudly announced that someone had given him a biscuit and that if it would help he would declare his acceptance of the gift in the Register. Unhappily for him, his careless tongue led to support from his own colleagues draining away. Defying the golden rule in situations like this, which is to keep your mouth firmly shut, he likened his predicament to that of John Major, when he was falsely accused of having an affair with Claire Latimer. The comparison was not only silly but indelicate. No loving husband wants to be reminded of the days when his marriage was put under threat by merchants of scandal. The expected enforced resignation of Hamilton could not be long delayed.

There were so many questions that needed answers. Hamilton and Smith had asked twenty-two questions between them on behalf of Mr Fayed. At best this was deemed unseemly. It was, after all, their own government who had called in Inspectors to report on Mr Fayed's take-over of Harrods, and had damned him in their official DTI Report mercilessly for being a liar and for having misrepresented himself, his family, his origins and his wealth in the document backing up his take-over bid. Prestigious solicitors and merchant bankers were also criticised for not having made the necessary enquiries about Mr Fayed.

In the light of the report of the Inspectors into Mr Fayed's take-over of Harrods, some of Mr Hamilton's statements seemed to call into question his judgement and ability to exercise his critical faculties in other matters and fields. In a private letter to Mr Fayed he wrote: "Everyone knows the Al-Fayeds to be amongst the world's most significant businessmen. I have no doubt that were it not for the paranoia and personal vendetta pursued by Tiny Rowland, you would not now be enduring the indignity of this enquiry". Surely Hamilton could not be suggesting that Michael Howard, now Home Secretary, had been wrong as a Minister at the DTI to set up the enquiry, still less that he had been influenced by the fact that his second cousin, Harry Landy, had been deputy chairman of Lonrho's property company, London and City Westcliffe?

Even more bizarre was Hamilton's letter to Mr Fayed of 1 September 1988 in which he wrote: "I am glad to learn from Ian Greer that meetings are taking place with the DTI concerning the inspectors' report and I very much hope this matter will not drag on much longer. Perhaps it might be useful if the three of us get together shortly". For what purpose, one may ask. DTI Inspectors are imperiously impartial and even Ian Greer, a famous Conservative lobbyist, is not allowed to bend their ears when they draw up their reports.

Then Sir Robin Butler, the Cabinet Secretary, asked by the Prime Minister to carry out "an independent and full investigation"

into the allegations against Hamilton, was made to look a fool. The Prime Minister's office volunteered the false information that the Cabinet Secretary had been told that Mr Hamilton's non-declaration in the Register of his stay at the Ritz had already been investigated and cleared by the Select Committee on Members' Interests. In fact the Select Committee had not undertaken any such investigation. Sir Robin's enquiry was astonishingly sloppy, so much so that constitutional experts questioned the wisdom of the Cabinet Secretary inadvertently acting as an apologist for the bad conduct of Ministers.

Worse, the Prime Minister had himself raised the question of whether Mr Fayed had directly or indirectly attempted to blackmail him, and had passed on a note of his meeting with an "informant" to the Director of Public Prosecutions, who had in turn passed it on to the Metropolitan Police. In the end it was the Prime Minister, not Hamilton, who cracked when he declared that the combined impact of unsubstantiated allegations against Hamilton "disabled" him from carrying out his responsibilities as a Minister.

Surely only a wimp of a Prime Minister would force a colleague to resign because of unsubstantiated allegations. Hamilton and his colleagues were furious. The Prime Minister's suggestion that Mr Al-Fayed might have been trying to blackmail him was contemptuously dismissed by the Crown Prosecution Service. The Prime Minister had in effect been found guilty of seriously abusing his privileged position in the House of Commons.

As hidden persuaders, lobbyists are a despised breed in Parliament. Some MPs hate them because they believe that they have real power; contrariwise, others believe that they hopelessly over-exaggerate their powers and therefore con their clients.

Nobody knows how much power Ian Greer, a parliamentary lobbyist, wields. He is clearly a big player with strong links to the Conservative Party. The youngest Tory agent, he provided John Major with a Jaguar and chauffeur when he was campaigning to become party Leader, paid for Major's collected speeches to be published, and apparently knows him personally. In June 1994 104 Labour MPs launched a vitriolic attack on him in an Early Day Motion in Parliament when it emerged that Central TV failed to put out a 'Cook Report' into his activities.

Approached by American businessmen with $40 million to invest, Greer and one of his colleagues from Ian Greer Associates claimed personal friendships with the Prime Minister, Cabinet Minister Michael Portillo, and former Chancellor of the Exchequer Norman Lamont. They promised to arrange meetings with DTI Minister, Neil Hamilton, David Amess MP, PPS to Portillo, and Graham Bright MP, PPS to the Prime Minister. Greer also produced a list of fourteen Conservative MPs whom he said he would contact to discuss the proposed venture, which was to use money obtained by former Russian communists from the sale of some of their national art treasures and invest it in the privatisation of the Insolvency Service. Alas for Greer, it was all a TV sting to test the nature of the services which his consultancy provided.

Ian Greer's lobbying seems to be, if not the kiss of death, then the cough that leads to death from lung cancer for MPs. His lobbying on behalf of killer tobacco manufacturers in 1994 ended up with allegations that Keith Mans MP, PPS to the then Secretary of State for Health Virginia Bottomley, advised the killers to keep up pressure on her so that they would be allowed to carry on advertising their products which killed. Mans told Bottomley that his actions had been misunderstood and that he was innocent of the charges.

MPs who sit on the boards of lobbying firms seem to have taken fright at the growing criticisms of the activities of parliamentary lobbyists. Menzies Campbell, the Liberal Democrat MP, paid £5,000 a year for his services by Westminster Communications, a public relations and lobbying firm, announced he was severing financial links with the company. So too did Ann Taylor MP, a Labour frontbench spokesperson. She had the cheek to try to justify her actions to the Nolan Committee. Labour MPs sniggered as she did so. So did Keith Speed MP and another Tory, Sir Marcus

Fox, Chairman of the Tory back-bench 1922 Committee and one of those who investigated the 'Cash for Questions' affair. Westminster Communications had to sever their links with MPs to enable them to join the Association of Professional Political Consultants (APPC), which believes there is a potential conflict of interest in having MPs on the boards of its members. The wonder is that the MPs could not see this for themselves.

In an effort to improve their public image, the various umbrella groups for lobbying firms have set up registers of parliamentary consultants. The Institute of Public Relations and the Public Relations Consultants' Association still allow MPs to be on the boards of lobbying firms. In 1994 MPs David Mellor, Simon Burns, Charles Hendry, Nigel Forman, Sir George Gardiner, Roger Gale, Sir Fergus Montgomery, Michael Jopling, Peter Fry, Paul Tyler and Dame Angela Rumbold represented lobbying or PR companies. All except Paul Tyler, a Liberal Democrat, were Tories.

Of these, Dame Angela Rumbold, a former Minister and Vice-Chairman of the Conservative Party, sprang to fame when a spectacular row broke out over her work for the lobbying firm, Decision Makers Ltd, which led the campaign on behalf of the company Blue Circle to site a key international railway station at Ebbsfleet in Kent rather than at Stratford in East London. Dame Angela insisted that her resignation during the row was not an admission that she had a conflict of interest. Decision Makers Ltd insisted that Dame Angela did not use her influence to enable them to see senior Ministers. The Prime Minister admitted to meeting the Ebbsfleet campaigners at a "social occasion", but insisted that the decision was left to other Ministers.

The fact remains that Decision Makers had access to senior Ministers which was denied to the Stratford campaigners, who are also thought to have used lobbyists. Dame Angela's influence, therefore, may only have been indirect, no more than her noted presence on the Decision Makers' board. Decision Makers, of course, were not lobbying either in the national interest or in the interests of Dame

Angela's constituents, who live not in Kent but in Mitcham and Morden, and few of whom will benefit from the development of a Channel Tunnel railway station at Ebbsfleet.

Lobbyists are here to stay but MPs do not have to facilitate their trade. If MPs are serious about the problems concerning them, the least that they could do would be to (1) make it unlawful for any MP to be paid by a PR or lobbying firm and to treat such payments as bribery on the part of the lobbyists, and (2) prevent any lobbyists from having House of Commons passes so as to stop them using and abusing the facilities of the House of Commons, i.e. getting papers and reports free of charge, having the use of the library facilities, hiring rooms, physically nobbling MPs.

It should also be unlawful for MPs to employ lobbyists as part-time secretaries or researchers, which is often a guise behind which lobbyists get passes. A private House of Commons Register which has to be filled in by MPs' research assistants showed that in 1995 thirty-seven research assistants of MPs were paid in whole or part by lobbyists or were lobbyists themselves.

Quangos

Quangos have been variously described as non-governmental public bodies whose members have been appointed by Ministers, or semi-autonomous bodies connected with government Departments. Although they've been in existence for well over 200 years they have become the subject of intense scrutiny over the past twenty years because of their number, the huge resources that they control, questions of accountability, and the suggestion that there may be political corruption in the appointment of many of their members. Writing in 1981 in *The Governance of Quangos*, Philip Holland said that the Labour government of 1974-79 had abused its power of appointments to Quangos (Quasi-Autonomous Non-Governmental Organisations) by limiting them to dedicated supporters of the Labour Party. He went on to suggest that through appointments to Quangos a political party could create a one-party totalitarian state. Maybe he was psychic.

More Abuse

In recent years there has, it is claimed, been even more abuse than there was when Labour was in power of the appointment by Tory Ministers of Tory placement. In 1993 the *Financial Times* reported that Chairmen of the ten largest NHS Quangos and the thirty non-NHS Quangos showed that if they had an identifiable political affiliation, it was Conservative. None of the top forty was a known Labour Party member or Liberal Democrat, while eight were Conservatives. When Labour was in power in 1978-79, while twelve of the top forty chairmen were known Labour Party members, three were known Conservatives and one was a known Liberal.

In 1993 Baroness Denton, a Junior Minister at the DTI, let the cat out of the bag, saying: "I can't remember knowingly appointing a Labour supporter". Then, realising that she was not supposed to make such a public admission of bias through the misuse of the patronage system, she claimed that she had been misunderstood and had meant to say only that she did not ask appointees about their political affiliations. Of course not. Such an exercise would be pointless where known Conservatives were being offered jobs.

By now in something of a muddle, Baroness Denton went on to say that the system would only work if Ministers gave jobs to those who believed in the Conservative revolution, apparently oblivious of the fact that this is what happens in corrupt one-party states which do not recognise the idea of pluralism.

There was also evidence that political appointments to Quangos had in recent years been linked to political donations to the Conservative Party. That seemed like corruption on the part of Ministers, multiplied by two. Over sixteen years the government had, it was claimed, built up a 'New Magistracy' of placemen, an unelected secret army of toadies doing the government's business, clean or dirty, instead of criticising, where appropriate, principles and practices that were damaging the interests of those whom the Quangos were supposed to serve. The mutual backscratching that has accompanied the establishment of the 'New Magistracy' is summed up in the equation 'political donations = political appointments'. At least two former venal Prime Ministers would have appreciated the sophisticated nature of this new spoils system had they been alive today – Sir Robert Walpole and David Lloyd George.

George Haworth, who studied 100 Quangos covering thirteen Departments of State, found that 157 individuals who had been appointed had ties to firms which had donated funds to the Conservative Party. However, Mr Haworth is a Labour MP so his evidence needed to be treated with cynicism and, if possible, corroborated. *The Observer* newspaper did so in 1994. Their study showed that 150 firms which had made donations to the Conservative Party had directors appointed to top Quangos. Many of these directors sat on more than one Quango, getting salaries and generous expenses, whilst many firms were represented on several Quangos.

Secretive System

Subsequently in 1994 the Labour Research Department (a body which has nothing to do with the Labour Party) carried out research for the GMB trade union into the composition of 482 NHS Trusts in Great Britain. It found "a closed and secretive system of political patronage". Sixty-eight Trusts had a Chairman who was a Tory or a leading figure in a company which had donated to Tory funds. Only three Chairmen had a similar connection with the Labour Party. The research also found that 149 Chairmen plus non-executive directors had strong links with the Tory Party or were leading figures in a donor company. This figure of 149 contrasted with that of twenty people with similar links with the Labour Party, eleven with the Liberal Democrats and twelve with other political parties.

Just seven per cent of all the Chairmen and non-executive directors had a medical background, whereas forty-three per cent had a

---

SO WHO'S COUNTING ANYWAY?

Although counting Quangos has been likened to counting the number of stones on the sea-shore between the tide marks, official data shows that there are some 2,000 Quangos in Britain today, employing some 40,000 people and spending over £40,000,000,000 annually. Included in the figure of 2,000 are advisory bodies, tribunals, prison boards of visitors, NHS Trusts and other bodies such as the Consumers' Council, the Broadcasting Standards Council and the Arts Council, etc, etc.

Appointments are supposed to be made on merit and not on the basis of party political affiliation. A Public Appointments Unit keeps a central list which is colloquially known as the list of the Great and the Good. It is through this list that top people look after each other, especially when they retire, ensuring a flow of income for, shall we say, not a lot of work. Currently there are some 5,000 names on the central list. There is also a reserve list of some 20,000 culled from the press, Ministers writing to each other with a third of the people nominating themselves in 1994. As ever, there are disproportionately small numbers of women and black people on the list.

Eight of the twenty-one members of the British Overseas Trade Board were directors of companies which had donated £242,000 to the Conservative Party in 1992-93.

Eight of the nineteen members of the China Britain Trade Group were directors of companies which donated £492,000 to the Conservative Party in 1992-93.

Six of the twelve members of the Court of Directors of the Bank of England were members of companies which gave over £200,000 to the Conservative Party in 1992-93.

Five of the twenty-two members of the British Museum Board of Trustees were directors of ten companies which gave £614,000 to the Conservative Party in 1992-93.

The Chairman of the Broadcasting Standards Council was Lady Howe, the wife of a Tory peer and director of three companies that passed £260,000 to the Conservative Party in 1992-93.

And so on and so on. Moreover, the BBC programme 'Here and Now' reported in 1994 that twenty-one wives of Tory MPs and peers and three husbands of Tory MPs and peers had been given jobs on Quango committees. This compared with the wife of just one Labour MP getting a job on a Quango. The programme claimed to have compiled a directory of 25,000 people sitting on 1,500 Quangos. The Chairman of the Conservative Party variously summed up the accumulating evidence as McCarthyism and a witch-hunt. Mr Haworth replied: "A witch-hunt is perfectly in order when there are witches to be found. It is a highly unlikely statistical co-incidence that on every Quango there are people donating to the Tory Party".

business background. Tory wives were again prominent. Trust Chairmen earned up to £20,000, whilst non-executive directors received £5,000 for their brief appearances. Directors from companies such as United Biscuits, Dixons, Sun Alliance, Tarmac and other companies who had been big donors to the Tory Party were named. More McCarthyism or more cause for concern?

Then another survey undertaken by the BBC TV programme 'Here and Now' in November 1994 looked at the boards of the 100 top companies in the FTSE index. It found that amongst 450 directors whose companies had given to the Conservative Party 150 had Quango appointments; whereas amongst 480 directors whose companies had not donated to the Conservative Party there were only fifty Quango appointments. Directors of Marks and Spencer and Dixons, both Tory supporters, did well.

Problems

Some of the problems might be solved or the allegations rendered baseless if (1) Ministerial patronage was restricted by the establishment of an impartial body, or series of bodies, to oversee appointments to Quangos. Exceptions might be made in cases such as appointments to Royal Commissions where Ministerial inputs might be deemed essential; (2) appointments to Quangos were advertised competitively; (3) board members of those Quangos which have executive functions and spending powers had to register their interests; (4) there was a code of conduct and ethics for people serving on Quangos; (5) political balance for non-executive directors was a requirement; and (6) Quangos were made accountable to Parliament.

The Nolan Committee on Standards of Conduct in Public Life called for a new Public Appointments Commission to ensure high standards, fair play and political impartiality for appointments to Quangos. Of course, not much will change. How could it be otherwise when Ministers have all along insisted that there is fair play and a lack of political bias in these appointments? A problem not recognised

is a problem to which there is no solution. Surely Nolan was not using scurrilous innuendo to suggest that the Prime Minister and his colleagues had not been telling the truth about the true nature of Quango appointments?

Honours for Politicians

Tory MPs who stay in the House of Commons any length of time get knighthoods for "political and public service" as surely as the sun rises every day. They really do have to do something terrible, like murdering their grandmother, to miss out. In December 1994 the Prime Minister, John Major, announced that 115 Tory MPs and 2 Labour MPs had received knighthoods since May 1979, when Labour was last in power. In 1966 Labour Prime Minister Harold Wilson announced that honours for purely party political purposes were to be discontinued.

The gravy train for MPs returned, however, when Edward Heath became the new Conservative Prime Minister, only to be stopped again in 1974 when Labour returned to power. Inevitably, Margaret Thatcher reintroduced the idea of making Tory MPs Knights of the Shires as a device for buying their loyalty. She asked the Leader of the Opposition to make recommendations for political honours, but he refused. John Major continues to award knighthoods to his own back-benchers.

Payment for Honours

Throughout this century honours have been bought, although the practice became illegal in 1925 with the passing of the Honours (Prevention of Abuses) Act. In the past, Prime Ministers used 'honour touts' to raise money for party funds. In 1922 public outrage backed by royal protests forced the Prime Minister David Lloyd George to set up an enquiry to look into the scale of the scandal.

Lloyd George had an understood, strict tariff – £10,000 for a knighthood, £30,000 for a baronetcy and £50,000 and more for a peerage. His chief tout was Maundy Gregory, who was eventually prosecuted in 1932. The scandal broke when questions were asked about the nomination of a peerage for Sir Joseph Robinson from South Africa. As someone who had just been fined £500,000 for corrupt practices, he hardly seemed an ideal nomination.

A debate ensued in the House of Lords where it was suggested that Lloyd George had personally made over a million pounds from the sale of honours. Letters were read out, one of which from Maundy Gregory said: "this really is an excellent opportunity, but there is no time to be lost if you wish to take it... It is unfortunate that Governments must have money but the party now in power will have to fight Labour and Socialism, which will be an expensive matter".

It then emerged that Lloyd George's Chief Whips – first Guest and then McCurdy – together with his press agent, Sutherland, had been responsible for building up the Lloyd George Political Fund by the sale of honours on a massive scale. Lloyd George dished out 294 knighthoods in eighteen months, so that London became known as 'The City of Dreadful Knights'. Having created the OBE, he distributed 25,000 in four years. He doubled the number of barons created each year. And all for a price! Lloyd George huffed and puffed, proclaiming a wounded innocence, but the upshot was a Royal Commission on Honours and the establishment in 1923 of the Political Honours Scrutiny Committee, which consisted of and still consists of three Privy Councillors to check that people recommended for honours are "fit and proper persons" to be recommended. The Political Honours Scrutiny Committee failed abysmally to do its work in 1976, when Harold Wilson presented his resignation honours list.

Allegedly written on tinted note-paper belonging to Wilson's secretary Marcia Williams, it became known as the 'lavender-coloured list'. In *The Politics of Power* Joe Haines, who worked for Wilson, confirmed that the list was originally proposed by her. Life peerages were announced for eight people:

Wilson's publisher, doctor, raincoat manufacturer, his former office manager, an academic, a property millionaire and two entertainment moguls. There were knighthoods for wealthy businessmen. Two members of the Scrutiny Committee had reservations about half the list and complained of being given insufficient time to investigate doubtful cases. One hundred Labour MPs signed a motion denouncing the list.

One of the recipients of a knighthood, Sir Eric Miller, later shot himself on the Jewish Day of Atonement in the patio garden of his home with a Walther automatic pistol, when his property company crashed. A DTI enquiry revealed that he had used the funds of Peachey Property to maintain an extravagant life-style, including Labour Party banquets and champagne for Wilson's resignation party, as well as providing filing cabinets for Downing Street.

Conspiring to Defraud

Another, Joe Kagan, the inventor of Gannex macs who helped Wilson with staff problems, was jailed for ten months after being convicted of conspiring to defraud the Revenue by paying £700,000 into a secret Zurich bank account. Stripped of his knighthood, he remained a Peer of the Realm. Wilson claimed he had rewarded real people, some of whom were engaged in "a really tough, almost piratical enterprise in foreign trade". Marcia Williams, now Lady Falkender, called the complaints of the critics "anti-semitic" and "a sanctimonious protest by the unimaginative half of the Establishment".

Today there is speculation about the links between honours for industrialists and contributions to Conservative Party funds. Nicholas Winterton, himself a Conservative MP, told 'World in Action' that some industrialists give money to the Conservative Party in the hope of getting knighthoods. So what's the evidence?

In *The Queen Has Been Pleased* John Walker analysed the peerages and knighthoods awarded by Margaret Thatcher to industrialists between 1979 and 1985. He found that eleven peerages had been awarded to industrialists whose companies had collectively given

£424,000 to the Conservative Party in the year they received their peerage and £1,800,000 in the preceding six years. Updating these figures, Labour Research in *An Honour to Serve* showed that during her whole period of office Margaret Thatcher awarded peerages to seventeen industrialists whose companies gave a staggering £6,500,000 in donations to the Conservative Party during her period as Prime Minister. John Walker also showed that from 1979-85 Margaret Thatcher gave knighthoods to forty-four industrialists whose companies between them donated £870,000 to the Conservative Party in the year in which their knighthoods were granted and no less than £4,300,000 from the period 1979-84.

Knighthoods

The *Sunday Times* Insight Team reported in 1992 that things were no different under John Major. It reported that seven of the twelve knighthoods given to industrialists under Major were given to directors whose companies had donated between £50,000 and £278,000 to the Conservative Party. It also concluded that "heads of companies which donated £50,000 a year over the past decade were ten times more likely to be honoured than heads of firms which give £5,000 on average".

Of course it's all co-incidence. Everyone awarded a peerage or knighthood has been a distinguished person in his own right. The fact that these people are directors in companies which donated money handsomely to the Conservative Party is surely proof enough of that.

Would it be any different if Labour were in power? Well, it would be an unwise person who would bet on Labour not rewarding its own, including some of the godfathers of the trade union movement. And who would bet against Tony Blair's millionaire friends in the media, who helped him with his campaign to become Leader, becoming life peers? Lord Barry Cox of Mapledene, Lord Greg Dyke of Putney Vale and Lord Melvyn Bragg of the Lakes – the names have a nice ring to them. Only time will tell.

Unlawful Acts

It's not often that two Prime Ministers and a Foreign Secretary are found by the Courts to have acted unlawfully in spending £234 million, but that's what happened to Margaret Thatcher, John Major and Douglas Hurd. By any standards this was wrongdoing on a spectacular scale.

In 1988 the British government signed an arms sales agreement with Malaysia. At the time, the British High Commissioner informed the Malaysian government that the British government were willing, through Aid and Trade Provisions, to offer "up to a total of £200 million for development projects to be agreed mutually between the two governments". Although Parliament was never told, Margaret Thatcher delivered the High Commissioner's promise of aid in return for the arms deal during a meeting with the Malaysian Prime Minister in London in March 1989. The scene was set for the Pergau Dam scandal.

In 1991 the dirty deal was completed when the Overseas Development Administration (ODA) in Britain decided to spend £234 million of taxpayers' money in aid on the Pergau Hydro-Electric Project in Malaysia. The government took the decision to go ahead with the project despite the fact that it was formally notified by its top adviser and civil servant that the project breached guidelines on aid expenditure, was "a very bad buy" for Malaysian consumers and was inconsistent with the "prudent and economical" use of the money of British taxpayers. The adviser also said there were cheaper alternatives.

The Foreign Secretary, knowing that something very wrong was being done, nonetheless obtained the consent of the new Prime Minister, John Major, to go ahead with the project. In 1994 two Committees in Parliament looked into the matter. One, the Public Accounts Committee, issued a damning report; the other, the Foreign Affairs Committee, issued a report full of weasel words. Their investigation revealed beyond any shadow of a doubt that the then Prime Minister, Margaret Thatcher, failed to tell the truth to Parliament in 1989, and that Chris Patten, then an MP and the ODA Minister, did likewise when he said: "the fact of the matter is that aid has not been used as a sweetener for defence deals anywhere". In order to satisfy the Conservative majority on the Foreign Affairs Committee these statements, which were calculated to mislead, were summed up as follows: "We have found, in the light of our evidence, that Ministerial replies to certain questions were literally true, though less open and less informative than the House has a right to expect".

But that was not the end of the affair. Under Section 1 of the Overseas Development and Co-operation Act 1980, the Foreign Secretary is empowered to authorise aid payments only "for the purpose of promoting the development or maintaining the economy of a country or territory outside the United Kingdom, or the welfare of its people". On November 10th 1994 the High Court ruled that since the project was "economically unsound", and known to be so, the Foreign Secretary had acted unlawfully. The Foreign Secretary, educated at Eton and Trinity College, Cambridge, believes that at all times he acted properly. So now you know that acting unlawfully is the same as acting properly, in the eyes of the Ministers. Did the Foreign Secretary resign over the affair? Don't be daft, you've been in politics too long to ask that question.

Victims of Crime

On November 9th 1994 the Court of Appeal held that the Home Secretary Michael Howard QC had acted unlawfully in cutting compensation payments for victims of crime. Specifically, the judges ruled that he had ignored a duty imposed on him by an Act of Parliament in 1988 and had then "acted unlawfully and abused his prerogative and common law powers". Under the unlawful Howard scheme to save money, a man left paraplegic after an attack by robbers who was previously awarded £689,000 would have received £175,000, while a woman of thirty-nine, widowed when her husband was stabbed to death, who was previously awarded £137,000 would

have received just £17,500. Did the Home Secretary who is responsible for law and order resign? Don't be daft, he simply appealed against the judgement to the House of Lords.

In May 1995 an unrepentant government gave the Law Lords a two-fingered 'V' sign when they introduced the Criminal Injuries Compensation Bill so as to get round their unlawful behaviour and return to being mean and nasty to the victims of crimes of violence.

Conclusion

The 1990s have seen MPs indulging in what is essentially a catching-up exercise. In the 1980s everyone else joined the loadsamoney, get-rich-

Peddling arms: Douglas Hurd and the Pergau Dam affair

quick, something-for-nothing society. As fraudsters in the City prospered as never before, as the self-regulation of financial markets failed to stop hucksters coming in, as merchant bankers, solicitors and accountants benefited from the declining standards of their professional worlds, as take-overs, some of which were financed legally, others illegally, produced overnight paper profits of millions, as the share prices of privatised industries doubled overnight, as rocketing house prices made people rich without effort, MPs looked on agog.

The 1990s have seen them act to redress the balance by taking a slice of the action for themselves. Those very MPs who had at first unbelievingly preached the philosophy that there is no such thing as society were surprised that people took them at their word. Then, having come to believe in their own rhetoric, they searched for theories to justify it and, ironically, found justification in the old-fashioned nostrums of eighteenth-century liberalism, devil-take-the-hindmost economics, social Darwinism, people getting on their bikes, the survival of the fittest and the notion that the one sign of earthly success was the accumulation of money.

Making Money

If making money was a moral imperative, MPs simply had to look to ways to make it for themselves. How else could they hold their heads up high in society? The wonder of it all is that, a few successful greedy buggers apart, they showed so little ambition and talent in their attempts to live up to the new monetised ideals which they had set themselves. The truth is that most of them have not become super-rich. Not by the Queen's standards anyway.

However, in their pursuit of an easy ride they had one unexpected and unintended success. They have poisoned the body politic and in the process made themselves the object of hatred, ridicule and contempt.

They thought in the 1980s that they had discovered a new vision which would bring about a state of nirvana for themselves and their constituents, only to find in the 1990s that those outside Parliament who are without standards and are quite prepared to ignore all the rules of decent behaviour themselves, nevertheless expect their elected rulers to behave differently. Can you wonder then that for most MPs this is the injustice of the world?

Why politicians should want to be loved is something of a mystery. Love is surely anathema to their trade. Why they should get angry, foam at the mouth and behave like demented hyenas when they are traduced is also a bit of a puzzle.

Take the payment of Jonathan Aitken's bill at the Ritz. That was pure pantomime and should have been enjoyed as such. Most of us have no difficulty in paying a bill when we check out of a hotel. We either sign a cheque or produce one of our many credit cards. But not poor Jonathan Aitken. For him there was inconclusive correspondence going back over a year between the Cabinet Secretary and the editor of *The Guardian*. Did he pay, didn't he pay; if so, all or part of the bill? Did an Arab friend pick up part of the tab? Did his wife slip back to the hotel with a bundle of greenbacks to settle up? What colour hair does his wife have? Was there a mysterious second lady? In whose name was the bill made out? What did it have to do with discussions on arms deals?

Why did Sir Robin Butler, the Cabinet Secretary, make a hash of yet another enquiry? Should we have even begun to believe the word of an Arab grocer over that of a Minister of the Crown? Was there anything to declare in the Register of Members' Interests? Was the orange really sucked dry?

Instead of having a good laugh MPs went into a frenzy of anger, not over the bill itself but over the fact that in his attempts to uncover its secrets, some investigative sleuth from *The Guardian* stole one sheet of notepaper with the House of Commons logo on it. Was there ever a more heinous crime? Suddenly Peter Preston, *The Guardian*'s editor and now chief witness for the prosecution became the defendant in the dock, and a trial was held before the Committee of Privileges. More hatred, more ridicule, more contempt for the MPs. Oh, dear! Oh, dear! That's the further injustice of the world for you. Will MPs never learn?

PARLIAMENT AND SEX

The General Theory

If the investigative journalists of press and TV are to be believed, then Tory MPs get a better deal than Labour MPs between the sheets and beneath the duvets. Some say that this is an illusion, and based on no more than the fact that Tory sex, often accompanied by the accoutrements of class and wealth, is inherently more fascinating than Labour sex. Others, whilst concurring with the illusion theory, put it down to the fact that sex on the part of Conservative MPs who are in power is bound to be more newsworthy because of the dangers to the government when it is shamelessly exposed in all its lurid details, the more so if Ministers are involved.

Then there are the purists who argue that the hacks from the Street of Shame will dig more deeply and more consistently to uncover Tory sex, because they are the party which has a Prime Minister who did not know what he was letting himself in for when he came up with 'Back to Basics' as the Big Idea. This enables journalists from the tabloids to take the moral high ground and level charges of hypocrisy at individuals, and the government more generally, when Tory MPs are caught with their trousers down. Particularly at risk are those Tory MPs who pontificate about morals, marriage and family life and who are seen holding hands and smiling beside their wives and children in photographs in their election addresses.

Such MPs who adhere to Victorian values, so beloved of Margaret Thatcher and John Major, have to be prepared to accept Victorian punishments when they fall short of their high ideals.

Of course hypocrisy in this field is not the preserve of Tory MPs. Knowing what I do about the past of one woman Labour MP, I was surprised at the vehemence of her attack on Tory politicians who were in trouble as a result of the exposure of their extra-marital sexual exploits. Sex as the confluence of two mucky dribbles is inherently absurd. Its detailed and graphic exposure must surely make the victims of the tabloid press squirm. The hurt done to them surely deserves our sympathy.

Another theory advanced by experts in the behavioural sciences relates to the fact that many Tory MPs spent their formative years at public schools, which until recently were boys only. This, say the psychologists, agony aunts and others, means that a number of these MPs found themselves sexually repressed or conditioned to enjoy sex with other boys when they should have been experimenting with the joys of heterosexuality. Apparently this can leave individuals with permanent psychological scars which may tempt them later in life to indulge in either an excess of sex or promiscuous relationships, including adultery.

Jim Prior MP, now Lord Prior, who was at the heart and head of British and Conservative politics for twenty years, summed up the somewhat odd and gauche way with which public schoolboys approach sex in his book *A Balance of Power*. Although a liberal by nature, writing about his schooldays at Charterhouse sex seems to have troubled him. First there was his account of the sex life of one of his contemporaries, Simon Raven, the well-known author and novelist, of whom he wrote:

Simon's proclivities are, I think, clear from his novels. They emerged at an early age and were unquestionably bi-sexual. He certainly regarded the prettier boys at Charterhouse as a challenge and although his romantic advances were no doubt accompanied by lust I don't think his seductions were evil.

Never reticent on these matters, it was not long before he began boasting that he had made his first female conquest. He had found a prostitute in Piccadilly. *Needless to say we were bubbling with interest and excitement. We wanted to know exactly how he had engineered his pick-up – after all, he was only sixteen. There was a ready answer: 'Oh, it was all quite easy. You have to put the end of your tie over your shoulder – that is the universal signal'.*

Then there was Prior's uneasy comment: "The corps, chapel and games were of course compulsory... Drinking, smoking and homosexuality were optional extras. They were strongly discouraged, if necessary by sacking, but sometimes went on in the woods round the playing fields".

Allowing for all this, there is probably more than a grain of truth in the assertion that when it comes to sex, the Tories basically out-play Labour. One Labour MP who used to be a member of the Young Conservatives and therefore had first-hand experience of Tory sex insists that the answer lies in the nature of the sex and love-making itself. He explained it to me as follows:

All of the studies on sex in Britain have failed to ask the respondents about their political preferences or affiliations. This means that they've missed one important point. That is that on the whole Tory women have less hang-ups about sex than their socialist sisters. They like it more and want more of it. Because Tory MPs tend to meet Tory women and Labour MPs tend to meet Labour women, inevitably more Tory MPs will be drawn into extra-marital affairs than Labour MPs and will stick at these affairs longer precisely because the sex is better. For Tory MPs therefore the risk of exposure, thoughts of which anyway tend to get lost in the passion, is a risk worth taking.

Assuming that the analysis is true it still begs the question – why do Tory women want more sex than their Labour counterparts? The answer to this question, so my colleague tells me, is that the kind of women that Labour MPs meet usually think that politics is more important than sex whereas for Tory women politics

Licked all over: Edwina Currie writes a blockbuster

and sex are indivisible. In addition, Tory women are not held back by the ideological impediments of Puritanism, Methodism and Marxism, all of which encourage Labour women to exercise their minds and their souls rather than their bodies. No sex, please, we're Labour!

Of course it takes two to tango, whatever political party you're in, and most women will rightly be deeply suspicious of any theory which sees sex in terms of them as the temptresses and men as the victims. That may be how it appears in the first novel of Edwina Currie MP, who admits she fantasises about the steamy sex romps of her characters, but she is surely out of touch with the real world. Shortly after I had read her blockbuster, I told her as we made our way to Whitehall to discuss the advice on sex education for schoolchildren which the government was about to publish that she should be obliged to hang a Sex Warning Sign on her breasts. By way of reply she said tartly: "I know why you men don't like my novel. It's because the female characters are powerful women who make men lie down on their beds and do things to them." Remembering the scene where a look-alike Edwina Currie plasters a man in strawberries and cream and then licks him all over, I replied smartly: "If that's your idea of a good night out – don't call me, Edwina. I'll call you. I didn't know you were into domination."

Conservatives Triumphant

For some Conservative MPs it is sex and money rather than sex and politics which are indivisible. The Hon Nicholas Soames MP, a Minister of the Crown and a former Equerry to Prince Charles, tells the story with the wit that often accompanies personages of ample girth, of how when he reached the age of maturity his father, a man of substance, took him aside and told him that when the time came to settle down he should find a woman who was well-endowed. Just so that there should be no doubt as to what he meant, his father explained delphically: "Get your cock in the till and keep it there". It was

in Washington in similar vein that Nicholas Budgen MP, barrister, small farmer who rides to hounds and is a right-wing paradigm of virtue, explained to his colleagues from all parties on the Select Committee on the Treasury that the Tories were "by tradition the party of cock and cash".

Of course there are the romantics, and they are usually the ones that come unstuck as they play out their fantasies. An aura of fantasy clung to the long-serving Leader of the party of cock and cash – Margaret Thatcher. A num-

ber of MPs of all political parties privately admitted that she was good-looking. For some of them she was an object of their desires. When I told some of my colleagues that part of her attraction lay in her raw sexual magnetism and asked them if they fancied her, they usually responded truculently, dismissively and guiltily. She, for her part, clearly had an eye for pretty youngish things and icons of mediocrity, whom she appointed to her Cabinet. Her Cabinet colleague Jim Prior MP accused her of not being averse to using "a bit of coquetry" to get her way, and said that amongst those whom she found "attractive" were Cecil Parkinson MP and Humphrey Aitkens MP, her Chief Whip.

Of course it was all innocent fun. Humphrey Aitkens was deeply in love with his wife while, as we all know, Cecil Parkinson's penis was pushing hard elsewhere. The anaemically good-looking Cecil Parkinson, now Lord Parkinson, was originally a member of the Labour Party, recruited into it by Labour MP Norman Atkinson. I well remember Margaret Thatcher's face dropping like a stone when Atkinson recalled the event while she and Parkinson were talking in the Members' Lobby of Parliament. Subsequently Parkinson became a Tory and a staunch supporter of centuries-old classical Liberal economic views.

He ensured himself a place in history not through his work in Thatcher's Cabinet but through his affair with his secretary, Sarah Keays. Parkinson told her he loved her, would leave his wife and marry her. She believed him.

When Keays became pregnant Parkinson proposed again, then cast her off, suggested an abortion and went back to his wife. All told, the vacillating Parkinson proposed three times. Thatcher said she would stand by her Minister. But when Keays responded like a woman scorned and published her version of events, Thatcher ditched Parkinson. It was all so hurtful, so predictable, like a stylised minuet, the human spirit at its worst.

Despite her initial support for him, Margaret Thatcher saw Cecil Parkinson's adultery as an act of betrayal. He was supposed to be a true believer in her moral revolution. She herself had launched a frontal attack on the "permissive claptrap of the Sixties which set the scene for a society in which the old values of discipline and self-restraint were denigrated". Now, just as she was producing her counter-attack here he was, a symbol of the post-war funk, which gave rise to the very kind of society which she despised.

Her successor at No. 10, John Major, felt bruised and let down too when a number of his officers turned out not to be gentlemen. For years David Mellor, an arrogant, ugly, fat, bespectacled man with teeth that don't quite fit, fantasised about putting on a Chelsea football strip and bonking a beautiful actress. Then along came the actress Antonia de Sancha, introduced to him by a teller of shaggy dog stories who wrote for *Private Eye*, as a result of which his dreams came true on a low-level bed, bugged and wired for sound. No, he would never resign and yes, the Prime Minister would back him. History was repeating itself. Of course many MPs empathised with him when he said on tape that after nights of steamy sex he felt too "knackered" to carry on the business of government.

Overnight, the Department of National Heritage where he was the supremo became the Ministry for Fun. Then Mellor made a fatal mistake by having his photo taken with his faithful, trusting wife and family by a farm gate.

After that the question of hospitality abroad came up, a free holiday in Marbella, Spain, from Mona Bauwens, the daughter of

HE SHOULD BE FREE IN ABOUT HALF AN HOUR

MP's DIARY

the financial director of the Palestine Liberation Organisation, which might, contrary to the Ministerial guidelines, have created a conflict with his public duties as a Minister. Exit Mellor. Later pantomime turned to farce when Mellor announced that he had become very close to Lady Penelope Cobham. For her part, Lady Penelope spoke of a deep bond between Mellor and herself and added, delphically, that her husband understood the situation. Mellor added: "I know this sounds a bit like Mills and

Boon but Penny and I are an item. Judith and I have been contemplating divorce for some time".

Taking everyone's breath away, he went on to imply that adultery was no big deal, and then excoriated a journalist who asked him if he felt he had treated his wife badly with the comment: "You are a pompous prat". He claimed that the press had taken away his dignity, but this assertion was met with a veritable volley of vulgar abuse. *The Star* called him a

"toe-rag" while *The Sun,* not to be outdone, described him as "a horny little git".

Then we had the story, tastefully told on payment of a large sum of money by *Hello* magazine, of the fecund Minister, Tim Yeo MP, who sired a love-child with a Hackney solicitor. After that there was Steve Norris MP, an amiable Minister with the convincing patter of a second-hand car salesman, who, but for his denial that he had five lovers in tow at the same time, would have become a legendary figure. The minds of most MPs boggled at the logistics and planning involved and the cost of the condoms, not to mention the energy required. A tragedy followed when Steven Milligan MP, a man said to be destined for high office, crossed over to the other side with the help of an orange, amyl nitrate and a piece of flax. Another high flyer, Hartley Booth MP, maliciously described by Tory Whips as "the maker of Hartley's seedless jam", admitted to sex of a kind in the Commons itself with his secretary.

Then there was David Ashby MP who, in a careless off-the-cuff remark, said that he had slept with 100 or so men, obviously meaning that from time to time he had shared a bed in hotels so as to avoid added expense – as rugby players on tour sometimes do. Rather stupidly, some chroniclers took his statement to be an admission that he was a voracious homosexual. Not unnaturally, and to protect his good name, he issued writs. Somewhere in between there was a gormless earl, a Minister in the House of Lords. Then... Then... Oh! how nice it was for the rest of us in Parliament to be chaste.

The blossoms on the cherry trees had just begun to appear in April 1995 when Richard Spring MP, Parliamentary Private Secretary to Sir Patrick Mayhew, Northern Ireland Secretary, was forced to resign. His resignation became imperative not because he had been caught three-in-a-bed with a tipsy Sunday-school teacher called Odette Nightingale and her lover from the City, but because of loose pillow-talk which amounted to gross insubordination to his superiors.

Whilst Spring had a contempt for the Prime Minister John Major, he had the hots for Norma Major. Asked by his mate how many times Major fucked Norma, Spring replied: "I should think probably about 1.1 times a year". But of Major's wife he said: "It's a shame... I quite fancy Norma actually". Of Cabinet Minister Michael Portillo, Spring commented: "I do know him quite well. I don't think he's gay for a minute. But he is rather attractive". Although some may smile disdainfully at this, can we forgive his vulgar, lower-than-vermin remarks about Prince Charles and Princess Di? "He's obviously potty... I don't know what he's doing shagging Mrs Parker Bowles", and of the Princess: "The thing is that he and Diana never hit it off in the sack. I know that from people who know her very well. He had a young virgin eighteen-year-old and had to give her the Penguin guide to sex".

The shock of these revelations by the *News of the World*, which surely gives us all a much-needed Sermon on the Mount each week, led to the calls by Tory and Labour MPs for the introduction of privacy laws – no doubt so as to save the Springs of this world from themselves. Spring was on a parliamentary jolly in the Canary Islands with seven other MPs when he learned that the story was about to break.

The breaking of the story was the first time the author, and probably most other MPs, had ever heard of Mr Spring. Naturally one feels sorry for him. Five minutes as a comedian, superstud and star are hardly recompense for a career in ruins.

All of these Tories had made it or were about to make it on the ministerial ladder. Yet all of them except Steve Norris failed. If they had been lawyers, estate agents or bishops would they have lived lives governed by the danger, fear and excitement of fatal liaisons? Perhaps there is something about climbing the greasy pole of power that is facilitated by the intense approach that only sex can bring. Perhaps there are just too many temptations and opportunities for powerful men, most of them far from home, from amongst researchers, secretaries and groupies. The House of Commons provides time and space, nooks and crannies, colleagues who know but will never tell, security staff and policemen anxious to preserve the reputation and dignity of Parliament, which pave the way for sex by courtesy of a tolerant establishment, providing only that you are not found out. For the aspiring MP that is the most sacred of commandments – do not be found out.

Whatever the motives of these MPs (and the peers) in allowing themselves, like most men, truthfully, to be ruled by their cocks rather than their heads, they certainly did the standing of John Major's government no good at the time. Whilst their indiscretions were certainly not the underlying cause of the government's deep and worsening unpopularity, their nakedness made it that much more difficult for the government to be taken seriously by a derisive public.

Sex Down Memory Lane with Conservatives

Scandals emanating from the bedchambers of Tory MPs and members of the House of Lords are nothing new. Tories have always preached and always sinned. In truth, the shenanigans of John Major's Ministers and PPSs do not rank

high in the scheme of things. Today's pigmies hardly bear comparison with the giants of yesteryear.

Viscount Castlereagh, a man given to psychopathic introspection and who, as Chief Secretary to Ireland, had dissidents flayed with a cat-o'-nine-tails in Dublin, inspired Shelley's famous poem, *The Mask of Anarchy*, written in 1819 after the Peterloo massacre, which includes: "I met murder in the way – he had a mask like Castlereagh."

In the poem, Castlereagh is seen feeding seven bloodhounds with human hearts. In real life, when Foreign Secretary and Leader of the House he fucked prostitutes. A blackmailer found out. So, using his own penknife, he committed suicide by severing the carotid artery of his neck. "People of England Rejoice: Castlereagh is Dead" screamed the headline of the *Weekly Political Register*.

The serious sexual scandals since 1945 summarised below have been mainly Tory ones:

John Profumo MP, 1963

The Profumo scandal was, by any standards, a classy affair. The basic story was simple. The Minister for War, John Profumo MP, had an affair with Christine Keeler, a high-class call-girl, who in turn had an affair with Eugene Ivanov, a Lieutenant Commander at the Russian Embassy and Soviet intelligence officer. The setting, the Cliveden estate of Lord Astor, was glamorous, and the sex exotic. Christine Keeler was good-looking but not as exquisitely so as Profumo's wife Valerie Hobson, a leading lady of stage and screen.

The first time Profumo met Christine he was in the company of Lord Astor. Profumo and Ivanov were introduced to Christine by Stephen Ward, a talented artist and Harley Street osteopath. Stephen would put a dog's collar around Christine's neck and he and Ivanov would go with her, collar attached, and talk as if nothing had happened. There were bit-part players from the underworld like Johnny Edgecombe, one of Christine's other boyfriends who was arrested for firing a shot at the door of Ward's house. There was even a

man in a black mask and there was a pompous Labour MP, Colonel Wigg, who had an axe to grind over a row about a military training exercise in 1961, and who forced the issue into the open behind the guise of security.

Profumo lied to the House of Commons about his affair with Keeler but was eventually forced to admit his involvement. The *New York Times* in a leader declared: "A political crisis even more profound than the storm over Suez... is now shaking Britain to its foundations". The *Washington Post* wrote: "a picture of widespread decadence beneath the glitter of a large segment of stiff-lipped society is emerging". Profumo resigned; Harold Macmillan, the Prime Minister, after performing badly in a debate on the subject in June 1963 and facing poor health, also resigned. In October, Stephen Ward, a convenient scapegoat for the establishment, had committed suicide after being found guilty of living off Christine's immoral earnings. Lord Denning, asked to report on the security aspects of the affair, blamed the press.

Anthony Courtney MP (1965-66)

Commander Courtney replaced Ian Harvey as the MP for Harrow East in 1959. A former Naval Intelligence Officer and fluent Russian speaker, his company, Eastern Trading Group Consultancy Services, did a lot of business in Poland and Russia. Almost certainly the company provided intelligence cover for work he was doing for MI6. In 1961 he had an affair in Moscow with Zinaida Grigurievna Volkova, an Intourist official. When the Labour government was elected in 1964 he attacked them for allowing the Russians to gain the moral ascendancy during the Cold War. In 1965 he asked the Prime Minister, Harold Wilson, if the government would stop behaving "like a lot of hypocritical rabbits in the face of the efficient Soviet espionage organisation".

How right he was. The Soviet espionage organisation turned out to be so efficient that it published an anonymous broadsheet with pictures of Courtney in a compromising position with a woman. Courtney was so inefficient that he allowed the KGB to monitor a telephone conversation with Volkova about the break-up of his marriage to Lady Elizabeth Trefgarne. His wife divorced him, citing Volkova. In the 1966 election he lost his seat and left public life.

Lord Lambton (1973)

1973 was a bad year for the government of Prime Minister Edward Heath. A rich man, an owner of racing horses, a good shot, an anarchic journalist and a man-about-town, Lambton took his marriage vows lightly. Perhaps this was a mistake for a Parliamentary Under-Secretary of State at the Ministry of Defence with responsibility for the RAF. His affair with Norma Levy, who ran an escort service, came to the notice of Commander Bert Wickstead, Head of the Metropolitan Police Serious Fraud Squad, and MI5.

When confronted about photographs of him with Norma Levy and deviant sexual practices, and asked questions about his use of cannabis, he resigned as a Minister. The Security Commission which subsequently looked into the affair thought that Lord Lambton's use of cannabis might lead him in a mood of irresponsibility to disclose classified information.

Lord Jellicoe (1973)

Lord Jellicoe, Winchester, Cambridge, Coldstream Guards and godson of King George V, resigned as a government Minister the day after Lord Lambton's resignation.

He hired women from two escort agencies which advertised in the *Evening Standard* but heroically never disclosed in pillow talk any of the Top Secret information to which he had access. The *Daily Express* took a spirited line, which would probably accord with public opinion today, when it asked the question of the resignations of Lambton and Jellicoe: "can we really afford to discard men of talent, wit and patriotism because their personal lives fall short of blameless perfection?" The Security Commission declared Jellicoe to be a thoroughly good chap and exonerated him of any wrongdoing.

Tony Marlow MP (1995)

For years Tony Marlow MP openly lived a double life with his wife Catherine and their five children and his mistress Jill Chambers and their four children. His wife's family lived at his farmhouse in Warwickshire; his mistress' family lived in another farmhouse at Mathry in Dyfed. Apart from his wife and mistress, Marlow did not seem to be all that keen on women, describing an Equal Pay Bill as an open invitation "to any feminist harridan or rattle-headed female with a chip on her bra strap to take action against her employer". A happy-go-lucky gentleman farmer, his life is full of contradictions. His two relationships sat uneasily with his condemnation of those immigrants who practised polygamy. His argument that Britain is overpopulated causes raised eyebrows amongst those who know that he had nine children. Surely they cannot all have been contraceptive mistakes. A prophet in his time, Marlow was the first MP to call for Margaret Thatcher's resignation as Prime Minister. He also told the world that John Major is terminally dead. Tragically, his wife drowned off the isle of Zante in an accident in 1994.

Labour on the Ropes

If masculinity is a virtue worth having, then Labour MPs can only be ashamed of themselves. Up against the ropes in the sex war with the Tories, their efforts to fight back do them little credit. In the tea-room of the House of Commons there is much talk but little evidence of real action. Frank Dobson, for example, has a limitless fund of fantastic dirty jokes, so many of which contain innuendo that one suspects that Dobson is fully capable of writing an encyclopaedia of sex.

In seeking out Labour MPs who are obsessed with sex one's mind turns naturally to two former members of the GLC – Tony Banks and Ken Livingstone. Tony Banks says that some women researchers and secretaries get jobs in Parliament with "the specific aim of bedding MPs". He adds by way of explanation:

"It's getting quite fashionable to shag an MP these days, I'm glad to say...". And according to the political columnist Sarah Baxter in the *New Statesman* of 18 February 1994, he says that there may be gay men in the House of Commons with the same aim in mind. Then on the floor of the House of Commons, much to the annoyance of Madam Speaker, Betty Boothroyd, he called for the introduction of condom machines in the Palace of Westminster. Since he has a happy marriage with a beautiful woman, one can only assume that all Banks' public talk about sex is for the benefit and edification of his colleagues.

The obsession of Ken Livingstone with sex actually destroyed his political career and his over-reaching ambition to become Leader of the Labour Party and Prime Minister, even before he entered the House of Commons in 1987. Livingstone, then a GLC Councillor, became an object of hatred and loathing amongst Labour MPs, when in an extraordinary outburst of political correctness, he wrote an article in Robert Maxwell's now defunct *London Daily News* saying that Labour's Northern MPs spent their evenings in Soho with prostitutes. It was a brilliant story but totally untrue. The MPs concerned were far more likely to spend their time in the House of Commons' bars and at Embassy dinners.

The lesson for Livingstone and any other new MP is: 'Don't bite the hand that one day you will need to feed you'. Alas for Livingstone, able, charismatic and sometimes convincing, he could not get the support of Northern MPs if he spent 1000 years in Parliament.

Livingstone got nearer the truth in an article which he wrote for Rupert Murdoch's *News of the World* on 12 June 1994. His advice that MPs are unwise to employ as researchers or secretaries their mistresses or toyboys is good. If it is true, as he wrote, that one MP got caught paying "a high-class prostitute £500 a throw for oral sex and charging it to his secretarial allowances as 'policy advice'", then clearly the MP was paying well over the going rate. His comment that some of the men are not very good on equal rights and can get a bit gropey is unexceptional. However, his

bizarre assertion that "a Tory paedophile ring is operating" questions his judgement in these matters.

One of Labour's sex-gods, Ron Brown MP, although he denied it, was spotted naked with a lover in the bathrooms in the House of Commons by two Labour MPs who, acting like school sneaks, reported him. Accident-prone to the last, his affair with his mistress Norma Langden found its way into Court when he was charged with stealing two pairs of knickers, a gold bar brooch, a picture and a pair of china earrings for Norma. Acting out of spite and fantasy, he was also charged with causing criminal damage to his mistress' flat, because, it seems, he loved her.

Acquitted of the theft charges, the judge said of his conviction on the charge of causing criminal damage that his conduct had been "a disgraceful exhibition of uncontrolled bad temper". Some thought this a harsh judgement on what was essentially what the French call a

Members in Soho: Ken Livingstone pays a high price in the North

crime passionel. Outside the Court, and despite his conviction, Brown, with the champagne fizzing, claimed "a moral victory". His wife stood by him. His political career was over. Some victory!

John Golding, a former Minister of the Crown, resigned his seat as an MP in 1986 when he became General Secretary of the National Communications Union. Just to show that there are Labour dynasties as well as Tory dynasties, his wife Llin Golding took over from him as the MP for Newcastle-under-Lyme. As an MP, Golding was on the moderate wing of the Labour Party. Today he would be described as a moderniser. Such warm words cannot hide the fact that he was a ruthless political operator. If hard times were ever to come to John few Labour MPs would shed a tear. And so it proved in 1988 when the *News of the World* published a revolting story alleging that Golding paid a prostitute for favours.

The story also called into account his manliness, a far worse matter for one so arrogant. To this day, Golding has never commented on the article, save to say that he discussed it with his wife because she was the person most concerned. Members of the National Communications Union took a rather different view. By a card vote at their annual conference they voted by 81,152 to 63,839 that he should resign as General Secretary because "he has lost credibility as our chief negotiator and brought the name of the NCU into disrepute". For Golding it was the end.

In 1994 Dennis Skinner, a friend of the author, was spotted in suspicious circumstances near the flat of his secretary, a US citizen. On 2 March David Evans MP, former manager of Luton Town Football Club and on the right wing of the Tory Party, described Skinner during a late-night adjournment debate entitled 'Back to Basics' as "a silly old fool – no fool like an old fool – who dresses in disguise, lurks in bushes in Belgravia and helps cement that special relationship between Britain and the United States". Sitting beside Evans and cheering him on during the debate was David Ashby, who, as we've seen, had only days earlier confessed that he had slept with 100 or so men.

Most Labour and Conservative MPs know about most of the relationships of their colleagues, but quite rightly we keep each other's secrets and hope that nobody finds out, on the basis of 'There but for the grace of God go I'. Of whose concern is it, except the people involved, that two front-bench Labour spokespersons were having an affair in one of the airless, windowless rooms upstairs in the Commons? And who cares a damn about Labour's leading front-bench spokesperson who had a five-year affair with a tall, slim blonde who said of him: "He was not very good in bed but I liked him and felt sorry for him". Unfortunately, the answer is that if they get caught out, such is the prurience of puritanical Britain that everybody will. If that happened, Tony Blair would have to drop them from his team.

Liberal Perspectives

History has taught us that whenever we get a new Liberal leader it's pretty certain that there is a sexual scandal in the offing. We look at four sample cases.

Lord Rosebery (1894-95)

If you asked 100 poets and writers today and 100 politicians who did most for society, Oscar Wilde or Lord Rosebery, who became Liberal Prime Minister in 1894, it is virtually certain that all 200 of them would plump for Oscar. Yet it may well be that Wilde, one of our greatest writers, was sacrificed to save a degraded band of politicians led by Lord Rosebery, to cover up a sex scandal.

Oscar Wilde, as everyone knows, went to Court twice over his homosexual relationship with Lord Alfred Douglas. His subsequent imprisonment produced the powerful poem *The Ballad of Reading Gaol,* but effectively destroyed him. In 1896 Douglas wrote in a French journal that it was the Prime Minister, Lord Rosebery, who told Asquith, the Home Secretary, that if the second trial did not go ahead (the jury failed to agree at the first trial) the Liberals might be damaged in the country and lose the forthcoming election. Douglas claimed that this was why the Solicitor-General embarked on the second prosecution, determined to get Wilde.

According to Douglas there were a number of homosexual Liberal MPs and peers at this time who were threatened by the "maniacs of virtue" with prosecution unless the case against Wilde was pursued. The story could be true. The Prime Minister, Lord Rosebery, was himself suspected at the time in political circles of being homosexual and of having had an affair with Lord Drumlanrig, Douglas's eldest brother. In a letter to his first wife's father in 1894 the Marquess of Queensberry referred to "The Snob Queers like Rosebery". Shortly before the letter was written, Lord Drumlanrig was found dead from a gunshot wound. A coroner's jury called it accidental death, but many thought that he committed suicide rather than face a public scandal resulting from publicity over his homosexual affair with Lord Rosebery.

It's also worth noting that Asquith had good reason to hate Douglas and Wilde at the time. This arose from the fact that Douglas was conducting a campaign at the time against Asquith, over Asquith's friendship with Wilde's literary executor Robert Ross, who according to Douglas, engaged in "depraved" homosexual practices.

Lloyd George (1863-1945)

Lloyd George was a man to whom almost any superlative attaches easily – a magnificent orator on a public platform, a superb debater in the House of Commons, a great social reformer, a brilliant Liberal Prime Minister, and of course an extraordinary opportunist and hugely successful womaniser. Although he had a handsome wife whose mental ability matched his own, he made adultery a way of life.

In his younger days his twinkling eyes, long brown wavy hair and unrivalled ability as a raconteur ensured him a constant supply of bed-mates from amongst a bohemian set of sopranos, young actresses, famous beauties and artists. His sexual liberalism, it seemed, knew

no bounds. But no one seemed to care. When found out, he would protest his innocence indignantly, then when that failed to work, evoke the sympathy of his wife with sadness and pitiful looks accompanied by his undying assurance that she was the only one he really loved. Better than any other Welshman ever born, he knew how to cheat on his wife heroically.

Like most rakes he lived dangerously. Cited in a counter-petition for divorce by a Dr Edwards as an adulterer with Mrs Edwards, he was acquitted for lack of evidence. He pushed his luck with Mrs Timothy Davies, whose husband knew about his wife's affair with Lloyd George but shrugged his shoulders. His affair with Frances Stevenson which began in 1912 when she was 23 and he was 50 began *after* her parents told him over lunch at Downing Street what a cad he was. When Frances Stevenson became his mistress, he lived a complicated double life with the knowledge of his wife and Miss Stevenson. Although he had two 'wives' and two homes, sometimes as his wife came through the front door Frances would go out through the back. Provocatively he would, to the knowledge of the two of them, still take Mrs Timothy Davies out for lunch or dinner.

In 1928 he had a daughter by Miss Stevenson, Jennifer Mary. On the birth certificate Frances, who was known as 'Pussy' by Lloyd George, who himself was called 'the Goat', was described as a lady of independent means living in the Coburg Court Hotel, Bayswater. In 1943 'the Goat' married 'Pussy', his wife having died two years earlier. Amid such a tangled web as this Lloyd George certainly had no need of apocryphal stories telling us that he once made love at the back of the Speaker's Chair in the House of Commons. When he died, young ladies of distinction were heard to say: "Lloyd George knew my father", reasonably safe in their assumption and hope that biblically he knew their mothers.

Jeremy Thorpe (1959-79)

On 4 August 1978 the Rt Hon Jeremy Thorpe MP, then Leader of the Liberal Party and the son of a Conservative MP, was charged with conspiracy to murder Norman Scott, a male model.

The co-conspirators who were to go into the dock with him were David Holmes, a one-time Treasurer of the Liberal Party, and two businessmen, George Devlin and John Le Mesurier. Additionally, Thorpe was charged

with inciting Holmes to murder Scott. Thorpe met Scott in 1960, felt sorry for him and, whilst emphatically denying any homosexual relationship, admitted to "a close, even affectionate friendship". Scott, for his part, claimed in outbursts that sometimes bordered on fantasy that he and Thorpe had a passionate homosexual affair. There was much talk of tears and biting the pillow. Blackmail threatened. A key player in the alleged plot was Andrew Newton, an ex-airline pilot who was convicted in 1976 of possessing a firearm with intent to endanger life.

The whole nation was stunned when they heard Newton shot dead Scott's dog, a Great Dane called Rinka, on Exmoor, but less moved when they learned that when Newton fired at Scott the gun jammed. One of the witnesses against Thorpe was another one-time Liberal MP, Peter Bessell, who said that Thorpe sug-

gested that David Holmes should kill Scott.

Even so, the case would probably never have reached the Courts but for the fact that *Private Eye* got hold of and published details of police interviews with Thorpe. The witnesses for the Crown at the trial – Scott, Newton and Bessell – were portrayed to the jury by the judge Mr Justice Cantley as the scum of the earth in his summing up. Fifty-two hours after they retired to consider their verdict the jury acquitted Thorpe and the other defendants. *Private Eye* had a field-day in satirising the woeful performance of Mr Justice Cantley, though no one doubts that, on the evidence, the jury reached the correct verdict.

At this point in time it surely does not matter whether Thorpe was or was not a homosexual. His counsel acknowledged at one point during the trial that Thorpe, a twice-married man, had had homosexual tendencies at one time. When asked by a BBC reporter if he had ever had any homosexual relationships, he replied: "That is not the major allegation... It may be that our priorities are different. It has been alleged that a man was hired to murder somebody. That is a very, very serious crime".

It was, and so was the killing of the dog, Rinka, who will forever be remembered in the annals of British political history because Auberon Waugh fought the 1979 General Election, which Thorpe lost, as the Dog Lovers' Candidate in Thorpe's constituency.

Still, his life had not been entirely in vain. When Thorpe left office he asked David Steel, his successor as Leader of the Liberal Party, if he could take away a memento of his period in office. Steel agreed, assuming that Thorpe would choose an item such as a paper-knife or pen. He was surprised to discover soon afterwards that Thorpe had arranged for the removal of Gladstone's desk.

Paddy Ashdown (1983 to present)

In his youth, as a boisterous Marine in training at Lympstone in Devon, Paddy Ashdown used to visit a dance-hall on Saturday nights just down the road in Exmouth. Somewhat infelicitously, he used to refer to it as "the meat market", a phrase used to connote women as objects who exist to be devoured by men. Later he went on to become Leader of the Lib-Dems, in which capacity he became the first major party Leader in British history to confess to adultery.

A headline in *The Guardian* screamed: "Action Man shows he is human". That may not be the way the mistress whom he dumped in great distress saw this Colonel's son, maverick from the Marines, fearless soldier who faced a gunman in Belfast and one utterly incapable of taking a joke at his expense in the House of Commons. And surely when it was all over he could have refrained from telling us that his perfect companion for his perfect weekend would be his wife.

Ashdown hates the House of Commons and in truth most MPs hate him, probably because he is self-educated, clever and charismatic. Few shed any tears when the *Sun* news-

paper headlines screamed: "IT'S PADDY PANTSDOWN"; rather there were sour grapes for the *Express* headline: "93 PER CENT OF VOTERS BACK PADDY". As so often with politicians who get caught at it Ashdown bitterly blamed everything on the press, the same press that for years had photographed him and his wife, at whom he looks "with soft focus eyes", together. His confession of adultery with

Tricia Howard was hardly voluntary.

He used gagging injunctions to stop the *News of the World* and others printing the story, bitterly angry that the paper considered paying £30,000 for a stolen document and then offered Ms Howard £100,000 for her kiss-and-tell story. She refused the offer. When Ms Howard left Ashdown she went to work for Ann Clwyd, where the author of this book saw her on several occasions looking upset and depressed. Eventually we discovered why, but kept our mouths shut. What a pity that Ashdown's glowing reference for Ms Howard said nothing about her terrible state of mind.

Gay Sex

Except when voting not to reduce the age of consent for homosexual men to sixteen, MPs probably respect sexual equality more than most groups in our society. Of course there are exceptions and contradictions.

A small number of Labour MPs are undoubtedly homophobic, by which I mean that they are tolerantly disposed towards homosexuals but believe that there is something wrong about it. In this category must be included David Blunkett MP and Ann Taylor MP, neither of whom would like their children to be gay. For many Tories, homosexuality is not an issue, but in deference to the prejudices and bigotry of their electorate in the shires they have to be seen to be against it. Yes, it's nauseating hypocrisy and vile political opportunism.

However, some Tories really do hate homosexuals, seeing them, in the words of the former Chief Constable of Manchester, James Anderton, as "people swirling around in a human cesspit of their own making". Some of these MPs have used well-founded worries about AIDS to ignite the old association of sex, disease and death. They see HIV and AIDS as nature's or God's revenge on the impure. One such was Geoffrey Dickens MP, the T-dancer who died in 1995 and who was in no position to lecture anyone on sexual morals. On 7 June 1988 he told the nation that if AIDS escalated and it could be proved that the root cause of "the disaster inflicted on the nation was homosexuality, then prison sentences for homosexuality could return". One imagines that gay Tory MPs in Parliament might take exception to this approach.

If, however, today most MPs believe that to be gay is to be human it has not always been thus. In 1964 when the *Sunday Mirror* suggested, without naming him, that Lord Boothby, formerly Bob Boothby MP and a Minister in Churchill's wartime government, was having a homosexual relationship with the leader of London's underworld, Ronnie Kray, the government was gripped by panic. The Prime Minister, Sir Alec Douglas Home, concerned that the government was about to be hit by another 'Profumo affair' so soon, ordered a secret government enquiry. The idea that a leading Tory MP should be having gay sex in Mayfair and elsewhere with a mobster at the head of a number of protection rackets was too much. So in July 1964 the Prime Minister met the Lord Chancellor at Chequers to discuss "the growing tide of rumours about the involvement of members of both Houses of Parliament in protection rackets and homosexual activities".

Later the Home Secretary, Henry Brooke MP, perhaps the worst Home Office Minister this country has ever had, confirmed that the Kray twins were involved in protection rackets but added that the problem was "less serious" in London than it used to be. The government Chief Whip warned that "one does not forget that the Profumo affair was seriously thought to have been based on Soviet subversion and I do not think this should be lost sight of in this case". The Private Secretary to the Prime Minister wrote that it was alleged that "Lord Boothby and Driberg [a Labour MP] had been importuning males at a dog-track". Like the good MP he had once been, Boothby lied both about his suppressed homosexuality and about his friendship with Ronnie Kray, took out a libel action against the *Sunday Mirror*, pocketed £40,000 in damages and received an apology. A relieved government called the police investigation off, thus allowing the Krays to

build up one of the biggest criminal empires ever seen in Britain – surely a small price to pay for preventing "a mushroom of rumour" bringing a government down.

Because many gay or bisexual MPs believe that their sexuality is a private matter and others believe that coming out can only cause them grief on account of underlying prejudices which exist in Britain at large, nobody has any idea of how many MPs are gay. A figure of sixty-five or so is sometimes touted, but this figure is based on the idea which has somehow gained credence that if one-tenth of the population is gay then one-tenth of the 650 MPs will be gay or lesbians. Unfortunately there is no reliable evidence that one-tenth of the population is gay.

Only two existing MPs have come out and declared themselves to be gay. One is Chris Smith, a highly talented MP whose majority in Islington South would probably have soared even if he had not come out. Clearly coming out did him no real harm, but it has to be said that people in inner-city North London are probably far more tolerant than those out in the sticks. The other MP who came out is Michael Brown, who resigned as a government Whip in 1994 as a result of revelations in the *News of the World*. In 1995 the gay rights group Outrage sent intimidating letters to twenty or so MPs in an effort to force them to 'come out' and admit publicly that they were homosexuals. It was said that Sir James Kilfedder, an Ulster Unionist MP, received one such letter shortly before he had a heart attack and died.

So far as gay sex is concerned within the precincts of the Palace of Westminster, gay penetrative sex that is, there is none so far as I am aware. Those MPs who are known to be gay keep their relationships private and discreet for the most part, and nothing much that goes on in the Palace of Westminster comes under that category.

Of course it has not always been thus. One of the saddest cases concerns Ian Harvey MP, a former President of the Oxford Union and a Lieutenant Colonel who became a Minister at the Foreign Office. He was undone on what H. Montgomery Hyde describes as a "dark and misty November night" in 1958 after a good dinner at the Polish Embassy. Harvey went over to the Mall, which leads to Buckingham Palace, and having picked up a Guardsman of the Household Cavalry, took him into St James's Park. When stopped by a policeman, he tried unsuccessfully to do a bunk. At Cannon Row police station he gave a false name. The House of Commons was informed. The next morning he was fined £5, not for a homosexual offence but for a breach of park regulations. Being an officer and a gentleman he paid the Guardsman's fine. This non-event ruined his life. "The gates were closed to me forever" he said, not referring to those of the park.

The story of Keith Hampson, a doctor of philosophy who is still an MP and the husband of TV star Sue Cameron, provides a cautionary tale for MPs. One evening in May 1984, with time on his hands, he went into a homosexual club called the Gay Theatre, just for devilment. There it was alleged he grasped the penis and testicles of a voyeur who turned out to be a policeman. Hampson's defence in Court was simple – the PC and WPC first entrapped him, then lied about what happened. The jury failed to agree on a verdict and the judge virtually ordered the Crown not to proceed with a re-trial. A week later Counsel for the Crown dropped the case and Hampson was formally acquitted. The stress caused by the case was said to be a factor in Sue Cameron's miscarriage. Hampson resigned as a PPS to a Defence Minister. He too may find that the gates are forever closed against him.

One member who flaunted his homosexuality was Labour MP Tom Driberg, a *bon viveur* and high churchman. In the House of Commons one day he accused the Foreign Secretary of "flirting" with kings. Anthony Eden retorted amid great guffaws: "I do not know how far the Honourable Member is an expert in flirtations, or in what kind of flirtations". Twice he was picked up by the police, once with a Norwegian sailor and once when he was cottaging in a public lavatory in central London, but on each occasion he talked his

way out of being charged. But of course he paid a price. A brilliant man in a party of much mediocrity, he retired from Parliament in 1974 without ever having been even a Junior Minister. As ever, he put his finger on the reason when he wrote that Attlee and Wilson, the Prime Ministers of his day, knew about his homosexuality – how could they not? – and "both were deeply prejudiced puritans".

Harvey Proctor MP was brought down by a rent boy called David. In an article in the Oxford undergraduate magazine *Twist*, Marianne Macdonald describes David as "the wild one, completely irresponsible, dangerous. Champagne, expensive meals, alcohol, alcohol. He brought out the sense of danger in other people... When he moved in with Harvey Proctor, Harvey would punish him for going out with other rent boys". According to David, "there was no sex involved. He'd start off with his hands, then move on to his slipper, then the cane. And it was horrendous". After a three-month affair with Proctor he spilled his guts out to *The People*. "There was," said Proctor, "and still is, a very strong sense of betrayal". It was betrayal which led Proctor to resign as a candidate for the General Election in 1987 after being accused of acts of indecency with two teenage boys, both aged seventeen. Proctor pleaded guilty and was fined £1,450.

His real bitterness was reserved not so much for David as for the hacks of the tabloid press whom he believes crucified him because of his political views on immigration, advocating as he did the voluntary repatriation of new Commonwealth immigrants. He tells us with venom: "One journalist from the *Daily Mirror* was caught snooping around my room in the House of Commons, and another got a story out of someone I know by plying him with drink and committing an act of gross indecency with him". This latter act sounds a bit like those secret service agents in films who are forced to fuck for their country. The man who was once called "the spanking MP" now runs his own shirt and tie business and campaigns for the rights of small businesses. In an act of great generosity, sixteen MPs invested money in Proctor's company to help him rebuild his shat-

Snooping for sex: Harvey Proctor attacks the hacks

tered life. Ten of them, including two Ministers, David Heathcote-Amery MP and Phillip Oppenheim MP, failed to declare their interest in Proctor's company in the Register of Members' Interests when they should have done. Were they all forgetful or did some of them not want to declare to Parliament the nature of their good deeds? Michael Heseltine did declare his shareholding in the firm, Cotton Rose Limited.

Alan Roberts MP, the talented and hugely engaging gay politician from Merseyside, died on 22 March 1990 of cancer of the bowel. Watching him wither away in the House of Commons was extremely distressing, more like God's stupidity than God's revenge. In the House of Commons he neither flaunted nor hid his homosexuality, and was a member of what became known as the 'Catering Committee set' because a few of them were gay. The *News of the World* clearly thought they had a cracking good story when they produced pages and pages detailing the most astonishing accounts, involving Roberts, of raw gay sex, orgies and much more besides, some of it taking place in that most corrupting of cities, Berlin.

Roberts denied suggestions that he had been whipped by men in SS-style uniforms while he was dressed as a priest in the Buddy Club, a gay haunt in West Berlin. He did, however, end up in hospital. Roberts sued the *News of the World* and won. In consequence they were forced to pay out substantial damages, with which Roberts bought a pub in the East End, apparently an old haunt of the murderous Kray twins. Now there's style for you!

Sexual Harassment in Parliament

Sexual harassment through innocent touching, gallant males taking women by the arm, and innuendo are commonplace in the House of Commons. Groping is less so, but not unknown in bars and on overseas trips when too much alcohol has been consumed. Not so long ago one Labour MP had occasion to complain to her friends about a colleague who visited her

hotel room in a maudlin state when they were abroad on official business. Virginia Bottomley, whose experience is presumably with Tories, went on record as saying that she only learned what sexual harassment was when she entered the House of Commons.

The main victims of sexual harassment may be women MPs, of whom there are few, or secretaries and researchers, of whom there are some 1,400. The advertisements for secretaries and researchers say nothing about *droit de seigneur*. The overwhelming majority of MPs' employees resent the claim of their bosses to this right. However, a lot of them suffer in silence and rarely speak out, even if scandals project them as bimbos.

Even hardened women journalists are at risk from the roaming hands and predatory activities of male MPs. Writing passionately on this subject Sarah Baxter, a former Lobby correspondent for the *New Statesman* and currently a journalist on the *Sunday Times*, records that even inviting an MP for lunch "can be fraught with ambiguity". Lunches are a time-honoured way of enabling journalists to talk to MPs in depth about current events or their beliefs, and for the MPs a chance to put across their own ideas. They are not meant to be the occasion for flattery and philandering. Sarah Baxter solved the problem at the Tory and Labour Party conferences, where alcohol is consumed by the bucket rather than the pint, by teaming up with a TV journalist for a rota of dinners with MPs.

It is inconceivable that women journalists would report MPs for sexual harassment. Indeed one or two good-looking ones know that by wearing a short skirt and talking intimately they can guarantee themselves exclusive stories. But for most women journalists it would be more than their job was worth to complain of sexual harassment. Supposedly hardened cynics, they would become laughing-stocks. However, it can only be a matter of time before secretaries and researchers start taking MPs to industrial tribunals for harassment if it turns out that the law allows them to do so. It's only an office, after all, so why should their employers be exempt?

SEX CODE OF CONDUCT FOR MPS

Any new MP would be well advised to adhere strictly to the following Sex Code of Conduct:

1 Don't. Let celibacy be its own reward.

2 If you want to unzip your trousers or take your knickers off, don't do it in the Palace of Westminster. However discreet you are the security staff will get to know about it. These chaps are professionals who can spot a bonk at 1000 yards. In 1994 they found two Labour MPs at it in a room off the Upper Committee Corridor.

3 Wherever you do it, use condoms or femidoms. This is more than a matter of healthy safe sex. Babies always ensure in the ensuing scandal that you will be shown up to be a bad egg. Little bundles of fun they may be, but they have in them the ability to destroy everything you've worked for.

WHAT MPS THINK OF EACH OTHER

Not a lot is the answer so far as Labour MPs are concerned when it comes to their colleagues. Welsh Labour MPs, most of them spawned in the valleys, have only one thing in common – they all hate each other. When Ann Clwyd embarked on a spectacular and unlawful sit-in at the Tower Colliery, which was to close, and defied management attempts to starve her out, you might have expected her Welsh colleagues back in Parliament to say, "Well done, Ann. We're 100 per cent behind you". Not a bit of it. Almost all of them were bitterly resentful of the publicity she was getting and went around the corridors muttering "That bloody woman's at it again".

It was left to a London MP, the author, to bring her plight to the attention of the Speaker. Scottish Labour MPs, when they do manage to put their thoughts into words that can be understood, show themselves to be deeply suspicious of their English colleagues. Perhaps not surprisingly, therefore, English Labour MPs talk about the existence of a Scottish mafia and the need to break up the Scottish hegemony so that English civilisation can get a look in.

For their part, Labour MPs from the North East of England find it difficult to come to terms with the fact that London Labour MPs are more intelligent than they are. But more significantly, a huge majority of Labour MPs join common cause in their hatred of the Prince of Darkness, spin doctor Peter Mandelson. The level of hatred is consistent throughout every geographical area and cuts across gender, class,

social background and occupation. Most Tories don't like him either. So there it is – the Prince of Darkness is the most hated MP in Parliament.

The only other MP who can even approach the Prince of Darkness as an object of hatred amongst Labour MPs is Ken Livingstone, and that for reasons you have already seen. The revelation that Livingstone was a tax-dodger who employed an accountant to help him avoid paying income tax on his substantial non-parliamentary earnings confirmed his status in the eyes of Labour MPs as a pillock. Those who have in the past genuflected to Red Ken as one of the most promising socialists of our time need not worry. In getting part of his income paid to him through an off-the-shelf company, Red Ken was only doing what fat cats in the City of London do, and it was quite legal. Unable to beat them, Ken joined them.

In his book *Loyalists and Loners* Michael Foot summed up beautifully how very good friends in the Parliamentary Labour Party express their undying loyalty to each other. In one short essay on Tony Benn, Foot accuses Benn of having calculated spasms, of creating an ignorant marriage of convenience between Christianity and Marxism, of unctuous pride, of false allegations of treachery against colleagues, of tomfoolery and Bennfoolery, and finally of lying.

A lot of hatred on the part of Labour MPs for their colleagues stems from envy and the culture of heroic failure which has accompanied many of them through life. Too many back-bench Labour MPs cannot cope with success themselves but none the less resent it in others, so they are jealous of many of those who make up Labour's hopelessly over-inflated front-bench team, a fair number of whom are creatures of the Leader's misuse of patronage. Contrariwise, Tory MPs tend to applaud success because they are confident that their turn will come next. They see the fruits of success as something to be shared rather than envied. Take the position of retired Ministers who get well-paid outside appointments in areas in which they were in charge when Ministers. In these cases Tory MPs don't whinge or say to themselves: "Hang about a bit, old man. Doesn't that create ethical problems?"; rather they think: "Gosh. I'd like to have the opportunity to do something like that".

For them, Lord Tebbit (formerly Norman Tebbit MP), the Secretary of State for Trade and Industry who became a director of the privatised BT, is a man to be looked up to. And so it is with Norman Fowler MP, former Secretary

for Transport, who joined the privatised National Freight Corporation. And well done Lord Wakeham, the former Energy Minister who gave work to Rothschilds because they deserved it and then got a job with them because he deserved it.

Other former Ministers who have picked up rich pickings in the outside world – Kenneth Baker, Archie Hamilton, Tom King, Tim Renton, Peter Walker, John MacGregor – are also much admired by Tory MPs mindful of the lush beckoning pastures outside Parliament. Frankly most Tory MPs are horrified at the thought that retiring Ministers could be put in quarantine for two years before they are allowed to join firms whom they've helped in the past. They also consider the idea of a statutory code of ethics for Ministers and ex-Ministers to be an insult to those who seek to serve the jobs and money markets profitably and nobly.

Salivating with Envy

The lips of many Tory MPs salivated with envy when they heard that their colleague Winston Churchill MP stood to benefit from a staggering National Lottery grant of £12.5 million to enable the nation to purchase the private papers of his grandad Winston Churchill. "Lucky bugger. He's won the lottery without even buying a ticket" they said, with no thought of Gladstone's contemptuous observation: "There never was a Churchill from John of Marlborough down that had either morals or principles". Young Winston would no doubt reply that Gladstone was a seedy old Liberal of gross sexual appetites, happily long since dead and whose *bon mots* were a despicable attempt to traduce the good name of our country's most beloved family.

Naturally MPs from one political party will attack MPs from the other in a way which suggests intense dislike. Sometimes they will mean it, before they exchange jokes on the Terrace and in the tea-room. When attacked viciously by a member of the other party in the Chamber of the House of Commons one of two courses is appropriate. Either you should intervene immediately with a flashing, witty put-

down, or if that is too difficult or too risky you should sit back with a fixed, disdainful grin on your face. Tony Blair is a master of this latter defensive ploy.

On 23 November 1993 in an unreported speech John Patten MP, the Secretary of State for Education with bouffant hair who was later sacked, accused Tony Blair of what in the Labour Party amounts to original sin, saying:

The Hon. Member for Sedgefield [Tony Blair] clearly is not a stupid person. Because he does not believe in anything he says, he does not say anything of substance about Labour's policy on law and order. Indeed, I do not think that he actually believes in Labour Party policy any more. This afternoon we have seen the beginnings of an early middle-age political crisis – someone who has realised that he is in the wrong party. I have the authority of the Government Whip, the Hon. Member for Stevenage [Mr Wood] to say that we would happily consider an application from the Hon. Member for Sedgefield to join us on this side of the House. I think that the Hon. Gentleman is really a Tory – and by the look on the face of the Labour Party Chief Whip, the hon. Member for Jarrow [Mr Dixon], he thinks so too. The Hon. Member for Sedgefield should have seen the faces of those behind him when he was speaking this afternoon. They could see the words 'Tory, Tory' coming out in bubbles around his head.

As the debate was about to come to an end there was no time for Blair to intervene, even if he had wanted to. Instead he relied on his intuition and sat immovable in his seat, his face radiating a smiling innocence as though he pitied Patten's poor attempt at humour. In fact it was a clever attack by Patten because although he himself did not believe what he was alleging, he knew that a significant number of Labour MPs did. All this of course was in the days before Blair became Leader of the Labour Party. Once that happened and Blair became Labour's dispenser of patronage all Labour MPs, apart from a few oddballs in the left-wing Campaign Group, instantly realised that Tony

was the wisest and fairest socialist ever to be made Leader of the Labour Party.

With the rise of the managerial class in both parties, and with technocrats replacing politicians, the House of Commons is in danger of becoming a House of Bores. No one, however, could attach that description to Nicholas Fairbairn MP, the former Scottish Solicitor-General who died in 1995. He was undoubtedly both the most quixotic MP in Parliament and the most offensive. His House of Commons garb consisted of double-breasted jackets, tartan trousers and antique waistcoats. On other occasions watch-chains and tie-pins were prominent. Occasionally there was a full-length caftan and even a bow-tie which once belonged to Compton Mackenzie. Descended from the Dukes of Gordon, he carried off his screaming clothes with aplomb. Not always loyal to his colleagues, he once described Peter Temple-Morris MP as a "waxwork wet", whilst when commenting on the idea of Michael Heseltine taking over as Prime Minister from Margaret Thatcher, he said: "Why do we want to change her for junk?" When Edwina Currie interrupted him in a speech in the Commons and asked: "Is my Honourable and Learned Friend seriously saying that no one ever died under general anaesthetic for dental treatment?" he replied: "If that is the basis of my Honourable Friend's argument I can say only that I hope she will take anaesthetics frequently". Obviously turned on by Edwina Currie, he later described her as "a hag" in the *Spectator*.

In 1992 in the pages of the *Antique* magazine Fairbairn and Clare Short MP took opposite sides on the feminist issue. Clare Short wrote: "Men rape women. Men consume pornography in vast quantities... Almost all women have been badly hurt by men". Fairbairn responded: "I declare my unquenchable interest in any woman, although not in any woman in the House of Commons, some of whom like Clare Short are nevertheless interesting... I have a primeval urge to rescue damsels from the sadistic distress of feminism". He concluded of men and women that "Their attraction to one another is inevitable, inevitably wonderful and inevitably stormy. Dr

Boteles said of the strawberry 'God could have made a better berry, but doubtless God never did'. And so I say of women *Glorificamur, te*; no, on second thoughts, *Glorifico vos*". His former girlfriend and secretary, Pamela Milne, committed suicide when their affair ended. His continued Ministerial prospects were not enhanced when, in a savagely cruel scene in the House of Commons, he took the blame which could not properly be laid at his door, for not prosecuting a rapist. Metaphorically, Labour's feminists screwed his balls off.

Few MPs are without vanity but Dr Jack Cunningham, known to his colleagues as Alderman Vanity, takes it to extremes. In one broadcast Cunningham, who is Deputy Lord Lieutenant of Cumbria, spoke of his delight when he was made a Privy Councillor at kissing the hand of the Queen, and how he valued the memento of the occasion, which consisted of a book of the New Testament inscribed "the Rt Hon Dr J Cunningham MP". Alderman Vanity, then Shadow Foreign Secretary, went on to tell the listeners that he was so important that he often met visiting statesmen and Prime Ministers to Britain alone in his room. Hardly the stuff of a man of the people, you may think. Certainly Dr Cunningham's Labour colleagues could not contain their mirth. Yes, Cunningham is the vainest MP in the House of Commons.

Vanity for Ron Davies MP, who is on the

Labour front-bench, is very much a practical matter. Davies used to have fading, yellowish teeth with a gap in his top set. Now they're gleaming white and the gap has disappeared. The offending teeth, it seems, have been capped in anticipation of the achievement of high office by Davies as Secretary of State for Wales. There was a time when Davies kept his mouth shut as often as possible but now he smiles at every conceivable opportunity so that we can all appreciate molars which have become an expression of the seriousness of Labour's modernising mission, whatever that might be.

The House of Commons abounds with gluttons, but few can match the bad table manners of Rhodri Morgan MP, a Taffy from Cardiff. In full flight, as he hurls food down his throat like a stoker on the old Great Western Railway line shovelling coal into the boiler so as to generate maximum speed, Morgan is a sight wondrous to behold. One assumes that Morgan's taste buds have long since given up on him, and that his aim is merely to stockpile fuel for renewed political activity.

You can tell a lot about MPs from their hair and the way in which they treat it. Tarzan (Michael Heseltine) has a brilliant shock of blonde hair through which he constantly runs his fingers as though he is in love with himself. On a public platform, you know that Tarzan's rhetoric is reaching orgiastic proportions when you see his flowing mane and foaming mouth acting in unison. Dennis Skinner, on the other hand, has a positively beautiful shock of black hair, with each individual strand telling its own working-class story as the Brylcreem of the 1950s has given way to the natural flow of the 1990s. It's very much hair that Looks Back In Anger. If Michael Fabricant's wig is designed to pass off for a gift of God it is the only gift that God has bestowed on him. There is, however, no question of the Speaker's wig being a fake. Made from horse hair and similar to the wigs worn by judges, it sits easily on the head of Madam Speaker. All that is missing is a whip, which she so desperately needs to give vent to her exasperation over the increasing naughtiness of her charges.

Most Labour MPs abhor the very idea of

The mane man: Heseltine knows how to knock them in the aisles

corporal punishment but not Allan Rogers, MP for the Rhondda. He practised it as a schoolmaster in the Welsh valleys. Civil servant, Chief Petty Officer 'Taffy' K Dunn from the Royal Navy Reserve, had Labour MPs and peers agog with horror when he revealed that one day at school he and thirty-one classmates were all beaten by Rogers, who thwacked each of them on the hand with a cane. Rogers, it seems, mistook exhaustion for malingering when the class was returning from exercise. His taste for aggression was also seen in boxing rings and can still be seen today in the way in which his shoulders move.

And what about the MP who should have been charged with wasting police time? That's Ann Clwyd. When she reported that her car had been stolen from the underground House of Commons car park, a frisson went through the security guards. How could a thief break security and get into the car park unseen? With batteries of closed-circuit cameras on every floor, how did he avoid detection as he broke into her car? And how could he drive out unnoticed? A few days later Clwyd's car was found at Paddington Railway Station – not dumped there by some mythical thief but parked where she had left it.

The most insalubrious MP is surely Rupert Allason, alias Nigel West, the House of Commons spy-writer. Pissing away merrily in the Members' loo at 10.45 pm on Monday 28 March 1994 he told a Tory colleague: "I'm just practising my white flag procedure", a reference to what he considered to be the cowardice of his own Prime Minister, John Major, over his surrender in changing the rules governing majority voting in the European Union. That's as may be, but why was he spilling out his innermost thoughts in such questionable circumstances?

The most disrespectful Tory MP, so far as his colleagues are concerned, is undoubtedly Nicholas Budgen. As Quentin Davies MP annoyed the Governor of the Bank of England at a hearing of the Select Committee on the Treasury, Budgen commented: "Even when he tries to ingratiate himself with someone, he's offensive".

Tony Banks, a star of television, might have been considered the funniest MP were it not for the fact that in 1988 he lost his sense of humour and blithe spirit when he moved a motion to report Andrew Rawnsley to the Committee of Privileges so as to get him slung out of the Lobby, merely because Rawnsley had described 200 Labour MPs as being "incompetent, lazy drunks". After a three-hour debate Banks was forced to withdraw his motion when other Labour MPs, led by the author, accused him of being po-faced and censorious.

The expert in black comedy is Robin Corbett MP who, as he went into the Division Lobby to vote for Austin Mitchell, one of his colleagues, to be put on the new Select Committee on Northern Ireland Affairs said to a Tory: "You must vote for Austin Mitchell because whoever is on the Committee will be on the death list".

Bore of the Year

The two greatest bores in the House of Commons are both driven people, made mad by their hatred of the European Union. They are of course Bill Cash MP (Conservative) and Nigel Spearing MP (Labour). In full flow with their white coats flapping they are both impossible to shake off. Many MPs still gleefully recall the day when Nigel Spearing trapped the Prime Minister, Margaret Thatcher, in the Members' Lobby with some minuscule, obscurantist point on Europe and slowly moved around as she tried to escape this way and then that. Spearing is the author's candidate for the 'Bore of the Year' contest, in which he would be asked to explain in not less than three hours why it would be wrong in principle for the European Union to give every man, woman and child in Britain £10,000 in cash each year with no strings attached. He would have no difficulty in coping. The best that can be said for Bill Cash, civilised by cricket in his youth, is that he has a lovely moll called Biddy for a wife and a wayward journalist for a son, whose skin is as sensitive as that of a rhinoceros.

And then of course there are the 'psychopaths', by which I mean not those who have a defined psychiatric illness but those whom one would hate to cross and then live to reap the consequences. For the 'psychopath', the quality of mercy certainly is strained. Labour's 'psychopath' is my good friend Gerald Kaufman, a man with a tongue so sharp that it hurts just to see his mouth open. The Tory 'psychopath' is their Deputy Chief Whip Greg Knight. The only advice that one can give is that you should stay away from him.

A close runner-up for the title of principal Tory 'psycho' is David Lightbown MP, another Whip hired by John Major to bring recalcitrant Tory MPs into line. Known as 'The Terminator,' Lightbown is a lumbering man of enormous girth, with shoulders that droop menacingly. One imagines that in his spare time he plucks out the finger-nails of those of his grandchildren who misbehave. One of his distressed constituents who threatened to commit suicide at his surgery took exception to his reply: "If you're going to jump out of a window, jump out of your window at home and not mine". Lightbown is, as they say, a direct, simple sort of a person with a vacuum where others have minds.

MPs who hand out abuse have to be able to take it, as Bernie Grant discovered when Richard Littlejohn, a low-life journalist from *The Sun*, responding to some of Bernie's comments on the police, reacted by calling him a "gutter politician... I wouldn't urinate on him if he was on fire".

"True Blue Tony"

The Real Who's Who of Politicians

MPs write their own entries for *Who's Who*, the bible of important people. Obviously they put themselves in as good a light as possible within the format to which they have to adhere. If their entries were written by their political enemies they would appear as follows:

John Major (Conservative)

The first captain of a ship to throw himself overboard during a storm and then call on the crew to dive into raging seas to save him. Different name from his brother Terry Major-Ball. Did not live at the home of Rose Oliphant but gave it as his address. Unsure of his academic achievements. Although he did not have an affair with the cook, Claire Latimer, did have an affair of passion and of sorts with a divorced woman called Jean Kierans whom he threw away like an empty husk when the greasy pole of politics beckoned. Streetwise. Owned a female rabbit and established a joint commercial venture with his friend, John Brand, the owner of a male rabbit. Bred mice for sale too, and offered a piece of cake as a bonus to anyone buying three of the varmints. Told a reporter he was neutral as regards peas. Like Mussolini wants to make the trains run on time. Counts the cones and the loos on motorways. Forced British Rail to make train journeys longer so they would avoid paying compensation under the Citizen's Charter for late arrival. His brother says his ideas are not fleeting fancies of the moment. Will be remembered for describing three of his Cabinet colleagues as bastards. Nickname: Toytown Tory.

Tony Blair (Labour)

Educated at Scotland's foremost public school, Fettes, a replica of a sixteenth century French castle, and St John's College, Oxford. A moderniser who believes in the old religion. Learned his Christianity from a nutty antipodean at school who seduced his mind over cups of coffee. Face distorted by a fixed grin. Poxy undergraduate rock star. Eminently forgettable barris-

the husband of Cherie Blair who believed 10 Downing Street was not a suitable residence for her family. Nickname: True Blue Tony.

"Fatman from No.11" (left)

Kenneth Clarke (Conservative)

Fat. Sinks pints of beer in the Strangers' Bar. Wears brothel-creepers and a stained Garrick Club tie. Insouciant. As an undergraduate at Cambridge strove to keep women out of the Union. Political bruiser not afraid to upset teachers, doctors, nurses and policemen. Makes up statistics as he goes along, pretty sure that his ignorant audiences will not notice. Presents economic pain as though it were divine pleasure. Poor speaker with quick mind. Nice wife. Described by his namesake Alan Clark in his diaries as a "butter ball", "a wanker" and "a podgy life-insurance-risk". Traitor to Margaret Thatcher. Will be remembered as someone who liked jazz and hated the professional middle classes. Nickname: Fatman from No. 11.

John Prescott (Labour)

Likes jazz. Pseudo class-warrior instincts stem from the days when he was a ship's steward on ocean liners cleaning up the sick of disgustingly rich passengers. Succumbs easily to flattery. Graduate whose sentences sound the same when spoken backwards or forwards. Snappy dresser. Male chauvinist. Big ego. Difficult to work with. Regular visitor to the tea-room. Will be remembered for writing Labour's socialist credo – Clause IV – out of the script. Carries little clout. Sneered at behind his back by the modernisers. Nickname: Thumper.

Paddy Ashdown (Liberal)

Politically incorrect. Once lived on a pedestal. Tried to live down the Paddy Pantsdown episode but found the Prime Minister pouring scorn over his blameless past. Warmonger. Dreams he is three in one – Eisenhower, Rommel, Monty. Humourless. Refuses to drop the slovenly habit of speaking with his hands in his pockets. Empties the Chamber faster than any other MP. Amazing ability to think up a new policy in the morning and drop it in the afternoon. Nickname: Paddy Backdown.

ter who hijacked a political party in the pursuit of personal power. Campaigned in the Queensbridge Ward of Hackney for Tony Benn to be Deputy Leader of the Labour Party in 1981. Once CND, not any more. Supporter of selective education for his own family. What you see is what you get. Hides himself away with his nappy-rash advisers. Accepts money to run his private office from a slush fund, the Industrial Research Trust, whose benefactors are unknown. Backed by millionaire friends in the media. Gauche at parties. Will be remembered as

"Ginny"

"Pretty Boy"

Rev Ian Paisley (Democratic Unionist)

Demagogue and bully. Operatic performer. Frightens God and the Speaker and women who want abortions in Belfast with his thunderclaps of bigotry. Gives his listeners GBH in the ear. Dismissed like a small boy from Downing Street after implying that the Prime Minister was a liar. Now out in the cold. Nickname: Pussykins.

Edwina Currie (Conservative)

When the AIDS scare broke, suggested that women who travelled abroad should take their husbands with them and use them as mobile condoms. Brash but erotically desirable. Judged by her first novel, spends her time mentally undressing MPs and examining their private parts when not studying the Kama Sutra. Expensively wrong about salmonella in eggs. Refused to work as a Minister under Fatman (Kenneth Clarke). Would do anything for a photo-call. Living proof of Winston Churchill's tart remark that in the House of Commons it is not the Opposition but your colleagues behind you who are your enemies. Nickname: Wonderwoman.

Harriet Harman (Labour)

Human being who turned into a man-eater. Now politically correct but not always so. Superior feminist of good breeding. A sister with few friends amongst the other sisters who

THE ART OF DESCRIPTIVE ELEGANCE

The House of Commons is still searching for a political orator who could match the descriptive elegance of the Australian Prime Minister, Paul Keating. He called one MP "a piece of criminal garbage" and another "a gutless spiv", while collectively he referred to the Liberal Opposition as "sleazebags", "perfumed gigolos", "boxheads" and "stunned mullets". However, perhaps Lord Sandwich and John Wilkes saved the British from the charge that they were short of political invective with the following exchange:

Lord Sandwich: "Pon my honour, Wilkes, I don't know whether you'll die on the gallows or of the pox."

Wilkes: "That must depend, my Lord, upon whether I embrace your Lordship's principles or your Lordship's mistress."

That exchange took place in the eighteenth century. More recently (23 November 1994) two former Tory Ministers, Tristan Garel-Jones MP and Edward Leigh MP, in a heated bust-up over Europe which took place in the Members' Lobby just outside the Chamber of the House of Commons, showed that the art of plain speaking on the part of MPs has perhaps lost some of its humour and elegance. Garel-Jones asked Leigh if he were plotting to overthrow the Prime Minister, John Major. Leigh, by way of reply, snarled: "Why don't you fuck off – fuck off, you cunt." "Obviously you aren't denying it then," replied Garel-Jones, only to add later as he pointed an accusatory finger at Leigh, "It's cunts like him who are going round trying to get votes against the PM."

If this public schoolboyish exchange was meant to demonstrate that parliamentary debate can still be virile, most of those trained to use the English language as a weapon of beauty saw it as so overtly sexist and tawdry as to be out of place even in a House of Corruptibles.

are Labour MPs. Presentable and media friendly but has suffered from trying to little avail to master the complexities of economic analysis. Married to former red-revolutionary, now a middle-of-the-road trade unionist. Nickname: Harridan Harbottle.

Virginia Bottomley (Conservative)

Well bred. Beautiful but sexless. Gave birth to love child born out of wedlock. Member of a Cabinet that hates single mums. Married beneath her. Source of much merriment at parties when she admits to having two degrees in sociology. Deemed by the public in an opinion poll to be the least sincere member of the Cabinet. Determined to close the world's best hospital – St Bartholomew's. Mission to abolish the NHS almost accomplished. Her career having been destroyed by the *Evening Standard*, she was demoted to Heritage Secretary where she can turn her attention to closing art galleries, museums and the Royal Shakespeare Company instead of hospitals. Nickname: Ginny.

Michael Heseltine (Conservative)

An honourable man who fights Prime Ministers of the day through his friends in the corridors, behind the scenes and down in the bowels of the underground car park – anywhere but in the open and to their face. Euroturd. Became the object of much merriment when he lost his job and became Deputy Prime Minister, a position in the constitution which has long since fallen into desuetude. Made a statement in the Commons on the export of arms to Iran which left his Cabinet colleague Alan Clark, a director of the company concerned, clinging by the tips of his fingers to a rock at the top of a gorge. When the control goes, acts as well as looks like Beelzebub.

    Maverick with flowing mane and foaming mouth when at his best. Naughty boy who forced the Speaker to suspend a sitting of Parliament. Flounced out of a Cabinet meeting while it was in progress. Destroyed a Prime Minister, destroyed the coal industry and then had a heart attack in Venice when he realised what he'd done. With Virginia Bottomley at large, would be advised not to have his next heart attack in Britain. Described at the time of the Westland affair by Alan Clark as "almost off his head with rage and – to my mind – persecution mania". Nickname: President of the Apes.

Gordon Brown (Labour)

Tortured son of a manse. Failed to tell the truth about not standing against Tony Blair for the Leadership of the Labour Party. Uneasy in the company of MPs. Angers his Shadow Cabinet colleagues because of his friendship with the Prince of Darkness. Tendency to rant on the floor of the House of Commons. In the wrong

job. Shadow Chancellor who believes that there is no such thing as economics. Nickname: Pretty Boy.

Michael Portillo (Conservative)

Invisible assassin with all the courage of a Heseltine and the charm of Vlad the Impaler. Nonplussed by the concept of loyalty and quite unable to understand that regimental spirit which enables an Englishman to throw himself in front of machine-gun fire to save the Leader. Man who will never be. Nickname: The Arrogant Bastard.

John Redwood (Conservative)

Treacherous bastard who decided he'd rather be on the outside of the Cabinet pissing in than on the inside pissing out. Carries an ideological torch to scorch the earth when the Vulcans take over the galaxy. Made classic mistake of zealots down the ages by going into battle with a Barmy Army behind him. Lover of Shakespeare with a lean and hungry look who wanted to play Cassius behind Heseltine's Brutus. Lusts for the return of the rope and punishment for those who procreate outside marriage. Unable to speak the language of the natives, he was despised as Secretary of State for Wales. Fellow of All Souls College, Oxford, who proves that in politics being terribly clever is a crippling handicap. Nickname: J. V. (Just Visiting the earth) Redwood.

"Paddy Backdown"

"The Arrogant Bastard"

WHO REALLY RULES BRITAIN?

The Candidates

As the British constitution is unwritten, nobody knows who is supposed to rule Britain or who, as a matter of fact, does rule Britain. This means that the power is there waiting for those best able to seize it. Amongst those who from time to time have tried to grab it are:

- ❖ MPs representing Parliament
- ❖ The Cabinet
- ❖ Civil servants
- ❖ The Prime Minister
- ❖ Sharks in the outside world in cahoots with Ministers and civil servants

MPs

When you first entered the House of Commons you were told "Parliament Rules OK", but warned that things are not always as they seem. Now you are in a position to know that Parliament's omnipotence is a myth put about by constitutional theorists, and that only two things can be said with certainty about parliamentary democracy in Britain today. First, effective power does not reside in Parliament or with MPs. Secondly, there is little that is democratic about the exercise of that power. Knowing now what you do about MPs, you may well respond along with the public:

"Thank God for that. We don't want to be ruled by a bunch of cretins, lechers and people who see their role as that of helping themselves rather than helping others".

Today, Parliament has taken over from the monarchy as the dignified part of the constitution. Take away the pomp and circumstance, the mystery and the theatre of state openings and there is not much left. The men in Parliament are emperors without clothes, while the women are Lady Godivas who ride naked on horseback not to remove exactions on the people but to remove exactions on themselves as they flaunt their vanities.

Having long since ceded its power to control the purse-strings to the Cabinet, our venerable, ancient, dying parliament seems incapable of reforming itself, let alone our daft constitution, and incapable of keeping its own house in good order. The establishment of the Nolan Committee to tell MPs how to behave was the ultimate insult.

Surely it is for the elected rulers of the Kingdom to set standards and not to be told by placemen on a committee how to behave? Improbably, nay impossibly, the Nolan Committee thought that MPs should be guided by seven deadly virtues – selflessness, integrity, objectivity, accountability, openness, honesty and leadership. Not a bad list for boy scouts, you may say, but for MPs – surely not! The establishment of a parliamentary Commissioner for Standards giving MPs advice and investigating misconduct could be worrying but for the fact that final judgement and sentence would rest, as now, with the Committee of Privileges. MPs were grateful that Nolan was scornful of the idea that they should devote themselves full-time to their work in Parliament and on behalf of their constituents, and pleased that paid parliamentary consultancies were to be allowed to continue, pending further thoughts by themselves. The red card for MPs who sell their services to firms engaged in lobbying on behalf of commercial clients – yes, that could hurt and empty a few wallets.

But truth to tell, no shock waves went through the Palace of Westminster with the publication of the Nolan report. And, glory be, Nolan made it clear that in any investigation of Ministerial impropriety the Sir Humphreys and Sir Robins should be protected from their own stupidity by keeping their advice to Prime Ministers secret. Despite all this, and amazingly, some Tory MPs, having been given the green light to carry on regardless, actually complained about Nolan, most of them deeply upset that they might in future be asked to declare the amounts they earned from their consultancies. Some people are so ungrateful.

Only in Britain, the home of hypocrisy, could a Committee charged with examining standards of conduct in public life fail to comment on a single instance of wrong-doing by any MP. In naming no names, failing to admit that there was anything awry other than the public's perception that everything was dreadful, and in sparing the wrong-doers from amongst our corruptible political class any feelings of guilt or shame, the Nolan Committee sought to make a virtue out of its cowardice.

They had, they argued, carried out a searching enquiry; nobody had squealed; and the government had accepted most of their recommendations. What could be better than that? Yet the cognoscenti, that is to say the professional wrong-doers from amongst MPs, quickly sussed out the fact that the new rickety framework which Nolan recommended was hardly likely to prevent Rt Hon and Hon Members from exercising their imaginative faculties in pursuit of late twentieth century noxious notions of greed.

The parliamentary gravy train is likely to speed ahead because too many MPs have become guardians without nobility, rulers without public purpose and representatives of a profession whose growing avarice is proportionate to its increasing irrelevance. Or as one Tory MP put it prosaically to a colleague in the tea-room: "No-one can seriously expect me to stay in this place for £33,000 a year". The rules of the club prevent me from naming him. Another MP, Alan Duncan, took to the streets to plead the case of greedy buggers from the professional classes whom he claimed would not become MPs if their snouts could not stay in troughs. Former Prime Minister Edward Heath produced even more hot air when he moaned that it was unhealthy that every MP, including himself, should now be under suspicion. How sad it was, you may say, to see Sir Edward Heath, the statesman, turning into Ted Heath, the grocer, behaving like an exploding old fart.

One matter not considered by Nolan, which erupted with fury just after the publication of his report, was the 'name-swap-amendments' scandal. Centre stage in this revelatory story was Sir Jerry Wiggin – plain Jerry to his friends, "Junket Jerry" to his detractors. Jerry used the name of another MP, without telling the Member of his deceit, to table amendments to a Bill which were designed to help a company in which he had a financial interest. Even the cynics amongst MPs were stunned. Unbowed, Jerry responded: "I generally find it more tactful if possible to find who are interested in the subject than to do it oneself".

Meanwhile, the low-lifers from the Tory Whips' office blamed not Sir Jerry but Sebastian Coe, the MP whose name had been used without his consent, for sneaking on Sir Jerry. When the Speaker accepted Wiggin's apology and decided to take the matter no further, much odium fell upon her and Parliament, whose servant she was. It seemed that she had established a new procedure akin to the confessional in the Catholic Church – redemption by getting things off one's chest. In future, all that Knights of the Shire like Wiggin would have to do to absolve themselves of their sins would be to make a less than fulsome apology, and that would be that. The fusillade of criticism fired at the Speaker by MPs on this issue was unprecedented in modern times.

Another issue which Nolan ducked was the cesspit from which political parties raise funds. Nolan thought that this was too delicate an issue to deal with – one that in the run-up to a General Election might offend the very Prime Minister who had appointed him.

If this is the case, then who can rule the rulers? That is the question to which we now turn.

The Cabinet

Most major decisions in British government are taken or at least approved by the Cabinet, which consists of twenty or so senior Ministers. As we have already seen, because modern governments take so many decisions a lot of them are delegated to sub-committees of the Cabinet. The full Cabinet normally meets on Thursday

Daily Mail
MONDAY, DECEMBER 16, 1985   20p

Minister's tactics 'are distasteful'

HESELTINE HELICOPTER STORM

By CLIVE EDWARDS and ROBERT PORTER

DEFENCE Secretary Michael Heseltine was bitterly attacked yesterday as he fought to keep the Westland helicopter firm out of American hands.

The chairman of the ailing British firm
...his tactics as 'aston-

Feeling great after the Dynasty massacre

mornings. With the establishment of a Cabinet secretariat in the First World War, Cabinet government grew immeasurably in importance. Some say it has never looked back.

Under the doctrine of 'collective Cabinet responsibility', whatever a Minister's personal views, once the Cabinet has taken a decision they must all stand by it. Privately, a Minister may seethe with indignation at a decision taken by the Cabinet, but publicly he must give it his whole-hearted support. It follows from this that Cabinet Ministers must not attack each other in public. To do so would be to suggest that government is something other than a seamless process, a gossamer thread that never snaps.

The practice is sometimes a bit different from the theory, as the Westland Helicopter Affair showed in 1985-86. Westland, the only major UK helicopter manufacturer, was having discussions about a link-up with an American company, Sikorsky, or alternatively a link-up with a European group. In December 1985 Westland announced it had come to an agreement in principle with the American group. The government said that as a private-sector company Westland had to decide on its own future. That's when the trouble started.

On 3 January 1986 Michael Heseltine, then the Secretary of State for Defence, wrote to Westland saying that European orders might be lost if it went ahead with the American deal. Effectively he was only repeating what the Prime Minister had already said in a letter herself. Then on 6 January the Press Association carried a story which contained a part of a letter from the Solicitor-General to Heseltine suggesting that Heseltine's letter to Westland had contained inaccuracies which he should correct.

It was the start of an astonishing political row between the Prime Minister and two Cabinet colleagues, Heseltine from Defence and Leon Brittan MP from the Department of Trade and Industry. While Heseltine supported the European deal, Brittan backed the American one. On 9 January Heseltine stormed out of a Cabinet meeting, resigned and accused the Prime Minister of bias towards the

American deal. All hell was let loose about who had leaked the Solicitor-General's letter. Suspicion fell on Brittan. Effectively, what had happened was that the Prime Minister set out to destroy Michael Heseltine, her Cabinet colleague, using her own press office and that of the DTI. Then, with the Opposition baying for blood, and in one of the most cynical manoeuvres seen in politics for a long time, she asked the Cabinet Secretary to hold an inquiry to find out who had leaked the Solicitor-General's letter, knowing that the one person he dare not blame was the culprit, herself.

With due majesty and deference the ludicrous Cabinet Secretary fudged the issue. Eventually Brittan, who was only doing her bidding, was forced to resign too. Despite the cover-up, Thatcher thought she might have to resign as well but the then Leader of the Opposition Neil Kinnock made a truly awful speech in the House of Commons and let her off the hook. Eventually, Thatcher repaid her debt of dishonour to Brittan by making him a European Commissioner. In retrospect, this affair showed precisely how the Cabinet system is not supposed to work for, as two Select Committees who looked into the affair showed, the national interest had been suborned by the disreputable personal conduct of members of the Cabinet.

The role of the Cabinet Secretary, Britain's top civil servant, in this affair, and that of the two government press offices which were staffed by civil servants, leads us naturally to the next candidate – the Civil Service.

Civil Servants

Anyone who has watched 'Yes, Minister' on TV may conclude that Sir Humphrey governs Britain. While always bowing obsequiously and saying "Yes" to his Minister, Sir Humphrey manoeuvres, manipulates and fixes things so as to get his own way.

How true to life is the series? Is there a real-life Sir Humphrey? Well, yes, and he is Sir Robin Butler, the Cabinet Secretary, about

whom more later. Every Wednesday the top civil servants who head up each government Department and who are called Permanent Secretaries hold their own Cabinet meeting, with a view to seeing that Ministers do not go astray at the real thing the next day.

In theory, top civil servants are paid to advise Ministers and then, when the policy has been settled, to see that it is carried out according to their Ministers' wishes. But as we now know, political life is not always what it seems. When I was a civil servant I worked in the then Ministry of Housing and Local Government. The Cabinet Minister in charge was the Rt Hon Richard Crossman. He soon realised that civil servants like Sir Humphrey were trying to circumscribe his power. Writing in his diaries he said:

At first I felt like someone in a padded cell, but I must now modify this. In fact, I felt like somebody floating on the most comfortable support. The whole department is there to support the minister. Into his in-tray come, hour by hour, notes with suggestions as to what he should do. Everything is done to sustain him in the line officials think he should take. But if one is very careful and conscious, one is aware of secret discussions between civil servants below. There is a constant debate as to how the ministers should be advised or, shall we say, directed and pushed and cajoled into the line required by the ministry. Each ministry has its own departmental policy and this policy goes on while ministers come and go.

Joe Haines, a press officer to Prime Minister Harold Wilson, noted how Sir Humphrey's boys (few top civil servants are girls) tried to get their own way by pursuing Departmental policies whatever Ministers might think, when in *The Politics of Power* he wrote:

Defence represents the military establishment against the people, instead of the other way round, and the Foreign Office prepares new orchestrations of 'I surrender, dear' to every demand or demarche made to it. The Treasury

Power personified: The effortless superiority of Sir Robin Butler

for its part reflects the power of capital, business, finance, industry, foreign exchange and commodity markets, economists, monetarists, shareholders, stockbrokers, the City of London and the Bank of England. If there is an ignorance greater than that of the politicians for the complexities of finance it is that of financiers for the simplicities of politics.

In his book *How To Be A Minister* Gerald Kaufman, who served under two Prime Ministers, put it another way when he wrote:

You will find that civil servants are very versatile performers. One day they will tell you that something must be done that cannot be done; the next they will insist that something must be done even though you do not want it to be done. They can be very persistent.

Sir Humphrey came to the Civil Service knowing that he was superior to most politicians by way of education, background and upbringing. That self-anointed superiority led him to invent a role for himself – that of governing the country. Sir Humphrey is a politician writ large who seeks to govern the country according to his own interests, tastes, Oxbridge education and upper-class background. He relegates Ministers to the second division, belonging as he does to a Trade Union which calls itself The First Division.

In real life as well as in the TV series, he uses a variety of devices to bring Ministers to heel, including delay, keeping Ministers busy with trivia, interpreting minutes and decisions in ways not wholly intended, slanting statistics, giving Ministers insufficient time to take decisions, going behind Ministers' backs to other Ministers and taking advantage of Cabinet splits and politically-divided Ministerial teams.

Two of his favourite devices are the 'Appendix H Solution' and the 'Three Options Syndrome'. Sir Humphrey's 'Appendix H' scam

THE NEXT STEP TO PILATISATION

In the last few years a large slice of government has been handed over to a new breed of civil servants who run what are called Next Step agencies. These agencies, set up by Ministers, have been hived off from central government and are outside parliamentary control and accountability. This means that Ministers do not have to answer for the misdeeds of this new breed of civil servants, still less resign if their agencies make a mess of things. The civil servants who run these agencies wield great power but exist in a political vacuum, answerable neither to the public nor to Ministers nor to Parliament. They set themselves targets and pay themselves handsomely. So naturally Sir Humphrey and Sir Robin are as enthusiastic about the creation of these agencies, which include amongst their number the Benefits Agency, the Child Support Agency and the Prison Service, as are Ministers. The agencies provide a perfect mechanism for undemocratic practices and bypassing Parliament.

The system works like this. The Home Office used to be responsible for the Prison Service. But now the Home Office, once it has set this policy, washes its hands of the Prison Service, which has become an Agency. Then things get so slack that at Whitemoor jail the prison officers go shopping for the prisoners, allow Semtex and guns to be brought into the prison, and fail to prevent top-security IRA terrorists from leaving when they get bored with the room service. An enquiry reports that Mickey Mouse could run a prison better than the civil servants in charge of the Agency.

The man who should be in charge, the Home Secretary, Michael Howard, comes to the House of Commons like a latter-day Pontius Pilate and says that whoever is responsible it is not him. Yet even as the Home Secretary makes his excuses, the Director General of the Prison Service glows at the prospect of receiving a performance-related bonus for all the good work he did, according to his own performance-related criteria, in the previous year. Then there is another breakout from Parkhurst, aided by a ladder made in the prison workshop. Life imitating 'Porridge'.

MPs laugh hysterically and that's that – a perfect example of modern government set up with the approval of Ministers and civil servants. Nice one, Sir Humphrey! What next, Sir Robin? The answer to this latter question seems to be more prisoners escaping from more prisons with great ease.

is as follows. Ministers take home scores of papers in Red Boxes which they have to read, or at least to initial as though they've read them. This means that when something goes wrong Sir Humphrey can point to the Minister's initials and put the blame on him. Sir Humphrey's wicked trick is to put the points with which he thinks the Minister will disagree in 'Appendix H', knowing that no Minister has time to read Appendix A, let alone Appendix H. So when the storm breaks and the Minister screams "You never told me that", Sir Humphrey replies: "Oh, yes I did. You must remember, Minister, it was in Appendix H".

Sir Humphrey's 'Three Options Syndrome' works as follows. The Minister is told that an immediate decision is needed and that there are three options – A, B and C. A and B, says Sir Humphrey, are impossible, so what does the Minister think of C? Of course it's an offer which the Minister cannot refuse. These scams really do happen.

How good is Sir Robin Butler at being Sir Humphrey, you may ask. Certainly Sir Humphrey would have been proud of Sir Robin when he developed his theory of the right of civil servants and Ministers to lie. Like Sir Humphrey, Sir Robin is a master of the use of language that takes the sting out of wrong-doing. So Sir Robin, as we have seen, made the right to lie acceptable by calling it, in true Sir Humphrey-speak, the right to mislead, to give half an answer, to present an incomplete answer, to tell a story that contains accurate points but is false. The fact that Sir Robin sought to sustain these arguments before a Lord Justice of Appeal in the Scott Inquiry was something which Sir Humphrey would have appreciated enormously.

Sir Robin also became Sir Humphrey incarnate when he conducted his enquiries on behalf of the Prime Minister into allegations of wrong-doing by Ministers. Whilst old-fashioned, fuddy-duddy civil servants were shocked, the new breed could see the brilliance of it. By only interviewing the defendants, i.e. the Ministers themselves, and refusing to take evidence from witnesses for the prosecution, Sir Robin ensured that every Minister would be acquitted of wrong-doing. This not only helped the Ministers concerned. It enabled Sir Robin to tell the Prime Minister that he could justly claim that the integrity of government was intact. To be able to make that claim is important when all around there is evidence of sleaze, misdemeanours and high crime.

One can even see the beauty of it, as Sir Humphrey did, if one considers a hypothetical judge at the Old Bailey who, on hearing the defendant plead 'Not Guilty' to a charge of murder turns to the jury and says: "Members of the jury, you have just heard the defendant enter a plea of 'Not Guilty' to the charge on the indictment. In this Court we take the views of the defendant very seriously indeed. I therefore direct you to bring in a verdict of 'Not Guilty'."

Of course it should be understood that Sir Humphrey and Sir Robin are not acting from base motives or hope of personal gain, but from a proper appreciation of what is in the national interest. In this sense Sir Humphrey and Sir Robin are very different from politicians.

The Prime Minister

Because the media concentrate their coverage of politics on personalities, everyone is aware that the Prime Minister is the most important public political figure in our society. His power derives from and is sustained by patronage, his control of the government administration, and our unified system of government, which is buttressed by the existence of political parties in Parliament which are controlled by his Whips. His power to hire and fire Cabinet Ministers at will is important, and a reminder to would-be recalcitrants on which side their bread is buttered. In all, he appoints 100 or so Ministers to office, and if one assumes that for every back-bench MP on the government side who is made a Minister there is another who would like to take his job, this means that Prime Ministers can rely, without effort, on the existence of some 200 sycophants. That's a good start for the brutal exercise of power on the part of someone whom we have already described as an elected monarch or benign dictator. Prime Ministers usually buttress their power by the establishment of Policy Units or Think-Tanks, the latter more colloquially referred to as wank-tanks.

Prime Ministers certainly think they rule Britain, with or without the aid of their Cabinets. In the end, the thought of their omnipotence gets them down and they all go mad, precisely at that point where they have convinced themselves that they are indispensable. My own view is that for the sake of their personal health as well as for that of the country, Prime Ministers should be more prepared to see therapists and shrinks to deal with their recurring problem of obsession, paranoia and guilt.

That said, the concept of Prime Ministerial government in which the Prime Minister was untouchable took a bit of a knock in the 1960s and 70s, when MI5 and its acolytes decided that they ruled Britain. In 1968 the *Mirror* tycoon Cecil King, a lifelong MI5 agent, together with a bunch of nutters, plotted a 'coup' in which the Prime Minister, Harold Wilson, was to be kidnapped and spirited away to Scotland, with his government replaced by a coalition led by Lord Mountbatten. The 'coup' fell apart when one of those approached refused to join in, and commented ominously that what was being proposed amounted to "treason". It says much for the corrupt resilience of British politics that although top people knew of this bizarre plot, no one was ever brought to justice.

In 1974 and 1975 traitors at MI5 were at it again, preparing a dirty tricks campaign to discredit the Prime Minister. A member of MI6 who spoke to Harold Wilson reported to MI5: "I was called in by the Prime Minister yesterday... Apparently he's heard that your boys have been going around town stirring things up about him and Marcia Falkender, and the Communists at No. 10". Shortly afterwards Wilson resigned, though no one is quite sure why. Whatever the reason, even the most hardened cynic would most likely feel sick at the thought of MI5 governing our country either then or now under its head, Stella Rimington.

For years Parliament tried in vain to bring the security and intelligence services, MI5 and MI6, under some sort of democratic control as they laid claim to licences to kill, bug and steal. In theory MI5, who search for traitors in Britain, was accountable to the Home Secretary, whilst their cousins from the fortress at Vauxhall Cross, MI6, who spy in foreign countries, were answerable to the Foreign Secretary. The trouble was that in practice neither the Home Secretary nor the Foreign Secretary would admit to the existence of MI5 or MI6, let alone answer MPs' questions about either their efficiency or their wrong-doings. Rather pathetically, the former Home Secretary, Merlyn Rees, now Lord Rees, complained that MI5 kept him in the dark about their criminal activities at the time of the Wilson government.

It was only in 1989 that MI5 and in 1994 that MI6 and GCHQ were placed on a statutory basis. The 1994 Act also set up an Intelligence and Security Committee, composed of six members from the House of Commons and the House of Lords, and appointed by the Prime Minister. The function of the Committee is to examine the expenditure, administration and policy of the Security Service, the Intelligence Service and GCHQ. As a result of the work of this Committee, Parliament and the public are none the wiser or the safer in relation to the activities of MI5 and MI6. Perhaps this is because the Committee is composed for the most part of a combination of cretinous creeps and old fogeys who could no more measure the consistency of a blancmange with the aid of a billion-pound laboratory and a team of research chemists than they could uncover wrong-doing, even if the clues were stuck to their eyeballs. Meanwhile, with the ending of the Cold War MI5 has lost a role and is searching for something to do. Does it matter if, as has been suggested, MI5 takes over many roles previously assigned to the police, such as the fight against terrorists, drug-trafficking and organised crime? Well, yes is the answer, because if that happens the police under the guise of MI5 will increasingly become an unaccountable, secret and undemocratic force. Don't say I didn't warn you!

Moreover, even before Harold Wilson became Prime Minister, civil servants had made it clear that in those days the status of Prime Minister was constrained, when the former Prime Minister's Principal Private Secretary wrote: "Harold Wilson's head, big though it is getting, is not quite big enough yet to enable him to have talks with the Civil Service". Whilst one can imagine civil servants disparaging Prime Minister John Major in a similar fashion, one cannot imagine them doing the same of Margaret Thatcher.

Sharks, Ministers and Civil Servants

To a large extent, the governance of Britain is outside anyone's control. Wars, failed harvests, famine, the trade cycle, booms and slumps and migrations are events over which governments have little influence. Governments also find that quite often might is right, not morally but because it imposes itself on others. In Darwinian terms, sharks survive at the expense of others.

At the top of British society is a vast array of successful sharks from the worlds of finance, commerce, industry, science and religion. The political establishment treats these sharks with the kind of reverence normally given only to endangered species, because they are what enables the world to survive. They constantly make voracious demands on governments, and are pleasantly surprised when notice is taken of their demands where others are left disappointed. Daily they lobby and harass Ministers and civil servants, and they've created a vast corporate apparatus to enable them to do so. Governments succumb to their wishes and even define their objectives as good and true because their values are survival values. Ultimately, their culture has to be defined as our culture, their morality as our morality. Perhaps it's silly to believe that it could be any different. Who can conceivably imagine our country not being governed by, and in the interests of, its sharks? Certainly that is not a thought which would occur to any of our MPs, a good number of whom not only have the highest respect for the sharks, but are desirous of representing their interests.

From what you know and what you have read in this book you may conclude that many MPs are themselves sharks. How times, tides and fortunes change! Not so long ago, MPs were so jealous and protective of their reputations that they used to complain bitterly to the Speaker that those who traduced their good name were 'in contempt of Parliament', and the Speaker would rail against the offenders as though they had committed the most terrible felony and abused the good Lord himself.

Today it is not possible to be found to be 'in contempt of Parliament', because Parliament is in contempt of itself.

THE AUTHOR

Brian Sedgemore's colourful career includes working as a civil servant, as a barrister at the criminal bar, as a researcher for Granada TV, as the MP for Luton West and since 1983 as the MP for Hackney South & Shoreditch. He has written three novels and a number of non-fiction books, including 'The Secret Constitution'.

At Private Eye he wrote under the sobriquet Justinianforthemoney.

Brian Sedgemore shaking hands with John Major

ACKNOWLEDGEMENTS

My thanks are due to the following for their wisdom and knowledge: Louis Allen & Others *Political Scandals and Causes Celebres Since 1945;* H Montgomery Hyde *Sexual Scandals in British Politics and Society;* Martin Durham *Sex and Politics;* Antonia Fraser *Cromwell – Our Chief of Men;* CV Wedgwood *The Trial of Charles I;* Macaulay *The History of England in the Eighteenth Century;* AJP Taylor *Essays in English History;* Arthur Bryant *The Age of Elegance;* Roy Jenkins *Asquith;* Peter Rowland *Lloyd George;* Wayland Young *The Profumo Affair;* Jim Prior *A Balance of Power;* Alan Clark *Diaries;* Andrew Adams *Parliament To-day 1990;* Maureen Mancuso *Parliamentary Affairs 1993; The Ethical Attitudes of British MPs: A Typology;* Rodney Brazier *Constitutional Texts;* F Benemy *The Elected Monarch;* Paul Welsby *How the Church of England Works;* Michael MacDonald *The Speaker of the House of Commons;* Christopher Jones *No 10 Downing Street;* Michael Cockerell & Others *Sources Close to the Prime Minister;* John Newman *The Buildings of England:West Kent and the Weald;* Terry Major-Ball *Major Major;* Michael Foot *Loyalists and Loners.*

Special thanks are due to Sidgwick and Jackson for permission to quote from *How to be a Minister* by Gerald Kaufman, Hutchinson

for permission to quote from *Diaries 1979-80* by Tony Benn, to Jonathan Cape for permission to extract from *The Politics of Power* by Joe Haines and to Penguin Books for permission for use of *The Crossman Diaries* by Richard Crossman.

My thanks are also due to the unstinting help I received from the staff of the Library of the House of Commons, including the Research Division of the Library. The views expressed are of course my own.

PICTURE CREDITS

Associated Press: 6, 48, 65, 81
Hulton Deutsch Collection: 10, 37, 62, 84
Network: Denis Doran 69; Justin Leighton 135 T; Neil Libbert 132; Paul Lowe 119; Martin Mayer 125; Judah Passow 21, 92; John Sturrock 14, 30, 41, 134 T; Andrew Wiard 130, 135 B
Parliamentary Copyright: 15, 70, 143
Press Association: 42, 55, 73, 75, 139
Rex Features: 18, 19, 33, 40, 85, 86, 90, 93, 95, 101, 109, 112, 133, 134 B
Newspaper headlines courtesy of John Frost Newspapers